8 00

POPULAR MECHANICS'

Picture History of American Transportation

EDITED BY

EDWARD L. THROM

CONTRIBUTING EDITORS: JAMES S. CRENSHAW, NICHOLAS G. GEANNOPULOS, ESTHER GARDUK, ALICE GORMAN, HELEN JOSEPH, BETTY M. KANAMEISHI AND RICHARD SIMONS

Simon and Schuster
NEW YORK
1952

To LORA LEE

FIRST PRINTING

PUBLISHED BY SIMON AND SCHUSTER, INC., ROCKEFELLER CENTER,
630 FIFTH AVENUE, NEW YORK 20, N. Y.
MANUFACTURED IN THE UNITED STATES OF AMERICA
PRINTED BY LIVERMORE & KNIGHT COMPANY, PROVIDENCE, R.I.
BOUND BY H. WOLFF BOOK MFG. CO., INC., NEW YORK, N.Y.

CONTENTS

A Note about the Editors

FOR THE most part, this book is the result of the efforts of what might be called the Chicago group of encyclopedists. Edward L. Throm, now editor of the Popular Mechanics Press, was formerly a department editor of *The World Book Encyclopedia* and a contributor to *Compton's Pictured Encyclopedia.* James S. Crenshaw, Nicholas G. Geannopulos, Esther Garduk, Alice Gorman, and Helen Joseph have contributed the various encyclopedias of which Chicago is the publishing center. Betty M. Kanameishi is an assistant editor of Popular Mechanics Press. Richard Simons is a member of the staff of the Sunday magazine of the *Indianapolis Star.*

INTRODUCTION

Better than any loyalty test is an American's reaction to the history of his country. We hope that the story this book unfolds gives you the same warming of the heart that it did for the editors who prepared the material. For this is the story of how a peculiar breed of men conquered, first the tangle of a wilderness, then the space of a sprawling continent.

For nearly a decade after the founding of Plymouth Colony in 1620, these first settlers hardly dared go more than a few yards from their settlements. From the standpoint of civilized transportation, the colonists were worse off than the ancient Romans—although there were wheelwrights among the early American colonists, they did not at first have a chance to ply their trade. In summer the colonists made their short journeys on foot or on horseback; in winter they used crude sleds.

Yet a hundred years later their grandsons were settling on the rim of the western prairies, and by 1830 wagon trains were rumbling from St. Louis to San Francisco in six months. By 1869 a man could cross the continent by railroad in seven days, and today his descendants can make the trip by air in the same number of hours.

The next time you're out seeing America, keep an eye out for evidence of the glorious story of American transportation. There are plenty of signs remaining. From an airliner flying over the Utah desert you can see, faintly but unmistakably, the wheel marks of the Oregon trail, ruts left by the heavy-laden prairie schooners after 1800.

A little knowledge and imagination can carry you back farther than that. Know, as you drive over Cleveland's Ridge Avenue or walk past the honky-tonks and second-hand clothing stores of Chicago's Clark Street, that beneath the layers of asphalt and stone lies ground over which Indian runners once sped along foot-wide trails through the Ohio and Illinois country.

Driving in the East or Middle West you may come across a long, straight, grass-covered ditch, its outlines softened by time. Here was a canal and towpath that once teemed with barges, straining mules, and shouting drivers.

Traveling the modern highway from Cumberland, Md., to Washington, Pa., you will be following the route of the old National Road, America's first highway worthy of the name. You will pass stone inns built before 1820 as stopovers for stagecoach passengers.

Taking the B. & O. out of Baltimore, your train will pass over a stone arch bridge, the Carrolltown Viaduct, built for the original B. & O. tracks in 1830, and you may think of the time when a steam locomotive raced a horse—and lost.

In Springfield, Mass., you can find the street on which the Duryea brothers ran the first gasoline automobile in the United States. On the beach near Kitty Hawk, N. C., you can walk on the historic dunes over which the Wright brothers soared in man's first powered, heavier-than-air flights.

At the riverside docks in Cincinnati, Louisville, or St. Louis you will see a few of the old-time sidewheel steamboats which had their gilded era on the Mississippi and the Missouri.

West of the Mississippi, automobile highways follow the trails of Lewis and Clark, Butterfield's stage line, and the covered-wagon routes to

California. In the rolling plains of the Dakotas and the mountains of Montana, you will pass through towns—Pierre, Bismarck, Williston and Fort Benton—terminals for venturesome steamboats which brought guns and clothing and hardware and groceries to trappers and miners. At Promontory Point in Utah you will find the stone marking the site where a golden spike joined the last rails for the first transcontinental railroad in 1869.

This, then, is the story we have tried to give you here—the inexorable march of a mighty people across a rich and beautiful continent, and the roaring pageant of transportation that followed the Westward Movement.

The pictures in this book have been selected from sources all over the country. In the latter half, however, they are drawn largely from the files of *Popular Mechanics Magazine*. No better pictorial record of the progress of transportation during the last half century exists. For it was in 1902 that *Popular Mechanics* was founded, and it has been dedicated to the new and the different in mechanical progress from then to the present.

If this book brings you some measure of appreciation of the steadfast purpose and the toil and the dreams of the men who developed our transportation, it will have served its purpose well.

Edward L. Throm

Behind the first lonely, coast-hugging colonies lay the magnificent wilderness of North America, where only the Indian hunters moved with any speed and sureness.

·I·

Colonial Days

THE FOREST began at the shore and extended a thousand miles to the west, an enormous expanse of giant trees, broken at random by sparkling lakes and streams, and by the great rivers and barren cliffs of rock; inhabited by wolves and bears and deer and reptiles and myriads of

The manner of makinge their boates.

THE manner of makinge their boates in Virginia is verye wonderfull. For wheras they want Instruments of yron, or other like vnto ours, yet they knowe howe to make them as handsomelye, to saile with whear they liste in their Riuers, and to fishe withall, as ours. First they choose some longe, and thicke tree, accordinge to the bignes of the boate which they would frame, and make a fyre on the grownd abowt the Roote therof, kindlinge the same by little, and little with drie mosse of trees, and chipps of woode that the flame should not mounte opp to highe, and burne to muche of the lengte of the tree. When yt is almost burnt thorough, and readye to fall they make a new fyre, which they suffer to burne vntill the tree fall of yts owne accord. Then burninge of the topp, and bowghs of the tree in suche wyse that the bodie of the same may Retayne his iust lengthe, they raise yt vppon potes laid ouer cross wise vppon forked posts, at suche a reasonable heighte as they may handsomlye worke vppon yt. Then take they of the barke with certayne shells: they reserue the innermost parte of the lennke,* for the nethermost parte of the boate. On the other side they make a fyre accordinge to the lengthe of the bodye of the tree, sauinge at both the endes. That which they thinke is sufficientlye burned they quenche and scrape away with shells, and makinge a new fyre they burne yt agayne, and soe they continne somtymes burninge and sometymes scrapinge, vntill the boate haue sufficient bothowmes. Thus God indueth thise sauage people with sufficient reason to make thinges necessarie to serue their turnes.

"The manner of making their boates" in the Colony of Virginia was accurately described by Hariot.

The tangled interior offered few open clearings like this ridge on the Muskingum trail in Ohio.

birds, and by unpredictable nations of Indians. In whole areas the sunlight never reached the ground. Here ordinary trees were 150 feet tall and two to five feet thick, and exceptional ones fifteen. Between the trees everywhere lay the ageless deposits of decayed vegetation, in which grew thick snarls of underbrush, and over this lay scattered the bodies of the fallen trees – felled by rot, or lightning, or by the violent windstorms that could turn the silent forest into a howling wilderness. Beyond the forest were the plains, where the prairie grass grew thick and tangled and high as a horse.

This was the backdrop against which the first North American seacoast colonies huddled. The settlers of St. Augustine (1565) were almost encircled by the sub-jungle of Florida. Farther north, the settlers of Jamestown (1607) for years never ventured far from their clearings at the mouth of the James River. It was equally rare when the Dutch at New Netherlands (1614) and the English at Plymouth (1620) and New Salem (1628) went out from their settlements. When they did it was only to go far enough to bring back game, wild fruits, bayberries for candles, and bark and roots for medicine.

There were wheelwrights among the colonists, but it was to be years before they would ply their trade, for there were no roads, the clearing of even a modest footpath was a backbreaking achievement. From the standpoint of transportation the New World colonists were worse off than the Europeans of the Middle Ages.

The only humans at home in the North American wilderness were the Indians. Even they had found travel by water the easiest way to go from one hunting ground to another. Only where necessary were the waterways connected by Indian trails. These primitive roadways were no more than 12 to 18 inches wide. In areas where travel was heavy, however, they were sometimes worn a foot deep! Over such trails Indian runners were able to travel as far as 100 miles between a sunrise and sunset. In contrast, the first extensive land movements of colonists, in parties including women and children, averaged only a mile an hour on foot.

Like the Indians, then, the white men found it much easier to travel over the lakes, rivers, and streams. The five principal New England waterways from which most travel movements began lay in the regions we now call Chesapeake Bay, eastern Massachusetts, New York Bay and the Hudson River, the Connecticut River Valley and Long Island Sound, Delaware Bay and the Delaware and Susquehanna rivers. Travel along all these waterways had begun by 1636, and colonial authorities were aware of the need to make overland travel easier. In Plymouth

Indian lore had much attraction for Europeans of the 1500's. This engraving of the burning of a dugout canoe appeared in a 1590 edition of Thomas Hariot's Narrative of the First English Plantation in Virginia.

Colony, governing officials ordered that creeks and streams be bridged by logs. Canoe ferries were set up for more convenient passage over larger rivers.

Just as the white man had followed the Indian's paths through the forests to the streams and rivers, he adapted for his own use the Indian water craft.

The simple and serviceable dugout canoe was made by hollowing out a log (15 to 30 feet long and about three feet in diameter). While strong and manageable, this type of canoe was too heavy to carry overland from one stream to another and was used chiefly on lakes and the major rivers.

More graceful and more mobile, the birch canoe, sung of by Longfellow, required more skill in construction as well as in navigation. Birch bark was peeled carefully from the tree in long strips, then laid over a framework of cedar or spruce. Sometimes the birch strips were sewed together with fibrous roots of larch or balsam, then formed on narrow elastic ribs of spruce. Cracks were sealed with hot pitch from the balsam or spruce. These canoes ranged from 10 to 60 feet in length and each tribe had its own individual variations of style. Because of its light weight, such a canoe could be carried many miles between streams.

A pack-horse train of the colonial period, after an original drawing by Louis Huard. Each horse was led by the one just ahead. Belled harnesses made the strays easy to find. Armed riders convoyed the pack-horse train to guard against Indian raids.

The difficulty of land movement and the availability of waterways of all types soon led the New Englanders to boatbuilding. Among the small sailing boats built by the early colonists were pinks, pinnaces, ketches, schooners, lighters, shallops, sloops and periguas. The name usually depended on a slight difference in rigging of the craft, shape of the hull, or local usage.

The first small ship launched in New England was the *Blessing of the Bay* in Mystic in 1631. By 1640 the shipbuilding industry was well established.

Two widely used types of river boats were developed by the colonists to fit their own particular needs. Both were a type of flat-bottom boat, popular because they would float in less than a foot of water even when heavily loaded.

The poleboat derived its name from the manner in which it was pushed upstream by means of long spike-tipped poles. These boats ranged from 20 to 30 feet in length. They were three to five feet in width and two to three feet deep. Traveling downstream in a poleboat required almost no effort, but upstream against a current was quite another matter. A tremendous amount of labor was required to make any progress. A crew of from four to eight men stood on each side of the boat, near the bow end and facing the stern. Sticking spike-tipped poles into the river's bottom, these men walked to the stern end and then back forward, repeating the process over and over.

The other early type of river boat, also widely used, was a larger model of the poleboat, equipped with a mast and sails. When the boat traveled against the wind, the sails were dropped and the poles used.

BECAUSE of the slow development of roads, travel by land continued to be a problem until well after the American Revolution. But even the American Indians found ways to make the land transport burden lighter. One of the earliest devices in use by the Indians was the travois, a kind of ground sled. It consisted simply of two poles, one end of which was attached to the back of a horse, a dog, or sometimes a squaw. The other end trailed on the ground. Sometimes a hide basket or a platform of sticks was put on the travois.

Thanks to the sled, land travel in colonial times was usually more extensive in the winter. Of course these hard-working pioneers had more leisure time then. But more important, the mudholes were frozen smooth. In New England the types of sleigh commonly used were called pods or pungs, a pod being drawn by one horse and a pung by two.

Farm families used such conveyances to haul their goods to the nearest market centers. Bundled in layers of good homespun coats, hoods, scarves and blankets, the farmer's wife and small children sat surrounded by cheeses, dried vegetables, flax and miscellaneous jugs. The man of the house usually walked or ran alongside.

Some historians claim that the first wheeled vehicles to rumble within the limits of what is now the United States were brought here by the Spanish in 1596. They were rough carts and wagons drawn by oxen and were brought to what is now New Mexico from Zacatecas, Mexico, by Juan de Onate.

Late in the 17th century, the appearance of a few sedan chairs on the streets of New York and Philadelphia excited awe and admiration. These European importations had boxlike seats and were carried either by servants or by a single horse. They were frequently of gaudy design. But the sober-minded Puritans of Boston would have no truck with such "Satan-inspired" contrivances. Even horse-drawn conveyances were frowned upon, and all travel on Sunday was prohibited.

The northern plains Indians used dog pack trains, a practice shared by the Indians and Eskimos of Canada. This was one native transportation device the white colonists did not borrow.

Snow and ice made a better roadway than summer's mud and rocks, so most traveling in colonial New England was done during the winter. Above is a crude farm sled of the colonial era. Later on family sleighs, many of dashing design and ornate decoration, were to appear in the region.

The Indian travois was a simple arrangement of two poles slung on either side of a horse. The poles supported a platform of branches which carried the household goods when the tribe was on the move.

Among other early types of wheeled vehicles for human transport was a heavy, two-horse model, similar to an English carriage. Two one-horse adaptations, better suited to local conditions, were developed. The "chair" was a two-wheeled carriage with a seat for two. Sometimes there was an additional small seat over the shafts for the driver. The "chaise," similar in construction, boasted the added luxury of a top cover of leather.

These early American carriages had no springs, but swung on braces of wood or leather. They were made by local blacksmiths and wheelwrights and were to suffer little change in essential design for the next hundred years. They did become gayer in color and more lavish in ornamentation. Wheels and bodies were painted red, yellow, blue, or brown with contrasting panels or trimmings.

The birch-bark canoe was used mostly by the northern Indians, since the great paper birch trees, from which they were made, seldom grew south of New York State. Although most white men considered them too tricky to be practical, they were truly delightful craft — light, easily driven, and remarkably tough and durable.

The Puritans frowned on display, and only a few sedan chairs like these 18th century English models ever appeared in the streets of the American colonies.

Wagons for the transportation of both freight and passengers came into use soon after 1700 and were frequently seen on the road between Perth Amboy and Burlington in what is now New Jersey. They were big-wheeled affairs with iron tires six to ten inches wide, drawn by from four to six horses, and covered with canvas tops.

But pack horses continued to be the chief carriers of freight because of the limited number of roads on which wagons could travel. The Indian trails had widened into the white man's tote path, and later into the wagon road. But they were still made of nothing but natural soil.

In an early effort to improve the wagon roads, small logs were placed side by side on the trail and covered with a two- or three-inch layer of dirt. It was then called a corduroy road, but the improvement was not very sig-

Conestoga wagons were developed by the thrifty farmers of Eastern Pennsylvania. They were enormous, with six-foot wheels and a 24-foot overhanging top of canvas. They were built exactly the same from about 1750 to 1850.

The prairie schooner was smaller than the Conestoga wagon and had less curve to the bed.

This Conestoga was hand-fashioned by John Studebaker in his smithy shop at Gettysburg, in 1830.

nificant. The labor involved in cutting enough trees to cover a sizeable stretch was staggering. Besides, when the rains came, the dirt washed down between the logs. It was doubtful which was to be preferred, having your wagon stuck in the mud or having it jolted to pieces bumping over the bare logs!

Pack-horse traffic rapidly grew into big business controlling many thousands of horses and mules and employing great numbers of packers and caravan drivers. The owners of the more successful companies contracted to move parties of people and their goods to any part of the country.

The first horse in a pack train was ridden by the driver. Each of the other horses in the procession was led by a rope tied to the one in front. Bars of iron were sometimes lashed to the backs of the horses and then bent around their middles so that barrels and kegs could be fastened on either side. The routes, variously called tote roads, pack roads or horse-ways, in many places were no more than paths two feet wide, winding tortuously over hill and down valley. This freight system was more widely used in Pennsylvania than in any other colony. Even as late as 1783, the pack-horse system was the only way of transporting goods from Philadelphia to Pittsburgh.

PENNSYLVANIA COLONY also was noteworthy in two other important related events in travel history: the cutting of Braddock's Road through the wilderness and the appearance of the famous Conestoga wagon. A simple situation called for an obvious solution: General Braddock needed wagons for his troops and a road for his wagons.

By order of the Pennsylvania Assembly in 1775 a force

This is the only example known to exist of a "coachee," a light family carriage used during the 1700's. It is believed to be the coachee owned by George Washington at Mt. Vernon and mentioned in his diaries.

of woodsmen was assembled to chop down trees to make a passage wide enough for wagon travel so that Braddock's forces could get through.

Maryland and Virginia failed to supply enough wagons to haul the troops and provisions, so General Braddock appealed to Benjamin Franklin for help in recruiting wagons from the Pennsylvania farmers, particularly those in Lancaster county. The thrifty and prosperous farmers of this rich region had developed a remarkable wagon with a canvas cover supported by hoops, variations of which played an important role in American transportation for a century, from 1750 to 1850. About 150 of these famous Conestoga wagons and 1,500 saddle and pack horses were rounded up by Franklin through advertisements in Lancaster county and in the *Pennsylvania Gazette*.

From the standpoint of size alone, the Conestogas with their six-horse bell teams were impressive. Team and wagon together measured 60 feet in length. The top of the front hoop was 11 feet from the ground, and the top ends of the wagon were some 16 feet apart. Rear wheels stood five to six feet high. Colors were almost a trademark: the underbody always a vivid blue, while the upper framework was bright red. It was topped with a dull white cloth cover about 24 feet long. The bells worn by the horses were almost as large as dinner bells.

Here is a description of the wagons, at the height of their popularity and fame, by John Strohn in the *United States Agricultural Report* (1863):

"The capacious wagons which the Conestoga farmers then had in use, were the best means of land transportation which the times and circumstances of the country

John Mercereau's "Flying Machine" made the trip to Philadelphia in a day and a half.

The Canadian calash came down into the American colonies in the 1790's. Note flaring mudguards and coiled rear springs.

A six-horse Conestoga wagon. The body of a Conestoga was tilted upward at the ends to keep the load in the center as the wagon traveled over rolling country.

Privately owned coaches were much more splendid and comfortable than the early stagecoaches. This illustration shows General and Mrs. Washington on their way to the White House in 1759.

Stage "waggons," forerunners of the stagecoaches, had a certain beauty, but they lacked the comfort and durability of the heavier and more generously springed coaches.

then afforded. These wagons and teams attracted attention and commanded admiration wherever they appeared; and hence the origin, as I conceive, of the horse and wagon to which the appellation of 'Conestoga' has been attached. The harness was constructed of the best materials, with an eye to show as well as utility. In the harness and trimmings of these teams the owners frequently indulged in expenses that approached to extravagance – It was, indeed, an animating sight to see five or six highly fed horses, half covered with heavy bear skins, or decorated with gaudily fringed housings, surmounted with a set of finely toned bells, their bridles adorned with loops of red trimming – prancing as if half conscious of their superior appearance, and participating in the pride that swelled the bosom of their master."

The Conestoga wagoner was the first American to drive from the left. Other vehicles of that time and later were driven from the right side. Not until after the introduction of automobiles with left-hand drive in the early 1900's did this national custom change.

Historical documents contain many references to feats performed by the Conestogas. George Washington's diary before the Revolution is filled with notes on his "waggons." During the hard winter at Valley Forge, supplies were brought to the hungry and shivering troops in Conestogas. In the spring of 1777, a sturdy Conestoga wagon, drawn by four horses and accompanied by a bodyguard of a full company of Continental soldiers, brought $600,000 in silver from Portsmouth, N. H., to the treasury at York.

Almost as famous as the wagons are the wagoners who drove them. To the small boy they were dashing, daredevil fellows, indeed.

A typical professional wagoner wore a wide-brimmed hat, homespun suit, high-top boots and a beard. In winter he added a huge topcoat, home-knit mittens and a scarf. For protection he usually carried brass knuckles and a blackjack, for fights were not uncommon.

As the wagon traffic grew heavier, numerous taverns and wagon stands sprang up at convenient intervals. At the end of the day's journey, the wagoner first attended to his horses, watering and feeding them. The wagoner carried his own bedding which he tossed carelessly upon the floor of the tavern where he slept.

Cost of a night's lodging, feed for six horses, meals for the teamster, and three shots of whiskey came to about 75 cents!

Wagoning was a young man's profession and its followers were a carefree lot who danced, sang, swapped stories, and enjoyed their liquor. Here is a description by Thomas B. Searight in *The Old Pike* of a night at a wagon stand:

Pungs (two-horse sleighs), and pods (for one horse) provided winter transportation in New England. The illustration shows British troops traveling through Canada in a pung.

Corduroy roads were laborious to build, and the soil with which they were usually covered washed away, leaving the bare logs to jolt the wheels to pieces, but they did keep the wagons out of the mud.

One of the earliest colonial routes was the Boston Post Road, a pair of ruts running to Providence. By 1672 it extended to New York. Today it is U.S. Highway No. 1.

The gig was a light carriage very suitable for poor roads, and therefore popular for long-distance travel. This one was built about 1775.

"I have stayed over night with William Cheets, on Nigger Mountain when there were about 30 six-horse teams in the wagon yard, a hundred Kentucky mules in an adjoining lot, a thousand hogs in their enclosures, and as many fat cattle in adjoining fields. The music made by this large number of hogs in eating corn on a frosty night I shall never forget. After supper and attention to the teams, the wagoners would gather in the barroom and listen to the music on the violin furnished by one of their fellows, have a Virginia hoe-down, sing songs, tell anecdotes and hear the experiences of drivers from all points of the road, and when it was all over, unroll their beds, lay them down on the floor before the barroom fire side by side and sleep with their feet near the blaze as soundly as under the parental roof."

STAGECOACHES were as much a part of the American travel scene as the Conestoga wagon and enjoyed a similar heyday. Forerunner of the stagecoach was the stage wagon, used for both freight and human travel until after the American Revolution.

The stage wagons had three or four wooden benches extending from side to side for passengers. There were no backs and no springs. The wagons had straight sides covered with a tunnel-shaped cloth top.

Improvements which transformed the wagon into a coach designed primarily for human transportation were a flat top and side curtains made of leather. Still later, seats were made of leather or wool and benches were

Postal service between the colonies, begun as a private enterprise in 1691, was taken over by the British government in 1706. Coaches were used for the longer trips but horsemen delivered along the shorter routes.

fitted with back rests of wood or leather. Still later, seats were set on wrought-iron springs or held up by pliable leather straps. Coaches were usually drawn by four horses and the teams were changed every few miles.

By 1771, the characteristic which was to become a national symptom, the urge for speed, was already in evidence. Rival stagecoach companies sought to shorten the journey by getting better horses or better drivers. One proprietor was inspired to name his stage wagon *The Flying Machine*, and advertised that the stage could make the trip from New York to Philadelphia in a day and a half. Fare, plus the cost of meals and lodging, brought the total cost of such a trip to about $6.50.

One of the earliest descriptions of a stagecoach journey is Josiah Quincy's, President of Harvard College, who traveled from Boston to New York a few years later:

"I set out from Boston in the line of stages of an enterprising Yankee, Pease by name; considered a method of transportation of wonderful expedition. The journey to New York took a week. The carriages were old and shackling, and much of the harness of ropes. We reached our resting place for the night, if no accident intervened, at 10 o'clock, and, after a frugal supper, went to bed with a notice that we should be called at three, which generally proved to be half-past two, and then, whether it snowed or rained, the traveler must rise and make ready, by the help of a horn lantern and a farthing candle, and proceed on his way over bad roads, sometimes getting out to help the coachman lift the coach out of a quagmire or rut, and

Benjamin Franklin, first colonial postmaster, pictured making a tour of inspection north of Philadelphia with his daughter.

One of Washington's coaches.

A heavy road coach by Brewster, now in the Edison Electric Institute.

A York mail coach built by Downing, of Concord, N. H. It carried mail between New York and Portsmouth, N. H. The body is suspended on leather thoroughbraces hung from short vertical whip springs.

arrived in New York after a week's hard traveling, wondering at the ease, as well as the expedition with which our journey was effected."

In the operation of the passenger and mail coaches, as in the operation of railroads later, competition and consolidation were characteristic. Rivalry between the large companies who owned many miles of lines was intense. When a new operator appeared, a fare-cutting war began, until one or the other was usually forced out.

One such memorable fight on the Boston-Providence Line finally reached the point where the two rival companies had done away with fares entirely and were serving free meals and a bottle of wine to the delighted passengers.

WHILE THE STAGECOACHES were extending their operations inland, the shipbuilders among the colonists were building up a thriving coastal trade. These early American ships were built for the most part for the use of the builder, either to engage in fishing or to carry passengers and cargo along the Atlantic Coast.

Passengers setting out on a journey by ship in those days undertook a voyage that was as unpredictable as the winds that sailed the ship. When a shipmaster set sail, he seldom knew his eventual destination or the length of time he would be at sea. A cargo would be put on board

The Recovery *of Salem, a typical merchant ship of the colonial period. The artist pictured her as "returning from Mocha on the Red Sea."*

and the ship would sail for its first port. There the captain-trader would sell his cargo. His next destination and sailing time would depend on what new cargo he could purchase and where he would be likely to sell it most profitably. It was not uncommon, too, for a ship to be becalmed at sea for weeks. For these reasons, the well-to-do traveler hired space on a ship much as one rents an apartment today.

The ships operated by the merchant traders were small, seldom more than 300 tons. Only a little capital was needed to build them and supply them with a crew and cargo. While vessels sometimes were co-operatively owned by groups of traders, the captain was almost always a trader himself as well as a navigator. Sometimes he would take on a little extra cargo for pay, but most often he and his partners bought and sold the cargo carried. While would-be passengers fretted in their cabins and partial cargoes deteriorated in the holds, shipmasters often spent weeks in port seeking to fill out their cargoes before setting sail.

There was no contract shipbuilding in North America until a few years before the Revolutionary War. In 1761 Captain William Swanton contracted to build a ship for a Scottish merchant. This marked the beginning of a new era of shipbuilding in the colonies, of which more will be said later.

The captain-trader loaded his ship with whatever cargo he could purchase, and his port of call was where that cargo would sell best. This typical dock scene shows the Arch St. Ferry landing in Philadelphia in late 1700's.

The Wilderness Road, otherwise called Boone's Trace and the Kentucky Road, was the first pathway for the westward movement. It began at an outpost called the Block House in Virginia, crossed the Powell Mountains, ran through the Powell River valley, then passed through the Cumberland Gap onto the plateau of central Kentucky. All along the road roved bloodthirsty bands of Indians, sworn to keep the white man out of their favorite hunting grounds.

·II·

The Westward Movement

GROUPS OF SETTLERS began moving away from the eastern seaboard about 1802. But the stage was set for these movements in 1773 by a famous American pathmaker – Daniel Boone, hunter, trapper, and former blacksmith and wagoner for Braddock, who had been through the Cumberland Gap into the country west of the Alleghenies as early as 1769. He returned with stirring tales of the rich "Caintuck country."

In 1773 Boone organized a party of seven families and 40 unattached men who were willing to leave the security of an established community. Some were on foot, others on horseback. Each man wore a leather belt to which was attached a tomahawk, a powder horn and leather pouches filled with homemade bullets and parched corn.

The women rode astride or in pillion saddles, and the children bounced behind them in wicker baskets. Behind

The Natchez Trace was flattened by the feet of flatboatmen walking back to their homes. The unwieldy boats could not be brought upstream and so were sold after delivering their cargoes at Natchez, Miss. The trail led back to Nashville,

the pack animals bearing the worldly goods of these travelers straggled a few cattle and pigs and a rear guard.

The average rate of travel was 10 miles per day, and by midafternoon the leaders were on the lookout for a place to pitch the evening camp. When a likely spot was found a makeshift shelter was thrown up for the women and children, the livestock was driven up and fed, the horses tethered and tended. Then the travelers themselves could rest and eat. The menu depended on what the forest had provided the riflemen that day.

Up to that time the Indians had permitted the white men to travel fairly unmolested. But when the settlers showed signs of moving westward, the Indians resisted. They had seen the game disappear from the eastern settlements, and now they knew the restless whites were moving into their prized hunting grounds – on which the Indians' whole civilization rested. It was along the Clinch River in Virginia that the Cherokees struck the party's rear guard, killing Boone's son in a brief engagement.

After the tragedy, some families returned East, but the remaining members refused to abandon the project. Instead, they halted for the winter while Boone negotiated with the Cherokees for title to the land bounded by the Ohio, Kentucky, and Cumberland rivers. Then, to make the second stage of the journey smoother, he blazed the trail which was first called Boone's Trace and later the Wilderness Road, cutting deep slashes in the trees to

The Michigan Road was a native trail continually taking up and leaving off again as it provided portage between waterways across the southern part of the Michigan peninsula.

A pack-horse train was the surest way to transport goods over mountainous territory. The sure-footed horses (or perhaps mules), worked their way over the roughest and steepest terrain with a minimum of guidance.

In the Spanish settlements of North America, well-traveled mule paths, or calzadas, were paved with flat stones.

mark the way. With Boone again at the head, the party resumed its march. Behind Boone came the axmen, who chopped down the smaller trees and cut the underbrush that blocked the path. Generally, however, they went around obstacles that could not be cut away readily. They slashed away at a rate that scarcely slowed their march. This first path was not intended to be a wagon road, but a pathway for horses. Later parties improved on Boone's trail-blazing technique; they painted numbers on the trees to indicate the miles traveled.

There was no attempt to keep a straight line; they followed the path of least resistance in the general direction they wished to travel. Thus they went generally west to the Cumberland Gap, then turned north to follow an Indian trail into Kentucky – the famous Warrior's Path. After another 50 miles, Boone left the Indian trail for a bison trail leading west to the Rockcastle River, then cut north to the present site of Boonesborough.

The only written record of those travels today is the diary of William Calk, who joined the Boone party at Boonesborough on April 20, 1775. Here are some excerpts from Calk's diary of the journey, begun from Williams County, Virginia, on March 13, 1775:

"*fryday 24th* (March) – we start early and turn out of the wagon Road to across the mountains to go by Danil Smiths we loose Driver Come to a turable mountain that tired us almost to death to git over it and we lodge this

The roadside tavern was the meeting place for wagons and coaches and the droves of cattle. This is the Fairview Inn, on the old National Road near Baltimore.

night on the Lawrel fork of the holston under a granite mountain and Roast a fine fat turkey for our suppers and Eat it without aney Bread.

"*fryday 7th* (April) — this morning is a very bad snowey morning we still continue at Camp being in number about 40 men and some neagroes this Eaven. Comes a letter from Capt. Boone at caintuck of the indians doing mischief and some turns back.

"*tuesday 11th* (April) — this is a very loury morning and like for Rain but we all agree to start Early and we cross Cumberland River and travel Down it about 10 miles through some turrabel cainbrakes as went down Abrams mair Ran into the River with her load and swam over he followed her and got on her and made her swim back agin it is a very raney Eavening we take up camp near Richland Creek they kill a beef Mr. Drake Bakes Bread without washing his hands we Keep Sentry this Night for fear of the indians."

Calk and his party reached Boonesborough on April 20th. Here they were received with a formal welcome of a volley of guns.

A few days later he noted:

"*wednesday 26th* — We Begin Building us a house and a plaise of Defense to Keep the indians off this day we begin to live without bread.

"*Satterday 29th* — We git our house kivered with Bark and move our things into it at Night and Begin house-

On established trade routes, wagon trains often met fleets of goods boats for a transfer of cargoes.

An early American chaise (about 1830), restored to fair condition.

A sleigh (1840) typical of those used throughout the North.

The popular Concord coach, of New England, reappeared, almost unchanged, in the West, during the middle 1800's.

keeping Eanock Smith Robert Whitledge and myself."

By 1784 there were already about 30,000 people living in Kentucky. Each year several thousand more marched over the Wilderness Road from North Carolina and Virginia. The church was the community unit, and sometimes entire congregations, led by their pastor, set out on foot for the bluegrass country.

These were unruly spirits, who left their communities because of the taxes those communities were beginning to impose, or because they were being surrounded by too many neighbors, and also because they had heard wonderful tales of the rich land to the west.

On reaching the promised land they had no choice but to become self-sufficient, for the conditions under which they had traveled permitted few belongings to be taken. They built cabins, cleared ground, planted corn, and made their own homespun clothing when what they had wore out. A few items had to be imported from the East – these were salt, lead, and gunpowder. These supplies were brought as far west as possible by boat, then hauled overland by pack horses.

Until 1800 the most important landmark for westbound travelers was Fort Chissel, about 200 miles east of the Cumberland Gap. It was the last link with "civilization." A half-dozen caravans might halt there in a day, with hundreds of foot pilgrims and a miscellaneous following of livestock and poultry.

In 1802 the United States Senate was given a firsthand account of travel conditions by Senator Otis Mason of Virginia:

"The pilgrim into those regions will have to pass

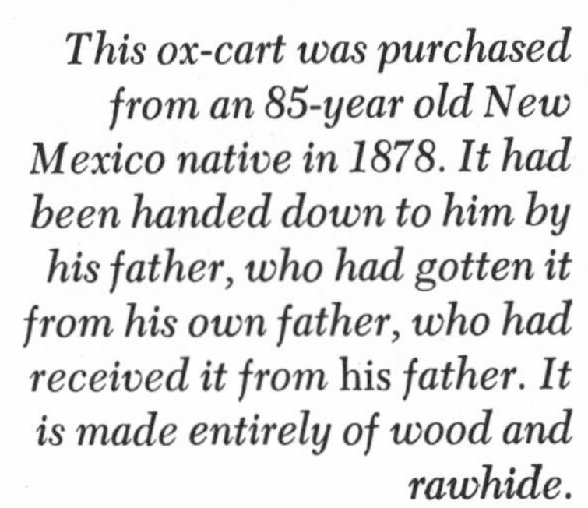

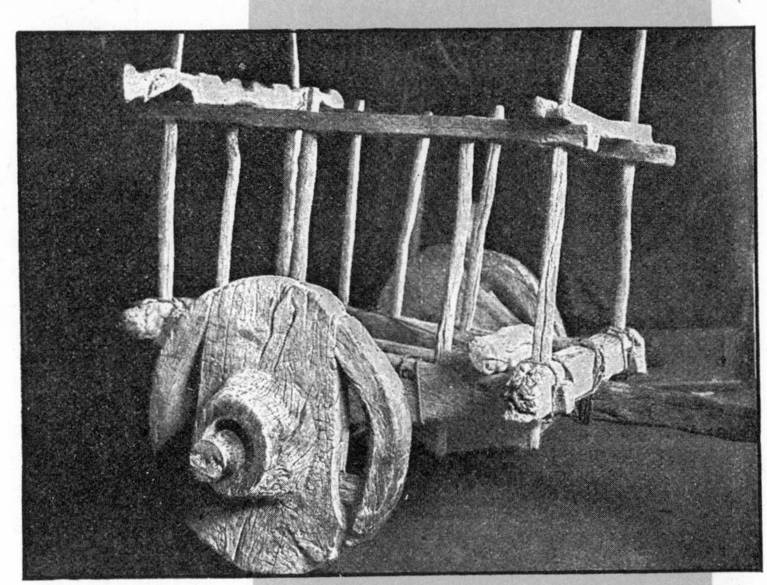

This ox-cart was purchased from an 85-year old New Mexico native in 1878. It had been handed down to him by his father, who had gotten it from his own father, who had received it from his father. It is made entirely of wood and rawhide.

through the country of the Cherokee Indian, nearly 100 miles over the Cumberland Mountains where he will be exposed to every inclemency of the weather without a shelter to retire to, for there is not a house nor a hut in the whole journey; a journey in which all travelers are obliged at all times and of unavoidable necessity to sleep one night at least, and from the fall of rains and rise of water courses many nights without a roof to cover them from the storm, and moreover where they are liable at every stop to be robbed by the Indians, as I myself experienced passing through that wilderness."

As the western horizon broadened, transportation by water increased. Pioneer resourcefulness modified the eastern river boats so they could be used on the "Massasip" and Ohio as far as the rapids near the present site of Louisville.

The old reliable dugout canoe was easily made, or one could be bought from an Indian for $3. Only one or two persons could travel this way. A larger canoe, called a piroque, could safely carry a family and several tons of household goods. A piroque was 40 to 50 feet long and six to eight feet wide. It could be purchased for between $5 and $10.

Another popular small boat was the skiff, first cousin to the present-day skiff. It had a wide, flat bottom and could safely carry a party of three. Big brother to the skiff was the bateau, which could neatly carry the average family. It was helped downstream by several pairs of oars called sweeps. Another sweep was used as a steering rudder. The bateau could be propelled upstream by poles.

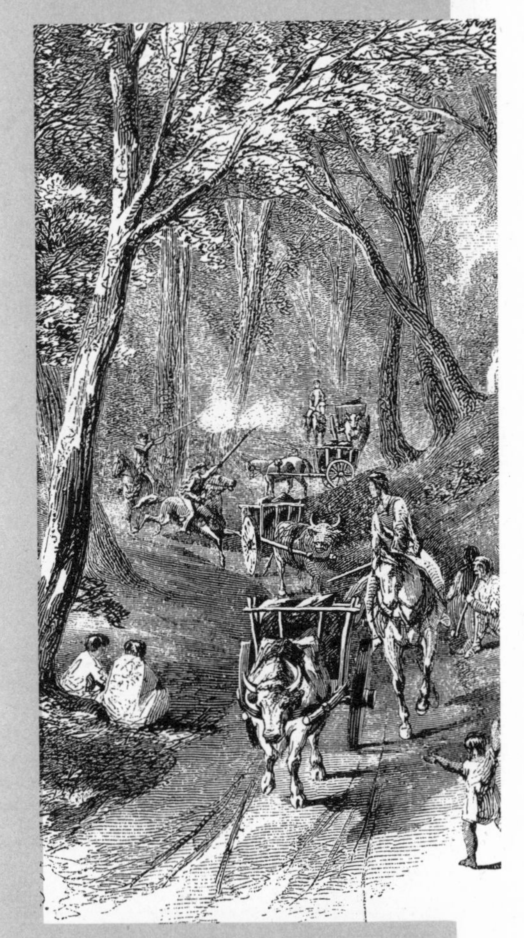

Oxen lent an Old World touch in some western settlements. Here ox-carts are hauling game after a hunt in the Red River Valley.

Traces of the old Santa Fe Trail may still be seen in the desert by passengers of modern air liners.

One of the last of the Red River carts (1882), used much earlier in the century in this famous valley.

The early 1800's saw the growth of coastwise travel of both packet sloops and various road vehicles.

One of these family-sized boats could be purchased for from $20 to $50.

The keelboat was one of the most widely used river boats. Its keel was a heavy timber which, in addition to serving as a stiffening member, extended beyond the bow to protect the hull from collisions with the submerged logs which infested the rivers. The typical keelboat was from 40 to 75 feet long and from seven to nine feet wide. It was equipped with a steering oar or rudder and sweeps. It also had a mast and sails.

Most large parties traveled on flatboats, which were like a house on a raft. The flatboat was awkward and almost completely at the mercy of the current, but it could carry a lot of people and goods.

It is a curious fact that we have the remains of many ancient forms of transportation, such as Roman chariots and Phoenician ships, but nothing remains of the crude river craft with which the first pioneers made their way into the American West. There apparently are not even any contemporary sketches. The reason is simple but little known: the pioneers pried their boats apart upon reaching their destination and used the lumber to help build and furnish their new homes. It is true they were in a magnificent virgin forest. But the labor involved in cutting down those trees and trimming lumber from the trunks was such as to make a piece of trimmed lumber almost as valuable as it would be in a treeless desert.

Once past the tree-studded Northwest Territories and into the open prairies of America, the westward-moving pioneers again turned to the wagon, which had been discarded for the pack horse and the river craft. The Conestoga of the East reappeared, with some changes in styling; it became smaller and trimmer, the curve of its bed was not so pronounced, and storage boxes appeared at its ends and sides. The new wagon was called a prairie schooner, and it creaked over the plains in isolated groups and in historic mass movements for the remainder of a century.

In the western settlements that sprang up in the wake of the prairie schooners, new and lighter wagons and carriages appeared. One favorite vehicle, the buckboard, represented a combination of both wagon and carriage.

Back on the eastern seaboard, the stage wagon had spent its short life and given way to the more elaborate and comfortable stagecoach.

As stagecoach travel increased, laws were passed for the protection and safety of passengers. One such law required lamps at night. Another imposed fines on drivers

The barouche used by Lafayette during his triumphal tour of the United States in 1824-1825. It was made by John Oulet of Baltimore.

who were found intoxicated while on duty, or who left their horses untied while still hitched to the coach. There were many opportunities for coach drivers to drink, and occasionally there was an accident.

Such an occurrence was reported in the *Maine Farmer* of April 3, 1835:

"The driver, on taking charge of the team at Groton, was observed to be not very well capable of managing his team, which was observed by several persons, one of whom remarked on his incapacity to drive. It is not pretended that he was drunk at the time, but laboring under the stupefying effects of intoxication. After the arrival of the stage at a place called Littleton he took his glass of grog. Mr. Bullard, proprietor of this line of stages, rode on the box with him and had occasion to arouse him from sleep twice after leaving Groton. Mr. Bullard was still on the box with the driver when they left Littleton. On arriving at the summit of the hill where the accident happened the driver was unable to control his team, four spirited horses, and they ran full speed down the hill, coming in contact with Mr. Powers' six-horse loaded wagon — which

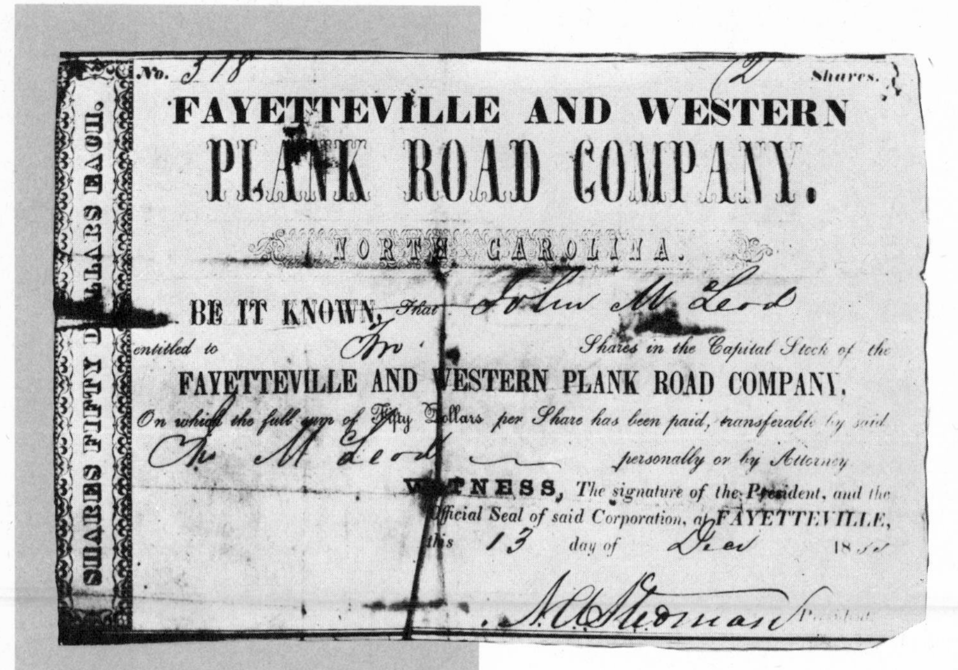

No. 318 (2) Shares.

SHARES FIFTY DOLLARS EACH.

FAYETTEVILLE AND WESTERN

PLANK ROAD COMPANY.

NORTH CAROLINA.

BE IT KNOWN, That John M. Leod entitled to Two Shares in the Capital Stock of the FAYETTEVILLE AND WESTERN PLANK ROAD COMPANY, On which the full sum of Fifty Dollars per Share has been paid, transferable by said Jn M Leod personally or by Attorney

WITNESS, The signature of the President, and the Official Seal of said Corporation, at FAYETTEVILLE, this 13 day of Dec 18

President.

Privately-owned toll road companies appeared throughout the country, but most of them were financial failures.

Stage drivers were a puckish and independent breed. This Allegheny route driver appeared in an early Harper's.

upset the coach. Mr. Bullard, holding on the railing of the coach as it turned over, swung around and under it upon his side. . . . Previous to expiring Mr. Bullard communicated to those in attendance the facts above stated."

The *Maine Farmer* editor added this comment:

"There is hardly a class of men whose sobriety and habits of carefulness are as of great importance as that of stage drivers."

Although travel conditions on the stagecoaches were far from luxurious or even comfortable, the customer seldom complained. There was usually a fine spirit of co-operation between driver and passengers. The fares often were asked to throw their weight from one side to the other to prevent the coach from tipping in deep ruts. "Now, gentlemen, to the right," the driver would call. The passengers would lean halfway out of the coach on that side.

The need for better roads was apparent to all. But the federal government and most of the new states were too poor to appropriate any money for the purpose. Private companies took over the road-making enterprises, and turnpikes and tollgates appeared throughout the East. The public paid tolls for the use of the roads every few miles. Thus the roads got built, but they proved not to be a money-making proposition for their promoters. Most turnpikes and toll roads lost money.

In 1806 Congress authorized a survey to select a route for a roadway leading west from Cumberland, Md., and five years later work was begun. By 1838 Congress had spent nearly $3,000,000 on the road, and it reached west

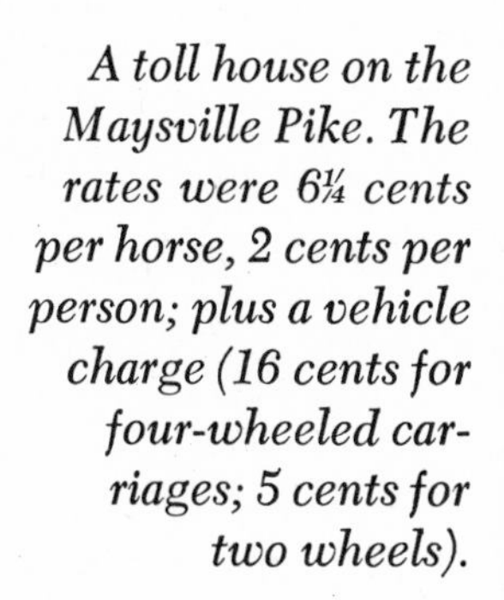

A toll house on the Maysville Pike. The rates were 6¼ cents per horse, 2 cents per person; plus a vehicle charge (16 cents for four-wheeled carriages; 5 cents for two wheels).

as far as Vandalia, Ill. For many years it was the chief line of travel for thousands of settlers on their way to the West.

One of the longest routes of the period before the railroads was the Santa Fe Trail. An expedition in 1821, led by Captain William Becknell, marked the beginning of wagon traffic on this trail running from Independence, Mo., to Santa Fe, N.M., a distance of 780 miles. There was a short cut, the Cimarron cutoff, but the long way was much safer. Even this way the danger from Indian attacks was such that wagons went together usually in trains of 26, and were accompanied by armed horsemen. Sometimes United States troops accompanied the wagon trains. Each wagon, drawn by ten oxen or mules, carried a load of about 6,000 pounds and averaged 17 miles a day.

Stagecoaches began to roll over the Santa Fe Trail in 1849, taking two weeks to make the journey. The fare was $250.

The Oregon Trail, sometimes called the Overland Trail, ran for 2,000 miles from the Missouri to the Columbia River, taking a general course through the present states of Nebraska, Wyoming, Idaho, and Oregon. In 1845 alone, more than 3,000 westward travelers passed over the Oregon Trail.

While the land pioneers went west, the trader-captains of the colonial period had given way to a new era, the beginning of the American merchant marine. Following the war of 1812, ocean trade and passenger traffic had increased to the point where shipping began to be a business in itself, distinct from trading. Shipmas-

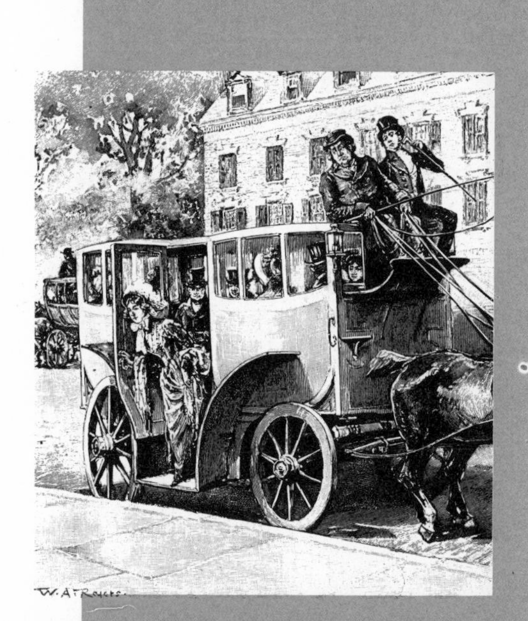

A New York City stage of the '30's held more passengers than the overland coaches.

Part of a trip over the Oregon Trail consisted of a raft voyage downriver with the wheels removed.

MILWAUKEE DIRECTORY. 150

WISCONSIN

STAGE LINES.

Leaves the General Stage Office, No. 13, Wisconsin street for Galena, via Prairieville, Delafield, Summit, Concord, Aztalan, Lake Mills, Cottage Grove, Madison, Dodgeville, Mineral Point, and Platteville to Galena.

With a branch running from Watertown, Beaver Dam, Fox Lake, Fond du Lac, to Green Bay.

Leaves the same office for Galena, via New Berlin, Mukwanago, East Troy, Troy, Johnstown, Janesville, Monroe, Wiota, Shullsburgh, and White Oak Springs to Galena.

With a branch running from Janesville, via Union to Madison, in due connection with the Galena line.

Also, a branch running from Janesville via Detroit, Roscoe, and Rockford to Dixon; connecting with the Chicago, and Galena Lines, at Rockford and Dixon.

Leaves Racine every Monday, Wednesday and Friday, for Janesville; Also, leaves Southport for Madison and Galena same days.

Leaves the same office for Chicago, via Oak Creek, Racine, Southport, Little Fort and Wheeling, to Chicago—connecting at Chicago, with the St. Louis and Michigan Stages.

Leaves the same office for Sheboygan, via Mequon, Hamburg: Saukville, Port Washington, and Sheboygan Falls to Sheboygan. JOHN FRINK & Co. Proprietors.

Milwaukee, 1848.

Wisconsin Stage Lines timetable, from Milwaukee directory, 1848.

ters advertised sailing schedules and embarked at the advertised time whether their holds were filled to capacity or not.

The first of the famous "packet" ships were those of the Black Ball Line, sailing between New York and Liverpool. By 1845 there were 52 transatlantic packets making regular voyages. At the same time, packet service was being established in the coastal trade. Small sloops of from 25 to 100 tons, usually single-masted, shuttled regularly between Atlantic ports from Maine to Virginia. Larger two-masted schooners and three-masted brigs carried on cotton trade with New Orleans and often visited South American ports. The packets carried mail as well as cargo, and because of their regular schedules merchants and editors were able to depend on receiving goods and news with certainty.

The packets took their clean lines from French luggers that had come to this country during the Revolutionary War, and the American versions first proved their worth as privateers and blockade runners. The packets were built increasingly larger and trimmer until about 1825, when a truly radical change in naval architecture was developed—the famed clipper ship.

The problem was to reproduce the lines of a small, swift vessel in a large one, and the approach was made with the building of the *Ann McKim* at Baltimore in 1832. She was

East Boston shipyard during the height of clipper ship building. From Gleason's Pictorial of 1855.

not an extreme clipper ship, however, and the experiments continued until 1843 when the 750-ton *Rainbow* was built at New York. Her stem was carried well forward, giving a concave bow, and the greatest breadth of the ship was put farther back than had ever been done in building a ship of such proportions.

Despite the ominous predictions of traditional naval architects, the *Rainbow* proved exceedingly fast and also exceptionally seaworthy even in the monsoons she was subjected to as a part of her run in the China Sea.

The *Rainbow* was followed by a host of these slim, trim clipper ships, knifing the water under huge clouds of canvas, sometimes attaining speeds as high as 20 knots, which exceeded that of any ocean steamships which appeared at the close of the clipper era. Before 1815 a crossing from Liverpool to New York took from 40 to 50 days, while the eastbound voyage took about one-third less. By 1848 the clipper ships had reduced the westward crossing to a little over 30 days.

There were drawbacks to the clipper ships: they were expensive to build and their huge toppings of sails required a large and well-trained crew. Had it not been for the rich China trade, which included such profitable cargoes as opium, and the discovery of gold in California, the era of the clipper ship might have ended earlier.

The gold rush beginning in 1848 created an insatiable

(continued on page 30)

Cotton was the cargo for the ships calling at southern coastal harbors.

Packet Morning Star, *painted as an artist saw her off Boston Light.*

The Franklin *of Boston was the first vessel to open trade with Japan under Captain James Devereaux of Salem, in 1799.*

The Washington Irving, *a Donald McKay packet of the Train line.*

The Antelope, *built at East Boston in 1843 for trade with the Orient.*

The clipper ship Coeur de Leon *in Hong Kong harbor, painted by*

Chinese artist Chong Qua. By tradition, all the extreme clipper ships were painted black to accentuate their clouds of white canvas.

John Fitch's first steamboat used engine power to operate a set of oars. This clumsy vessel operated on the Delaware River in 1786 at a speed of about eight miles an hour.

Fitch's continuing experiments included boats operated by paddle wheels and the first known screw propeller, in 1796.

Oliver Evans, another pioneer in steamboat trials, called this 1804 model the Orukter Amphibolos.

demand for clipper ships, since there was no other way to get goods and men to the gold fields at the other end of the continent speedily. The wagon trains were far too slow for men with gold fever. The owners of clippers earned fabulous amounts for voyages from New York to San Francisco. In 1850, for instance, the *Samuel Russell* carried about 1,200 tons of cargo at freight rates of $60 a ton, and her gross earnings of $72,000 for the one voyage were a little more than her building cost! Between 1843 and 1853, 270 clipper ships were built, and during one frantic year, 90,000 people were carried around South America to California. Crazy were the cargoes they carried: one ship bore thousands of cradles – not for babies, but for conversion to gold-screening devices.

When cargoes became more prosaic and less profitable, the earnings of the clipper ships began to decline. Their end was signaled on the ocean by the improvement of steamships, with their larger cargo-carrying ability, and in the coast-to-coast trade by the completion of the first transcontinental railroad line in 1869.

WHILE THE UNITED STATES led the world in building ships of wood and sail, the search for a more efficient means of marine transportation was underway in America as well as in Europe. In 1786 John Fitch of Connecticut built a steam vessel that reached a speed of eight miles an hour. He followed this with several other experimental steam-propelled boats. Little interest was displayed, however, and American shipbuilders concentrated on improving and refining their clipper ships. It

Launching of the steam frigate, Fulton the First, *in New York harbor Oct. 29, 1814. This 84-ton side-wheeled vessel was the first U. S. steam warship.*

was the British who made greatest progress in the marine engine. When Robert Fulton launched the *Clermont* in the Hudson River in 1807, it was the first commercially successful steamship in this country. But only the hull was made in the United States. The engine was imported from England.

A steamship operating on inland waterways, not requiring masts and sails, could have a higher superstructure so that there was ample room for carrying freight and passengers profitably. Seagoing steamships, on the other hand, were still basically sailing ships with full sets of canvas. Engines and paddle wheels provided auxiliary power which was useful chiefly during calms or against strong head winds. The space occupied by the machinery and fuel and the drag of the paddle wheels while navigating under sail hardly compensated for the added speed.

Although the general superiority of British steamships was unquestioned, it was the American *Savannah* that made the first Atlantic crossing. The ship, built by Francis Sackett in New York, sailed from Savannah, Ga., on May 24, 1819, and reached Liverpool 27 days later. Steam was used for a total of 80 hours on the voyage, but it had to be discontinued when the supply of wood being used for fuel ran out. Perhaps the best indication of public feeling about steamships was the humor current at the time. When the *Savannah* made her first crossing, one newspaper commented: "The engine hardly detracted from her sailing qualities." Another joke of the day was the suggestion that every steamship be followed by a fleet of sailing ships carrying fuel.

The Clermont, *famous as "Fulton's Folly," began to ply the Hudson River in 1807 between New York and Albany as the first successful commercial steamboat.*

The Savannah, *first steamship to cross the Atlantic. The engine was in use on only three of the 27 days of the voyage.*

Improved steamships of the 30's and 40's brought speedier crossings, but the public estimation of steamships continued to be low. The wooden vessels often caught fire from flying embers and overheated fireboxes. The engines, clumsy and unreliable, were equipped with few safety devices. Often the first indication of trouble came from a bursting pipe or boiler. To avoid corrosion of the boilers, it was necessary to blow out the brine deposited by sea water at regular intervals and then refill with cold sea water. Time was lost each time this had to be done. The increased size and strength required of the hull to carry the cumbersome engine and the fuel created new problems for naval architects. Along with other early ocean-going steamships, the *Savannah* eventually had her engines removed and ended her days as a sailing ship.

The first really satisfactory Atlantic crossing was that

Paddlewheel streamers of the U. S. Mail Steam Ship Company were famous in the coastal and river trade during the 1850's.

The Mississippi, which means "the great river," was named by the Ojibway. The great river had long served as a boundary between Indian tribes before the white men ventured into this territory. The Mississippi then became the main highway in the discovery and exploration of an inland empire.

of the *Great Western,* a giant of 1,340 tons, which arrived in New York on April 23, 1838, 15 days after her departure from Bristol, England. During that same year there were 11 more successful crossings, and the steamship began to find its place in ocean commerce.

The most significant advances to follow were the utilization of the screw propeller and the use of iron for hulls. But American shipbuilders, masters with wood, looked on iron with contempt and its use in shipbuilding fell largely to boilermakers and machinists. After the California gold rush was over and the clipper ships declined, American shipbuilding lost ground generally. This may have been due to the fact that the entire country did not share the seaward orientation of the eastern states. Attention had been turned to the opening of the West, both in overland and river transportation.

The number of flatboats on western waters actually increased after the coming of the steamboat. The freight business had been so stimulated by the advent of steam vessels that the steamboats could not handle all of it.

Keelboats, of which this is an impressive example, had a hull form that was adopted almost unchanged by steamboats.

The exploits of Mike Fink, the roughest and toughest of keelboatmen, became legendary.

FROM THE BEGINNING, the Mississippi River system played an important role in the westward movement. But the flatboats and the rafts and the canoes were not capable of large scale movement of passengers and freight. It was the river steamer that turned the Mississippi and the Ohio and the Missouri into great arteries of commerce.

The story of the steamboat starts with the historic maiden voyage of Robert Fulton's *Clermont* on the Hudson River in August, 1807. Although the *Clermont* never ventured into western waters, Fulton had built the steamboat with the possibilities of the Mississippi River system in mind. Having succeeded with the *Clermont,* Fulton received the financial backing of Robert Livingston to build another ship.

The result was the steamboat *New Orleans,* which left Pittsburgh on Oct. 20, 1811, on her maiden voyage. She made the 700-mile run to Louisville in 70 hours. This first successful steamboat on western waters had a capacity of between 300 to 400 tons and measured 138 feet long and 30 feet across the beam. She carried two masts equipped with sails and was driven by a stern paddle wheel. The freight was carried in the bow of the boat, the exposed engine and smokestack stood in the middle and the cabin was built in the rear. The boat is said to have cost $40,000 to build, with half of this sum earned during its first season of operation.

The *New Orleans* was probably considered a good ship during the 1810's, but she couldn't go upstream. The strong current of the river was too much for her weak

The Washington, *built by Henry Shreve, was the first real river steamer.*

engine and dragging keel. So she wound up with a regular route in the deep-water country between New Orleans and Natchez until 1814, when she was wrecked on a snag at Baton Rouge.

The success of the *New Orleans* led to the organization of the Ohio Steamboat Navigation Company with Fulton and Livingston as chief stockholders. To make sure that they would not be hampered by competition, this company obtained a monopoly from the state of Orleans which granted them "sole and exclusive right and privilege to build, construct, make use, employ and navigate boats, vessels and water crafts, urged or propelled through the water by fire or steam, in all the creeks, rivers, bays and waters whatsoever, within the jurisdiction of the territory, during 18 years from Jan. 1, 1812." The company then launched three more steamboats by 1815: the *Vesuvius*, the *Etna*, and the second *New Orleans*.

Another shipbuilder, Daniel French, brought out the 25-ton stern-wheeler *Comet*. French's boat made a few trips in 1813 and 1814, but she, too, could not make it past Natchez on the upstream trip from New Orleans, so she was dismantled and her engine was put in a cotton gin. However, French was not discouraged. He got Henry Shreve for a partner and formed the Monongahela Steam Navigation Company. Shreve, for whom the city of Shreveport was later named, captained French's second boat, the 45-ton *Enterprise*.

Despite the monopoly held by Fulton and Livingston on the lower Mississippi, the *Enterprise* became the first

St. Louis in 1832 was a growing town of 25,000 persons.

Cairo, at the point where the Ohio joins the Mississippi.

The Anson Northrup, *typical of the small, cheaply built, wooden steamboats of the early era.*

Fort Snelling was typical of the many military posts erected because of the friction between Indians and fur traders.

The United States bought the Louisiana Territory from France in 1803 to get control of New Orleans, which virtually commanded the Mississippi.

steamboat to ascend the Mississippi and Ohio rivers. She traveled from New Orleans to Louisville in 25 days in 1815. Shortly after her successful voyage, the *Enterprise* was seized for violating the monopoly. Henry Shreve then began his fight to open the Mississippi to all, and the monopoly claim was withdrawn in 1819.

Having solved one problem, Henry Shreve turned his attention to correcting the many flaws in the *Enterprise.* The result was the building of his own steamship, the *George Washington,* which has been considered by many as the first real steamboat. He threw out all accepted principles of shipbuilding and the *George Washington* became the prototype for some 5,000 or more steamboats.

SHREVE'S BOAT was built to run *on* the water instead of *in* it as had her predecessors. She was 136 feet long and 28 feet across the beam, and her hull resembled a keelboat. The resultant sacrifice in hold space had to be made up in deck area, which was more convenient for storage of cargo anyhow, because of the frequent loading stops and primitive docking conditions. Also, high freeboard was unnecessary in the comparatively waveless waters of the rivers. It was an extremely shallow and almost but not entirely flat hull, which sat just about flat on the water.

The engines, first of the high pressure type to be used in a boat, were placed on the deck instead of in the hull. Then, to compensate for the space taken away from the deck, another deck was added. Thus resulted the first double-decker steamboat. Two smokestacks were placed side by side on deck as on every western river steamboat since. Launched in June, 1817, the *George Washington* made the round trip between Louisville and New Orleans in 45 days and proved the practicability of upstream navigation for the first time.

After 1811, steamboats appeared one by one on the Mississippi, but the inhabitants of St. Louis were still waiting to see their first one in 1817. Finally, in August of that year, the *Zebulon M. Pike* arrived.

In 1819, the *Independence* became the first steamboat to navigate the Missouri River, going as far as Chariton, Mo. The upper Mississippi was not penetrated until 1823, when the *Virginia* left St. Louis on April 21 and arrived in Fort Snelling, Minn., some 800 miles away, 20 days later.

From 1817 on, the number of steamboats on the western rivers increased rapidly. Eight new steam vessels were launched in 1817. During 1818 and 1819, more than 60 new boats were built, which was four times as many as were constructed in the previous seven years. Even with

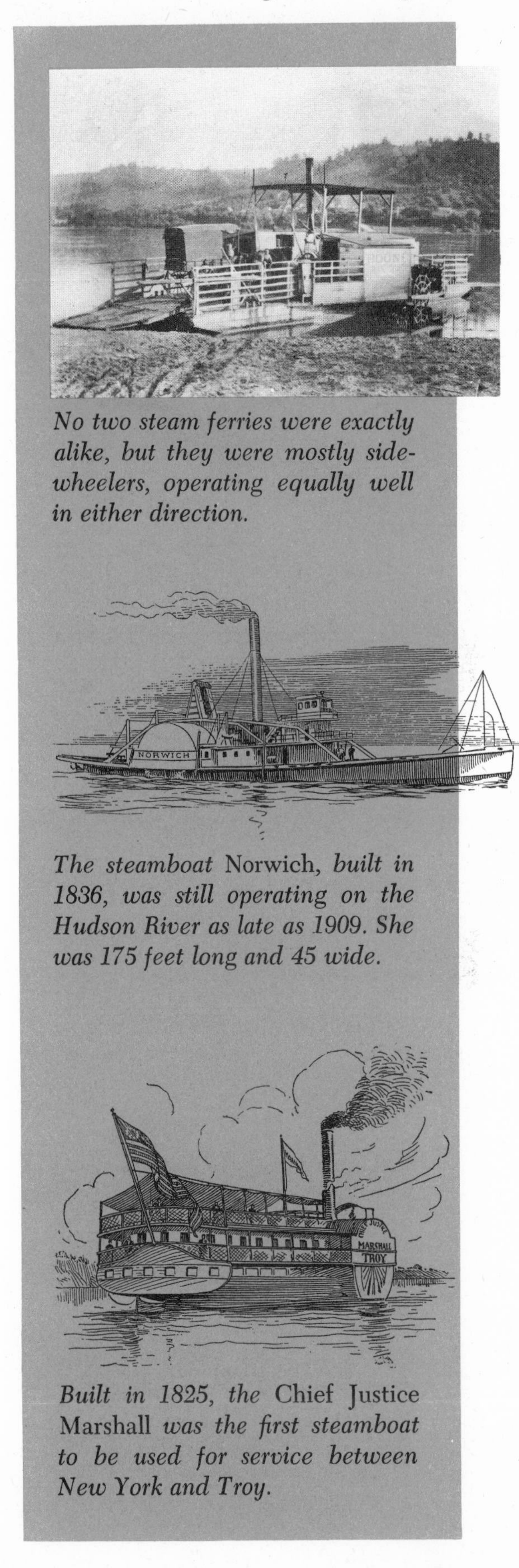

No two steam ferries were exactly alike, but they were mostly side-wheelers, operating equally well in either direction.

The steamboat Norwich, *built in 1836, was still operating on the Hudson River as late as 1909. She was 175 feet long and 45 wide.*

Built in 1825, the Chief Justice Marshall *was the first steamboat to be used for service between New York and Troy.*

In 1844, the steamer Missouri *made the trip from St. Louis to New Orleans and back in 4 days and 19 hours. This came close to breaking the record on this run, which was set by the* J. M. White *five years earlier.*

Even a small stern-wheeler on a small river put up impressive clouds of smoke and steam.

all these boats in use they still carried only about one-third of the total trade on western waters. This, however, was a substantial increase over 1817, when nine-tenths of the trade had been carried by other types of craft. In 1818, the United States Post Office made its first mail contracts with the steamboats.

Before the second decade of the nineteenth century drew to a close, steamboats had found their way into all the tributaries of the Mississippi and had penetrated as far north as St. Paul. Records show that by 1830 the number of steamboats in operation came to 296, measuring 31,506 tons. New Orleans reported that 2,300 steamboats had arrived in her ports during 1934. During that year, 304 steamers were built in Pittsburgh, 221 in Cincinnati, 103 in Louisville, 19 in Nashville, and 35 in other cities. Despite this rapid growth of the steamboat trade, the big day for the river queens was still to come.

THE EARLY STEAMBOATS were hardly visions of beauty. They had been built for the express purpose of taking passengers and freight from one point to another, and little attention was paid to comfort and ornamentation. Passengers had to pay more for quarters farther aft than those forward. The reason was obvious. If the boat blew up, which was likely, the passengers farthest away from the boilers stood a better chance of escaping death.

Accidents on the river were a matter of course, and the steamboat owners seemed quite nonchalant about them. When they built a boat, it was expected that it might last only two or three seasons. The engines were inefficient and cheaply built. Cordwood was used for fuel, and the inadequate stacks frequently showered the wooden decks with sparks and embers. The crews were poorly paid and mostly inexperienced or incompetent. This period of cheap construction and haphazard operation lasted till about 1838. There is no record showing exactly how many of the early steamboats went to an untimely end, but it is safe to say that very few died a peaceful and natural death. One source reports that between 1831 and 1833, 66 boats went out of commission, and only 15 of these ended their days on the scrap pile. The other 51 sank, exploded, burned, got caught on snags, or were lost in the ice. To make matters worse, many sporting captains raced their boats and ended up with burst boilers.

On the whole, the early steamboats were rather slow. The average speed was 12 miles an hour downstream and six or seven miles an hour upstream. Of course, this was considered quite fast to river travelers who had been accustomed to floating at the rate of the current, which might be two to four miles an hour except during floods when it would go as high as ten.

Steamboat schedules during the 1820's and 1830's were extremely flexible. It was not rare for a vessel scheduled to leave at 8 o'clock in the morning to depart late in the afternoon. Sometimes there was a wait of two or three days, until the captain felt that he had a payload of freight and passengers. The only compensation an impatient passenger had was that once he had paid his fare, the steamboat company had to provide accommodations and food as long as he was aboard.

Fares varied according to the accommodations requested. In 1833, cabin fare from Pittsburgh to St. Louis was $24 and deck passage cost $8. The cabin fare from St. Louis to Galena was $15 and deck passage $8. One could travel even more cheaply as a deck hand. Many immigrants traveled this way and paid only $10 to go from Pittsburgh to Galena. Although traveling on deck was inexpensive, it was an unpleasant and often unhealthful way to travel. Passengers had to share the deck with the cargo, which might be cattle, horses, wagons, plows, barrels of flour, and other miscellaneous items. The washrooms were usually untidy and as many as 50 passengers used the same towel, which was suspended from the ceiling. As for the food, it was hardly better than the "grub pile" fed to the crew. Because of the filthy conditions and coarse food, cholera often broke out and claimed many lives.

THE UPPER AND LOWER Mississippi can be considered as two distinct rivers as far as traffic was concerned. St. Louis marked the dividing point, and passengers and

Blazing braziers of pine knots were used to light the way through the treacherous, snag-filled bayous at night.

The steamboat Sultana *was well-known along the Mississippi during the peak years of steamboat racing.*

Trees along the banks rotted and fell into the water to complicate navigation. The ones which floated were bad, but the logs which barely floated, with one water-logged end resting on the bottom, were a real menace.

Collision was but one way to end a steamboat's career.

Rapids on the upper Mississippi, near Keokuk, Iowa.

freight that had to go all the way up or down the river changed boats there. The types of boats used on the upper river differed from those on the lower river. The shallow channel and rapids on the upper river created such an impediment during the low water stages that upper Mississippi boats had to be smaller than those operating south of St. Louis.

Steamboating on the upper Mississippi received its initial impetus from the presence of military forts at strategic points along the river. The traffic to the forts consisted of boatloads of troops and supplies. After the voyage of the *Virginia* in 1823, 14 boats followed in her wake by the summer of 1826, all with loads of troops and military supplies.

Transportation of troops during the wars with the Indians was usually more profitable than peacetime movements, as the former moves were made under pressure when no time could be lost in obtaining competitive bids. In the long run, however, more troops were moved during times of peace.

The steamboats reaped even larger profits from the transportation of military supplies and equipment. Even as late as 1853, the St. Paul trade in government supplies still exceeded the trade in goods needed by the settlers. It is estimated that the upper-river steamboats earned almost $3,000,000 because of the presence of military forts.

As the white men moved into the Indians' hunting grounds in the upper Mississippi Valley during the early part of the nineteenth century steamboats were called upon to move parties from both sides to the treaty grounds. This process became so expensive that the government switched to the policy of having small Indian delegations brought to Washington, D.C. Steamboats did good business in this way, too.

Treaty after treaty was signed, and more and more

A major tragedy in the history of steamboating was the great fire among the tightly packed boats at St. Louis on the night of May 17, 1849

territory was taken away from the Indians. All these treaties meant annuities for the Indians, and the steamboats were provided with still another source of income. A contract to deliver annuities in cash and goods was much sought after.

Then came the signing of the Treaty of Traverse des Sioux on July 23, 1851, which marked the beginning of the end of Indian land title in the upper Mississippi Valley. The Indians began to migrate westward, and of course the steamboats were ready and willing to take the red men to new hunting grounds.

The majority of immigrants settling in the upper Mississippi Valley were brought by steamboat. Between 1850 and 1870, the side-wheelers were jammed with immigrants heading northward. Steamboat captains reaped a rich harvest throughout this period. The mad stampedes to California and Oregon were almost insignificant compared with the huge waves of land-hungry pioneers that swarmed up the Mississippi. The statistics of arrivals at St. Louis of steamboats from the upper river testify to this. The number jumped from 647 in 1848 to 1,524 in 1860.

The beauties of the northland were exploited from the earliest days of the steamboat era. Perhaps the earliest pleasure-seeking trip on record was that of the steamboat *Lawrence* to the Falls of St. Anthony, Minn., in 1826. However, until the Black Hawk War had eliminated the danger of Indian attack, few passengers were found on the upper-river craft. Then along came George Catlin to propose his "fashionable tour" – an excursion trip up the Mississippi to Fort Snelling, where the passengers got off to gaze at the wonders of the St. Anthony and Minnehaha Falls.

Realizing the possibilities in such a tour, Captain Daniel Smith Harris and his brother Robert Scribe Harris launched in 1837 the steamboat *Smelter,* which was

Boats stopped daily to wood up.

Racing boats were familiar sights.

The arrival and departure of steamboats caused much excitement in the smaller river towns such as Warren, Pa. Men, women, children, dogs, cats and horses gathered along the river to witness the great event.

equipped with private staterooms. As the "fashionable tour" became more popular, the steamboat accommodations improved to compete for the excursion business. Captain Orrin Smith fitted his *Brazil* with two-berth staterooms having doorways leading into the saloon, which ran full length down the middle of the boat. Doorways also opened out upon the deck. Captain Joseph Throckmorton introduced spring mattresses on his ship, the *Malta*.

As the competition increased for the excursion trade, captains offered still other inducements. By the middle of the century, most of the passenger boats were provided with some kind of band or orchestra. Dining tables were supplied with the best food that money could buy, and passengers soon learned which boats served the best meals.

Although the "fashionable tour" was the most glamor-

The steamboat Jacob Strader *was openly advertised as being "low pressure." The distinction was made between high and low pressure because the more sensitive travelers regarded low-pressure crafts as less dangerous.*

Cincinnati in 1848 was typical of inland river towns, with a long sloping grade forming the loading area. This view shows the water at a fairly low level. If it rises the boats are merely tied up higher on the slope.

ous of the excursions, there were many other steamboat pleasure trips taking place all along the Mississippi and Ohio rivers. Captains engaged in this excursion trade usually made several profitable voyages each season. Many of the trips were sponsored by civic, political, fraternal, or religious groups. The Sunday School excursions held on the Fourth of July were extremely popular.

To climax this colorful era of excursions came the Falls of St. Anthony Excursion in 1854. This trip celebrated the completion of the first railroad to connect the Atlantic Ocean and the Mississippi River. Leading citizens from all over the country were invited to participate in a joint railroad and steamboat excursion to the Falls. There were many acceptances. The excursionists gathered at the Rock Island station in Chicago early on the morning of June 5, and shortly after 8 A.M. two trains of nine coaches each

The New Orleans of 1853 was a busy and prosperous city which seemed to be on its way to becoming the nation's greatest metropolis. All the through-trade steamboats eventually reached New Orleans.

The steamboats of the middle 1800's were gaudily decorated. The Phil Sheridan *is a good example with its mural-painted paddlebox, eight-sided pilot-house with gilded dome, and oak-leaf-decorated stacks.*

The floating theater contained a stage, footlights, scenery, a sloping floor with seats, a balcony and private boxes. A stern-wheeler, tied at the rear, pushed it from town to town.

left the city. At Rock Island, Ill., several hours later, the passengers boarded steamboats which proceeded up the Mississippi to the Falls of St. Anthony, Lake Calhoun, Minnehaha Falls and Fort Snelling. This was by far the most spectacular event of its kind that the West had ever witnessed.

MANY PRODUCTIVE INDUSTRIES, among which fur trapping, lead mining and grain raising predominated, sprang up in the regions served by the river boats.

The fur traders were most active during the early part of the nineteenth century when the Indians still held land in the upper valley. The steamboats carried supplies and equipment up the river for the Indian trade and large

The America *was a typical "cotton packet" with its lower deck flaring prominently beyond the cabin structure to allow loading of bales in tiers.*

quantities of furs were shipped downstream. The fur-trading communities became so dependent on the steamboats that the American Fur Company and other traders began to assume heavy financial interests in the upper Mississippi craft.

The presence of lead mines in the upper valley did much to develop steamboating in the first quarter of the nineteenth century. First of all, it encouraged many workers to migrate to this region. And once the settlements were established, ever-increasing supplies had to be brought to them. Then the lead ore had to be shipped out of the region, which gave the steamboat owners approximately two-fifths of the total revenue from upstream trade.

No other single factor during the period between 1823 and 1848 was as important in developing steamboating on the upper Mississippi as the shipment of lead. During this quarter of a century, 472,000,000 tons of lead, worth $14,-178,000, were mined and shipped down the Mississippi and huge profits were reaped by steamboat captains and owners from this traffic.

In the 1870's, when the passenger traffic on the upper river was declining rapidly, the grain trade reached enormous proportions. Most of the grain was shipped by steamboat, and once again captains were able to pocket profits and stave off for almost a generation the decline and ultimate extinction of steamboating on the upper Mississippi.

During the second era of steamboating, which lasted from about 1840 until the outbreak of the Civil War, the queens ruled the western rivers, especially the lower Mis-

Bales of cotton could be seen everywhere on the levees of New Orleans.

St. Paul, Minn., in 1855 was the river terminal for the boatloads of upper valley settlers.

Vacationists packed the steamboats to Lake St. Croix.

sissippi, in high fashion. The 1830's and 1840's were flush times for many American cities, and traveling between them were the steamboats, loaded with freight and passengers. To meet the demand for luxuries and comforts which the passengers could now afford, the steamboats went in for elaborate architecture, dependable machinery and lavish entertainment.

What lead was to the upper Mississippi, cotton was to the lower river and its many tributaries – the Red, Arkansas, Ouachita, Black, and Yazoo rivers and the countless navigable bayous. The steamboat provided an extremely useful tool for the cotton growers. A plantation owner, employing slave labor, could become rich quite simply by raising cotton, sometimes by the thousands of bales, and loading it directly from the river or bayou bank for shipment to New Orleans.

A particular type of steamboat was required to carry cotton. The boat had to be equipped with extremely wide guards held up by chains, on which the bales of cotton could be loaded. Space also had to be provided for passengers and other freight. With the steamboats to take the cotton to market, production increased from a total southern output of five million pounds in 1812 to 500 million pounds from Tennessee, Louisiana and Mississippi alone.

Among the popular steamboats after 1840 were the *General Brown, William French, Ed Shippen, Diana, Bell Key, Bostona I, Grace Darling, Peytona, Atlantic, Niagara, R. J. Ward, Eclipse* and *Shotwell*. Then there was the old *J. M. White*, the second of three steamboats bearing the same name. Built in 1843, the *White* was the fastest steam craft in the world. In 1844, she made the trip from St. Louis to New Orleans and back, which is about 2,436 miles, in

Here is Hannibal, Mo., the home town of Mark Twain. In the distance is Jackson Island where Tom Sawyer and Huckleberry Finn became pirates.

approximately a week. This accomplishment was not bettered for at least a quarter of a century. The wheels of the *J. M. White* were placed about 25 feet farther back than was the custom, and within a few years every new steamboat was built with side wheels placed far back of the center.

No other period in the colorful history of steamboating equaled the heavy passenger traffic of the decade between 1850 and 1860. Comfortable accommodations, tasty meals, lavish entertainment, and cordial hospitality became matter of course.

Steamboat builders competed to outdo each other in ostentation. Once the passenger got settled in the lounge with its thick carpets, cut-glass chandeliers, and oil paintings, it was as though he were in an ornate hotel lobby. There were white gingerbread work and gold leaf everywhere – on cabins, railings, hurricane roof and cornices of pilothouse and officers' quarters. Gaudy pictures, usually depicting home and pastoral scenes, were painted on paddle boxes, cabin ceilings, stateroom doors, and saloon walls.

The *Eclipse*, one of the most decorative of the packets during the 1850's, boasted of having at the ends of the main cabin gilt statuettes of Henry Clay and Andrew Jackson. There was a piano for use by the passengers and 48 bridal chambers were advertised.

These were large boats that ruled the western rivers just before the outbreak of the Civil War. Some of them were over 250 feet long. They accommodated three to four hundred passengers and five to seven hundred tons of freight. The peak year in the number of steamboats afloat was reached in 1859 when the approximate total was 2,000. Compare this with the 850 in service in 1850.

Flatboat-men and steamboat-men regarded each other with mutual fear and hatred.

St. Anthony Falls, Minn., attracted many an excursionist.

The life of a wealthy planter was a good life indeed. And the wealthiest of them all lived right on the river bank where cotton could be loaded directly onto the boats.

The steamboat with the fanciest menu often got most of the passenger trade.

Passenger fares were governed by the number of passengers and boats in the trade, the season of the year, and the stage of water. Competition often brought rates to a ruinous level with times when the captain could not pay for the wood bill after a trip. A representative price for cabin fare from New Orleans to St. Louis was $25. Deck passage was around $3 or $4 for adults and half fare for children. Deck passengers had to provide their own food and assist the crew in wooding up.

Although most of the thousands of boats on the western rivers were independently operated, there were a few organized lines from the very beginning. One of these pioneers was the United States Mail Line, which began operations with the launching of the *General Pike* in 1818. As early as 1847, this line was operating daily boats out of New Orleans to St. Louis. The first five years of service to Memphis were on a three-days-a-week schedule, but it became a daily run when the cotton trade was in full swing. The Mail Line prospered during the 1850's with such vessels as the *Jacob Strader, Moses McClennan, Fashion, Alvin Adams, Northerner, Southerner, High Flyer, Cape Caterlin* and *Telegraph III*.

The Lightning Line, operating boats on both the Ohio and Missouri rivers, established a fine reputation for regular service, comfort, speed, and cuisine. It began operations in 1856 between Jefferson City and Kansas City. It also served well the cities along the Ohio River. The *Robert J. Ward, Diana, Baltic, John Raine, Antelope, Fanny Bullitt,* and *E. H. Fairchild* were some of the vessels on the Lightning Line.

Also operating on the Ohio and Missouri rivers was the Union Packet Line, organized in 1858. It provided daily service from Louisville to Wheeling, W. Va., where connections were made with the Baltimore and Ohio Railroad. On the Missouri River, this line operated between St. Louis and St. Joseph. Owned and operated by Captain Tom Brierly, the Union Packet Line boasted of having one of the most pretentious arrays of side-wheelers on western waters. Among these were the *Morning Star, Evening Star,* and *Polar Star.*

The City of Vicksburg *was one of many steamboats built by the Howard Shipyard of Jeffersonville, Ind.*

A line of "short boats" was especially organized to squeeze through the canals built around the falls at Louisville and continue southward. This line was known as the Cincinnati and New Orleans Express Line. Before the formation of this line, all passengers and freight going either up or down stream had to be transferred at Louisville. The short boats were small and lacked speed, but prompt and reliable service, excellent accommodations, and fine food made up those shortcomings adequately.

Steamboating on western waters was as much a way

The Grand Republic *had one of the most elaborate cabins ever built on a steamboat. The chandeliers held clusters of oil lamps with glass bell-shaped deflectors to keep the oily soot from marring the woodwork.*

of life as a means of transportation. The side-wheelers became an integral part in the lives of passengers as well as of riverside inhabitants. Life on the steamboat was made interesting by such diversions as theatrical and musical entertainment, gambling, drinking, and racing other steamboats.

There were interminable poker games for those who chose to gamble. And the nonprofessional card players were usually fleeced, as the river gamblers were clever and often dishonest. The barroom was the favorite habitat of many a passenger. Those who cared neither for gambling nor drinking could content themselves merely with eating, for lavish meals were served aboard.

Informal musical entertainment was often provided by the vessel's crew on board and by stevedores at the landings. The larger boats carried full brass bands or orchestras. Individual musicians of wide renown were often featured to attract customers.

It was the second Robert E. Lee, *built in 1866, which was known for its great race against the* Natchez. *The original* Lee *was built and operated by Captain T. Rezin Belle, who named his ship after his lifelong friend.*

Steamboat hospitality became famous. Some passengers traveled free of charge as guests of the captain. This may seem like a lavish way of doing business, but it paid off in the long run. For only those who would eventually give business to the steamboats were treated so royally.

The grand hospitality was also extended to the river banks. It was a big event when a steamboat drew into a landing on the lower Mississippi, and a big crowd gathered about. As soon as the gangplank was lowered, a member of the crew would come ashore with a tray of delicacies for

those on the river bank. Nuts, ices, grapes, celery, pineapple, roast beef, and fish would be served to the women and children while the gentlemen went aboard for drinks with the captain. This again was public relations which usually brought dividends.

Steamboat racing became one of the most popular sports in the Mississippi Valley. Nothing could build up prestige faster than a steamboat winning a race from another vessel or against time itself. Such racers as the *J. M. White, Sultana, A. L. Shotwell, Eclipse, Natchez*

The steamboat Eclipse, *built at New Albany, Ind., had carrying capacity of 1200 tons. She was able to make 18 miles an hour in still water, and with a light cargo and high pressure could attain a speed of 24 miles an hour.*

Steamboats and flatboats shared the Mississippi during the middle 1800's.

Whether it be day or night, steamboats raced each other with the same vigor. The people ashore were just as interested in the outcome of the race as were the passengers aboard.

The Natchez, *a mail boat running between Vicksburg and New Orleans, was operated by Captain Leathers. Much of the course of the famous race was in strange waters for Captain Leathers, so the* Natchez *was at a distinct disadvantage.*

and *Robert E. Lee* were favorite topics of conversation up and down the river.

Of all the races, the one which gained the most fame was that between the *Robert E. Lee* and the *Natchez* in 1870. Both were fast boats capable of doing 18 miles per hour against a normal current and at least 25 miles per hour downstream. So the bets were laid and a crowd gathered at the river in New Orleans on June 30, 1870, to watch the two vessels leave at 4:55 P.M. Hour after hour the two steamboats raced side by side. Then they ran into a fog at Devil's Island. The *Robert E. Lee* kept on, but the *Natchez* stopped for six hours until the fog cleared. The *Lee* was the first to arrive in St. Louis, having covered a distance of 1,210 miles in three days, 18 hours, and 30 minutes. The *Natchez* arrived six hours and 33 minutes later. Because the *Natchez* had lost time in the fog, the friends of this boat never accepted the result as a decisive defeat.

The race against time itself was won over and over again as the steamboats became swifter with each succeeding generation. The *Enterprise*'s record of 25 days from New Orleans to St. Louis was cut to nine and a half days by the *General Brown* in 1826. By 1860 the same distance was covered in less than four days by many vessels. The record for the New Orleans to Louisville run was 25 days in Henry Shreve's day, but by 1853 the same distance was made in four days, nine hours, and 31 minutes by the *Eclipse*. The *A. L. Shotwell* beat this record by 12 minutes. The *Comet*'s five-day-and-ten-hour time between New Orleans and Natchez was a record in 1814, but both the *Natchez* and the *Robert E. Lee* lowered the time to 17 hours and 11 minutes by 1870.

Manifest of the ship North Alabama.

MANIFEST

JAMES HOWARD

E. D. PEGRAM, Master. J. H. CHASSAING, Clerk.

TO

RICHARDSON & MAY,

From Memphis to New Orleans

NOVEMBER 3d, 1875.

CONSIGNORS	No. Bales
King & Clopton,	632
W. E. & C. L. Moore,	491
Nelson & Hanks	218

The Martha Jewett *was one of many colorful packets which inspired the writers of popular songs.*

By 1850 accidents became so numerous that the federal government stepped in. Captain Davis Embree had made a survey which listed 618 steamboats lost from the date of the introduction of steam on the rivers through 1848. Forty-five were lost by collision, 104 by fire, and 469 wrecked on snags. This total did not account for the hundreds of ships lost through mechanical failure, such as explosion, collapsing flues and bursting steam pipes. In 1852, the government enacted statutes requiring steamboat inspection, governing construction and operation of steam engines, and providing for the removal of snags and sandbars from the channels.

THEN there were the showboats, the floating theaters famous in fact and fiction. These were great barges towed by steamers. (To "tow" a barge on the Mississippi river system means to push it, with the towboat lashed flush against the stern of the barge.) The showboat barges consisted of a lower deck for whites, an upper deck for Negroes, a stage, and dressing rooms which were also used as staterooms by members of the acting troupe. The galley, company mess hall, laundry and crew's quarters were located on the towboat.

The arrival of a showboat was heralded by its calliope, audible for 10 miles up and down the river. This instrument, termed by some music lovers as a cross-breeding of a fire engine with a pipe organ, was a series of steam whistles, pitched to produce the notes of the scale, and grouped together and operated from a keyboard. It was the invention of a Worcester, Mass., beekeeper, Joshua C. Stoddard. Patenting his idea in 1855, Stoddard formed the American Steam Music Company and in 1856 gave a

The Suwanee *is modeled after the small river boats which once plied the Mississippi. The engines were originally in a boat used by Thomas Edison.*

concert in New York harbor from the tugboat *Union.*

With more shrillness than an oboe, more overtones than an organ and the overall blare of a brass band, the calliope called together an enthusiastic crowd of patrons long before the showboat arrived at a river town. The spine-tingling qualities of the calliope still are recognized by circuses, although only a few now are steam-operated.

The bitter rivalry between steamboats and railroads began even before the outbreak of the War Between the States. The Rock Island Railroad built a wooden bridge across the river at Davenport and the first train crossed over it on April 22, 1856. Two weeks later, the packet boat *Effie Alton* tried to pass under the bridge and crashed into a central pier. The boat's galley tipped over and set fire to the packet and then to the wooden bridge.

Then the accusations began to fly. The railroad charged that the pilot of the *Effie Alton* deliberately wrecked his vessel in order to destroy the bridge. The steamboat company in turn sued the railroad for damages. The case ended in a compromise. However, bridge laws were enacted to guard against obstructions to navigation on the rivers. The steamboatmen also agreed to lower their smokestacks so that they could pass under the bridges.

The year of 1861 marked the beginning of the end for the steamboats. First, the federal government slapped on an embargo denying shippers the use of the rivers. Then the actual outbreak of war sent the vessels scurrying into the tributaries and bayous to seek refuge. By the dozens the packets were sunk, burned, or simply neglected.

The federal government, however, needed big packets on the Ohio and Mississippi to transport troops and supplies. To meet this need about 40 fine boats were built.

Originally a packet, the Conestoga *was converted to a gunboat to serve during the Civil War. The* Conestoga *along with the* Lexington *and* Tyler *were the first Union Navy gunboats used on the Mississippi.*

The gunboat Osage *was designed and built by Captain James B. Eads during the Civil War. A number of these propeller "monitors" were built but most of them appeared too late to be of actual service.*

Although the passenger traffic on the steamboats diminished as the railroads grew, many stern-wheelers remained in service as towboats for coal and freight barges.

On the whole, however, the Civil War played havoc with the steamboat business. The southerners suffered more than the northerners, since all of the fighting took place in southern waters. And many of the vessels that had fled into the tributaries had rotted during the war and were not worth reconditioning. The scarcity of capital after the war also made it difficult for the South to replace

The hulls, built to float flat in calm water, had not much stiffness.

The City of Louisville, *built during the closing years of steamboating, was not as elaborate as her predecessors. But she was still a fine ship – with 72 staterooms.*

When she went down in 1918, she closed 87 years of daily trade between Cincinnati and Louisville.

the lost boats. The lower river and its tributaries were completely devoid of anything resembling regular service.

To make matters worse, many of the shippers who had been denied use of waterways during the war had turned to the railroads. The relatively speedy and efficient service given by the railroads managed to hold most of their customers even after river traffic was able to resume again.

The Mohawk River, where it slants into the Hudson at Albany, was made navigable with locks as early as 1796. From this beginning came the dream of a canal to the Great Lakes.

Prime reason for the development of canals was the condition of the roads, over which freight wagons either slithered in mud or were shaken apart on rough plankways.

CANALS were not a new thing in this country when people began talking about an artificial waterway from the Hudson River near Albany to Buffalo on Lake Erie in the early 1800's. George Washington had headed companies organized to build short canals around the rapids on the James and Potomac rivers. The Carondelet Canal, giving New Orleans a short cut to the Gulf by way of Lake Pontchartrain, had been opened in 1794. That year also saw the opening of the South Hadley Falls Canal, which made the Connecticut River navigable. The Santee Canal, bringing trade to Charleston, S. C., from the middle

"Fast" passenger packets, pulled by two horses, slid through the canal waters at the rate of five miles an hour. Freight barges, usually pulled by a single mule, were much slower.

of the state, was completed in 1800. The Middlesex, connecting Boston with the granite quarries and timberlands of New Hampshire, was finished in 1803.

The idea for the Erie Canal can be traced to Elkanah Watson, who carried messages to Benjamin Franklin in Paris during the Revolutionary War. The usefulness of Europe's canals impressed Watson, and when he returned to this country he actively promoted waterways here. Especially did he like the idea of connecting Lake Ontario with the Hudson River by way of the Mohawk, which slanted into the Hudson above Albany. Under Watson's leadership, the Mohawk was made navigable with locks in 1796.

New York State leaders then began dreaming of a canal to the Great Lakes. In vain they sought Federal aid and urged Ohio and Indiana territories to co-operate. Finally, after the War of 1812, New York decided to undertake the canal alone.

The existing canals were short: the Middlesex, for instance, was only 27¼ miles long. The Erie Canal was to be 363 miles long! No wonder skeptics called it, "Clinton's Big Ditch," and "Clinton's Folly." De Witt Clinton, as mayor of New York, served on a commission to survey a route for the canal in 1810, and it was around him that the canal enthusiasts rallied. In 1817, as governor, he steered legislation which provided revenue to begin operations. A tax of 12½ cents was levied on each bushel of salt carried more than 100 miles by steamboat on the Hudson River. Thus the boats of Fulton and Livingston helped to build a new system of transportation.

A spadeful of earth turned over at Rome, N. Y., on July

On fine days, canal boat passengers went to the roof to enjoy the passing scenery. The more agile could jump off for a short stroll along the towpath.

Lockport, one of the New York towns that sprang up along the route of the Erie Canal, obtained its name from its function as a lock station on the waterway.

4, 1817, marked the beginning of construction. A large section of the canal route lay through dense forests. The resourceful engineers developed drum-and-cable rigs never before used for pulling down trees and uprooting stumps, and designed a plow with an edge sharp enough to slice through the tangled roots of virgin ground.

The route lay through a troublesome bog known as the Montezuma Swamp. It is almost impossible to dig a ditch in a swamp, but the Erie engineers surmounted the difficulty by digging that part of the canal in winter when the

This cable and gravity railroad, in Pennsylvania, carried canal boats from one waterway to another.

An old canal boat moves through a drawbridge on the Chesapeake and Ohio waterway.

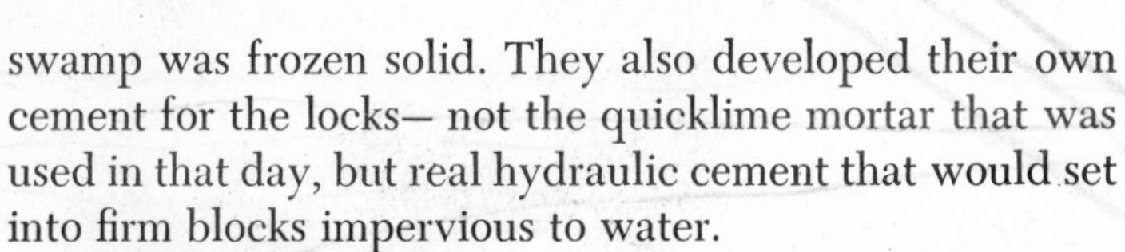

swamp was frozen solid. They also developed their own cement for the locks— not the quicklime mortar that was used in that day, but real hydraulic cement that would set into firm blocks impervious to water.

In October, 1819, water was turned into the completed section of the canal between Rome and Utica, and a boat carrying Governor Clinton and his party pushed off amid general rejoicing and the din of cannon and bells. By the spring of 1820 the first passenger packet came into Syracuse, a small town called into existence by the canal.

Anthracite coal from Pennsylvania was important cargo.

Whatever its drawbacks, canal travel was smooth and quiet.

Some of the canals were later dredged for riverboats.

By 1822 boats were operating over 220 miles and tolls were rolling into the treasury. In June, 1825, the gates near Buffalo were opened, and the waters of Lake Erie were let into the western end of the canal. The Erie Canal became a funnel through which freight and humanity poured east and west. Goods that had been rafted down to New Orleans—corn, pork, hams, beeswax, cattle, meal, chickens, fruit, lumber—now were transported eastward via the Erie Canal.

Although canal travel was slow—anywhere from a mile and a half to five miles an hour—it speeded transportation between eastern and western New York. The time from New York City to Buffalo was reduced from 20 days to six. Most important, the canal lowered the cost of freight. It had cost about $125 a ton to ship goods by wagon from Buffalo to New York. By canal the charge was $5. Flour from Lake Erie ports could be delivered to New York for about $1.50 a barrel. Prices like these opened up an entirely new market to the farmers and millers of Ohio, Indiana, and Michigan.

WESTERN NEW YORK, which had been a wilderness, rapidly became settled after the opening of the canal. Buffalo, a tiny village before 1825, built 3,400 new houses in that year alone. By 1840 it was a city of 18,213 people. Rochester, Syracuse and Utica, all on the canal, grew overnight into thriving towns. New York City, the ultimate terminal for most of the canal traffic, grew from 152,056 in 1820 to 391,114 in 1840. The canal guaranteed New York's position as the first city of the land.

Visualize, for a moment, this new highway of commerce along its serpentine length. It was 40 feet wide at the surface of water and 28 feet wide at the bottom. The channel was lined with clay to make it waterproof. The minimum depth of the water was four feet. Along one side ran a wide towpath on which a mule or horse walked and pulled the canal boat.

The canal was carried above rivers by means of viaducts. It coursed around the hills where possible, or through deep cuts if necessary. It rose to new levels by locks. At the cities it widened into basins which were the barge terminals. It passed through dense forests and pleasant farmlands.

Water was supplied from reservoirs, parallel rivers and lakes. Inspectors walked their boats along the banks, looking for breaks in the walls. In winter the canal was emptied, sandbars were dredged out and new clay lining plastered on where necessary.

The canal itself belonged to the state, but the boats and barges were owned by private companies who were

In 1875 promoters proposed the "New York Steam Cable Towing System," an idea for a cable extending the length of the Erie Canal to be gripped by clip-drums on steam-operated boats and barges. The plan died a-borning.

obliged to pay tolls to the state for the use of the waterway.

The builders had thought the canal would be used only for freight, but people insisted on passenger boats as well. The best passenger service was by packet. By hitching tow horses to a packet boat and changing teams frequently, speeds of five miles an hour were achieved. Soon the state was forced to pass speed laws because of the damage to the canal banks when packets bumped and gouged into the clay sides. The very names of the packets—*Flying Cloud*, *Greyhound*, *Lightning*, and *Whirlwind*—expressed speed.

A view of the Chesapeake and Ohio Canal at Georgetown, photographed about 1903.

Lift locks of the crudest type, operated by donkey engines, ropes and windlasses, served to pass the canal boats from one level to another.

The towpath ran along only one side, and when a boat passed another, one tow rope was slackened and allowed to sink beneath the passing boat.

The packets were from 75 to 80 feet long, 11 feet wide, and about eight feet from waterline to roof. The crew was quartered in the bow and behind the crew's quarters was a small cabin for ladies. Back of that was a large cabin that served as a lounging room during the day, a restaurant at mealtimes and the men's cabin at night. Passengers were free to go to the roof, where the air was better, and the more agile could even hop off the boat to the towpath and take a walk alongside for exercise!

When night came, porters brought in narrow frames of metal or wood with canvas stretched on them. One edge of these rude bunks was fixed to the side of the cabin by rods, the other by a rope to the ceiling. If there were more than 42 passengers, the extras were put to bed on the table or the floor.

In the 1840's you could, if you wished, go from New York to Cincinnati, a distance of 1,100 miles, almost entirely by water. You took a steamboat to Albany, a stage to Schenectady, canalboat to Buffalo, steamboat to Cleveland, canalboat to Portsmouth on the Ohio River and steamboat to Cincinnati. Total fare, $14.75. Time, one month. Many people did exactly that, but those in a greater hurry took the National Road to Wheeling and steamboat to Cincinnati.

As completed, the Erie Canal led from Watervliet, on the Hudson River eight miles north of Albany, to Buffalo on Lake Erie. In its 363 miles the waterway ascended and descended 500 feet by means of 83 locks. It was America's greatest engineering feat up to that time. For a state of a million and a half people, with a countryside largely wilderness, it was a remarkable undertaking.

In the next 20 years other canals were dug in Pennsylvania, Maryland, and North Carolina and there was even

The Oswego Canal at the foot of Sycamore Street in Liverpool, N. Y. In the distance are an old-fashioned ice house and a salt boiler.

Old locks of the Erie Canal at Waterford, N. Y. (right). A tow of modern barges (left) leaves the present-day locks.

First railway in America, built at Quincy, Mass., in 1826.

One of America's first crude attempts at a steam locomotive — the John Stevens.

The Stourbridge Lion *was built in England, shipped over here.*

a fever of "ditch digging" in Ohio, Indiana, and Illinois.

Today New York State has a canal system of 525 miles, and its barges and tugs haul 5,000,000 tons of farm products, ore, chemicals, lumber, and scrap iron every year. From Corpus Christi, Tex., to Mobile, Ala., power barges carry oil, rice, and lumber along a chain of inland waterways. To the southeast are other intracoastal canals. Descendants of the glamorous Erie Canal still serve our country.

A SHORT QUARRY LINE at Quincy, Mass., in 1826 . . . a railway over which cars loaded with granite were moved by gravity and horsepower . . . the building of the first track of the Baltimore and Ohio Railroad in 1828-1829 . . . these were the beginnings of the railway system of the United States.

The logic was simple. If steam could propel a boat through water, why could it not drag a wagon on land?

Even in 1812 when New York was actively promoting the Erie Canal, John Stevens suggested that the state build a railroad instead:

"Let a railway of timber be formed between Lake Erie and Albany," he wrote. "The angle of elevation in no part to exceed one degree. . . . The carriage wheels of cast-iron, the rims flat with projecting flanges to fit the surface of the railways. The moving power to be a steam engine, nearly similar to the one on board the *Juliana*, a ferry boat plying between this city (New York) and Hoboken."

For 1812, that was a fairly good description of a railroad. It specified tracks, flanged wheels, and steam locomotives. But Stevens was a prophet ahead of his time. It was 17 years after Stevens' vigorous proposal that the United States took railroads seriously.

People do not risk their money to build a railroad because they believe it would be a pleasant idea to have one around. There must be a pressing need for it, a need so great that it seems certain the line can earn money. The first railroad to provide public rides in this country was the Baltimore and Ohio, and it was started for the purpose of competing with the Erie Canal. The merchants of Baltimore had profited greatly from the western trade that came to them over the National Road, but now much of this trade was going to the northern route along the Erie Canal and the Baltimoreans were becoming concerned over their loss.

Baltimore first considered a canal, but decided that the task of running a canal through the Alleghenies was too great. Instead it was decided to build a railroad to the mountains, carry the cars over the divide by means of inclined planes and cables, and meet the Ohio River at

Wheeling. There was business to be done with the rapidly growing West, and a railroad would bring that business to Baltimore.

On Feb. 28, 1827, two years after the completion of the Erie Canal, the B. & O. was chartered. In 12 days the citizens of Baltimore and Frederick, Md., subscribed for $2,000,000 worth of stock and the city of Baltimore subscribed another $500,000.

The route was surveyed by Army engineers, while committees were sent to England to study the young railroads already in operation there. On July 4, 1828, the company laid its cornerstone, called "The First Stone," which may still be seen in Baltimore.

One of the first questions to be decided by the directors of the B. & O. was whether to use horses or steam power on the track. The track to Ellicott's Mills, 13 miles away, was completed on Jan. 1, 1830, on which day a single horse drew a car containing 24 persons at a speed of 15 miles an hour. Later that same day, one horse drew three cars containing 80 passengers at eight miles an hour.

All that winter, prominent Baltimoreans and members of Congress from nearby Washington rode the 13-mile stretch to Ellicott's Mills for the novelty of it, paying nine cents one way. This was the first public use of a railroad in the United States.

Before all this, however, a steam locomotive already had been operated on a track in this country. The Delaware and Hudson Canal Company, the line which was built to transport anthracite coal in northeastern Pennsylvania, had bought a seven-ton English locomotive called the Stourbridge Lion. In an experimental run on Aug. 8,

In 1829 the B.&O. used horses over a 13-mile route out of Baltimore.

Tom Thumb *was the first locomotive to pull a load of passengers.*

Tom Thumb *raced a horse-drawn car in 1830. The little engine was doing fine until its blower belt flew off and steam pressure dropped, allowing the horse to pull ahead.*

The Best Friend, *a small four-ton locomotive, began the first scheduled service in America on Dec. 25, 1830. It was built for the South Carolina Railroad, now part of the Southern Railway.*

The John Bull *was originally constructed in 1831 and operated on the historic Camden & Amboy Railroad in New Jersey, now a part of the Pennsylvania Railroad system.*

First locomotive headlight appeared in the 1830's. It was an open fire of pine knots burning on a sand-covered flatcar.

The DeWitt Clinton *was the third locomotive engine built in America. The cars were so much like stagecoaches that they maintained the driver's seat, or box, on the outside at either end.*

1829, the Lion had proved too heavy for the company's track. Furthermore, its four wheels were rigidly mounted so that they would run only on a straight track or a very gradual curve, which was satisfactory in England's flat countryside but not for a railroad built in the hills. The Lion was a failure in this country, but it did get people interested in the possibilities of a steam train.

Finally Peter Cooper of New York, who had property interests in Baltimore, offered to build an experimental steam engine for the B. & O. He came down to Baltimore with his engine, a tiny affair with a 4-inch stroke. He had made a boiler about the size of the average water-heating boiler in a home, setting it vertically on a flat-bedded, four-wheeled truck. He had then connected the boiler and engine and contrived a sytem of wheels, pulleys, and levers to turn the wheels. The resulting locomotive was so small that he dubbed it *Tom Thumb*.

This Rock Island ad of 1873 featured a contemporary sketch of an 1831 train. Above, right, is an 1833 advertisement.

Old Ironsides, *built by Mathias Baldwin, at the Ninth and Green depot, Philadelphia. First run: Nov. 26, 1832.*

Early cars were simply stage-coaches with flanged wheels.

Experiment, *built in 1832, for Mohawk and Hudson, was then the world's fastest loco-motive.*

In the summer of 1830 the little *Tom Thumb* made a speed of 18 miles an hour over the track to Ellicott's Mills. A performance such as that could not be ignored, and on one of its trips there occurred a memorable race with a horse.

The track between Baltimore and Ellicott's Mills was double, and halfway between the towns was the Relay House where fresh horses were put on the cars. At the Relay House the *Tom Thumb* met the driver of a horse-drawn coach, and the driver invited Peter Cooper to race him in to Baltimore. Cooper accepted.

In the first mile or so, while the *Tom Thumb* was getting up steam, the horse drew ahead. As steam pressure increased, the locomotive passed the horse and chugged down the track, smoke pouring from its stack.

Just as Cooper was congratulating himself that the race was won, the belt which operated the blower flew off its drum, and without the blower to force a draft through the furnace, steam pressure began to drop. Cooper tried to replace the belt while the car was in motion and lacerated his hand. The pressure dropped further, the engine slowed down, and the horse came from behind to win the race.

NEVERTHELESS, the performance of the *Tom Thumb* convinced the B.&O. operators that steam power was the thing. In January of 1831 the railroad advertised for locomotives, offering $4,000 for the best design and $3,500 for the next best. It was specified that the engine must burn coke or coal, must not exceed three and one-half tons in weight, must draw 15 tons of freight at 15 miles an hour, and the wheels must have flanges to run on the inside of the rails.

The *York,* built by Phineas Davis, a watchmaker from York, Pa., won the prize. It came within the weight limit, was mounted on a flatcar, and had a vertical boiler in which the fire came up through the hollow center. The *York* drew a train of five cars carrying 150 passengers at 15 miles an hour. Bystanders who saw the train pulling out of Baltimore in the summer of 1831 declared it one of the grandest, most inspiring sights ever to greet the eyes of man.

But Phineas Davis was not the first builder of a successful locomotive in this country. That honor must go to the West Point Foundry of New York City, which built two locomotives for the South Carolina Railroad in the fall of 1830.

The South Carolina Railroad never indulged in horse-drawn equipment. It received its first locomotive, the *Best Friend of Charleston,* in the fall of 1830. It operated satisfactorily until June 17, 1831, when the fireman, tired of

hearing the hiss of escaping steam, either sat on or tied down the safety valve. When the pressure became too great for the thin walls of metal, the boiler exploded, destroying the engine and breaking the fireman's hip. By this time, however, the line's second engine, the *West Point*, was in operation, and service was continued.

Upon completion of the line to Hamburg in September of 1833, the South Carolina was the longest railroad in the world—136 miles.

Conservative New England was also afire with the railroad fever. On June 8, 1830, Boston promoters organized the Boston and Lowell. The following year, the Boston and Providence was chartered and on the very next day, Bostonians chartered the Boston and Worcester, hoping that some day it would reach Albany where it could profit from the tremendous traffic flowing east and west on the Erie Canal. Between Albany and Schenectady, the Mohawk and Hudson line—later to become part of the New York Central—started laying track in the summer of

The Atlantic, *the second model built by Phineas Davis, went into operation on the Baltimore and Ohio Railroad in the summer of 1832.*

The Sandusky, *a locomotive of the Mad River and Lake Erie, first railroad chartered west of the Allegheny Mountains.*

The Pioneer *made railroad history when it pulled the first train out of Chicago on Oct. 25, 1848. This old locomotive is still in operating condition.*

This was the first locomotive of the Milwaukee Road, built in 1848 by the Norris Works, Philadelphia.

1830, and on this track the famous *De Witt Clinton* had its first trial a year later.

To understand the crudities of those early attempts at steam travel, imagine climbing into an open coach for the first trip behind the *De Witt Clinton*. The entire train, consisting of engine, wood-and-water car, three coaches, and several flatcars, was not much longer than a present-day locomotive. The engine was 10 to 12 feet long with a horizontal boiler and a high smokestack in front. The car behind the engine contained a barrel of water and a stack of wood for fuel.

The three passenger coaches were merely stagecoaches modified with flanged wheels to fit the rails. The flatcars

This one of many locomotives named Pioneer *was built in 1851 for the Cumberland Valley Railroad, now a part of the Pennsylvania Railroad.*

behind were fitted with benches to accommodate the overflow of passengers eager to make history. Each car was coupled to the other by a three-link chain nearly three feet long.

The engine started forward and as it took up the slack in the chain couplings, the cars started with a jerk that threw passengers off their seats toward the rear. When the train was properly lengthened out it rolled smoothly enough, but as the fire became hotter, sparks and burning embers began showering the unprotected passengers. For a few miles the privileged riders were busy beating out their burning clothes and putting up umbrellas to protect themselves.

The original Rocket, *ancestor of the present streamlined* Rockets *on the Chicago, Rock Island & Pacific Railroad.*

WIDE CARS AND FREE FROM DUST.

1857. CHANGE OF TIME JUNE 1, 1857.

THROUGH TO NEW YORK IN 31 HOURS.

THE

ONLY DIRECT ROUTE TO NIAGARA FALLS,

Buffalo, Rochester, Utica, Hornellsville, Elmira, Binghamton, Albany, Troy, New York, Philadelphia, Boston, Montreal and New England States, over the

MICHIGAN CENTRAL RAILROAD

AND

CANADA BROAD GUAGE RAILWAY.

The Michigan Central Railroad has the advantage of an EXCLUSIVE TELEGRAPH LINE, used entirely for the movement of all trains, thereby avoiding a possibility of collisions or delays, so annoying on other routes.

FIVE DAILY TRAINS LEAVE CHICAGO:

5.00 a m — EXPRESS MAIL: Making direct connections through to Niagara Falls, Buffalo, New York and Boston.

6.00 a m — LIGHTNING EXPRESS: Arrive at Niagara Falls at 11 P.M.; New York at 2 P.M. next day. Boston at 4 P.M.

7.15 a m — CINCINNATI EXPRESS: Making direct connections to Lafayette, Indianapolis, Cincinnati, New Albany, Louisville, Dayton, Columbus, Zanesville, Wheeling, Pittsburgh, Baltimore, Philadelphia and Washington.

3.30 p m — AFTERNOON EXPRESS: Arrives in New York at 9 A. M. second day, or Boston at 1 P. M. Philadelphia at 10.30 second morning.

8.50 p m — STEAMBOAT EXPRESS: Connecting with North Shore Line of Steamers at Detroit next morning, through without landing connecting with first morning Express at Buffalo, arrive in New York at 9 P. M., and Boston 1 at night. Also connects direct through by Railroad via Niagara Falls or Buffalo. Connects at Michigan City to Indianapolis, Louisville, Cincinnati, Dayton, Columbus, Wheeling, Baltimore, Pittsburgh, Philadelphia and Washington.

The Trains on the Chicago, Burlington & Quincy, Galena & Chicago Union, Illinois Central and Michigan Central Railroads run into the same Depot at Chicago, saving the expense to passengers of hack hire and transfer of baggage.

ALL TRAINS CONNECT AT DETROIT WITH STEAMERS FOR CLEVELAND.

The 5 and 6 A. M. 3.30 P. M. and 8.50 P. M. Trains make direct connections at TORONTO with the

GRAND TRUNK RAILWAY

to Kingston, Ogdensburg, Montreal, Quebec, and all points in Canada East, Northern Vermont, New Hampshire and Maine.

It is well known by the Traveling Public that this Road has no Competitor of equal facilities from Chicago to Niagara Falls, New York, Boston, Ogdensburg, Montreal &c. &c.

The only Train that leaves Chicago Saturday night is over this route, 8.50 P. M. One Train Sunday, at 8.50 P. M. No 3.30 P. M. Train Saturday.

Baggage Checked through to Niagara Falls, Buffalo, Albany, New York Boston, Elmira and Philadelphia.

THROUGH TICKETS GOOD FOR NINETY DAYS!

Allowing holders to remain over and resume their seats, can be bought at the different offices in the West; also at the Passenger Depot, foot of Lake Street, and at the General Ticket Office, Corner of Lake and Dearborn Streets, Chicago, opposite the Tremont House.

H. J. SPALDING, General Pass. Agent

THE QUICKEST TIME TO NEW YORK IS OVER THIS ROUTE.

The American Express runs over this route and no other.

Salisbery's Patent Duster is used on all Express Trains

Chicago Democrat Print, 45 La Salle Street

Schedules were usually not this exact in 1857. Railroads were mostly short lines connecting with stagecoaches and canals.

When the train stopped to take on water, the cars came together with a series of bumps that piled passengers in the forward ends. To prevent these jolts on the return trip, the riders tore down a rail fence, cut bolts of wood, and wedged them between the cars.

TRAIN SCHEDULES were not very exact. Railroads were merely short lines making connections with stage lines and canals, and the train patiently waited until the stagecoach or canalboat arrived before starting out. And since starting times were so indefinite, nobody knew just when a train would arrive at its destination. There was yet no telegraph to announce what station a train had reached. When it left one town for another, it was as completely lost as a ship at sea. Some stations erected high lookouts from which sentries could sight an approaching train.

While some early locomotives had wood-block brakes operated by a foot pedal, others had no brakes at all. When a train approached the station, a crew of men ran out, grabbed it wherever a handhold was available and pulled it to a stop.

Most improvements also came about as the result of experience. The maiden trip of the *De Witt Clinton,* for instance, proved that it would not do to couple cars together with links of chain. A rigid bar was substituted and finally the coupler and pin, which allowed a little play between cars, but not too much.

The cowcatcher was invented by Isaac Drips of the Camden and Amboy Line. After a few cows had been demolished, he decided to install on the front end of the locomotive a little truck bearing two iron bars thrust out like spears, but slanting down toward the track. These bars protected the engine, but sometimes impaled the cows, so he substituted a crosswise bar, much like the present-day bumper on an automobile. Eventually the V-shaped cowcatcher came into use.

In 1840 the United States had just 2,818 miles of rail-

The Tiger, *first Baldwin locomotive equipped with link motion, was built for the Pennsylvania in 1856.*

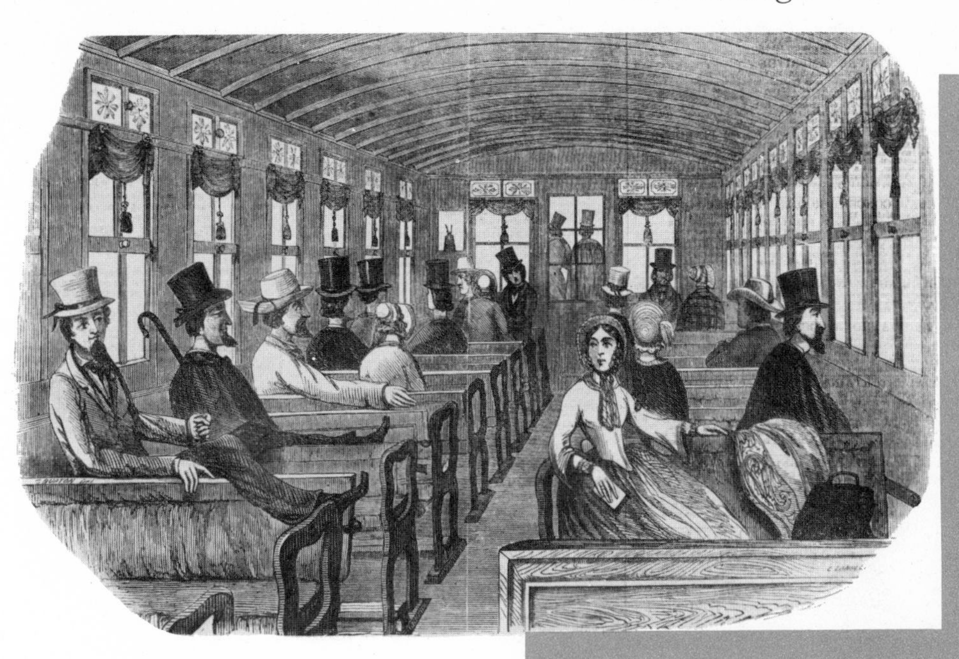

Passengers of the 1850's traveled in gaudily painted wooden coaches lighted at night either by candles or kerosene lamps. Small stoves provided heat in winter. Platforms were open.

road, most of it along the eastern seaboard. Up in New York, steel rails were reaching westward from the Hudson more than halfway across the state. In Pennsylvania, engineers were grading roadbeds into the Allegheny Mountains. The state of Michigan was ambitiously throwing iron rails westward toward Lake Michigan, and Ohio was building its first line southward from Lake Erie. Kentucky, Indiana, and Illinois each had a short line. And from Charleston, S. C., a railroad ran inland almost to Atlanta. Another ran from Savannah nearly to Macon.

Chicago was building its first line westward toward Galena, Ill. but still had no through connection with the East. If you wished to go from Chicago to New York, Great Lakes steamers and railroads got you there in six days.

By 1860 the railroad's conquest of the country east of the Mississippi was nearly complete. The New York Central and the Erie reached the Great Lakes in 1850 and 1851. The next year the Pennsylvania entered Pittsburgh,

The Lady Franklin, *in 1859, was used for railroad ferry service at Harper's Ferry. The boat was built to run on either water or ice.*

4-4-0 locomotive built by the American Locomotive Co. in 1860 had handsome proportions and elaborate ornamentation.

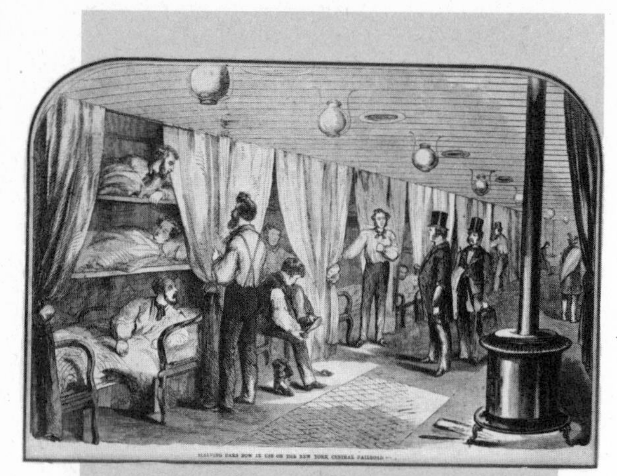

In 1859 lower berths made up by putting shelves between the facing seats. Double-deck uppers were soon abandoned.

Washrooms of the first Pullmans had tin basins, roller towels, common drinking cups, and not much room.

and in 1853 the Baltimore and Ohio was extended to Wheeling, W. Va. By the close of Pierce's term the railroads from the East touched the Mississippi at 10 points, furnishing transportation for the farm products of the West to the Atlantic ports in place of the long voyage down the river and through the Gulf of Mexico. West of the Mississippi, lines were tentatively reaching out into Iowa, Missouri, and Louisiana.

The period from 1840 to 1860 also marked the final triumph of rail over canal. While railroad mileage was increasing from 2,818 to 30,600, canal mileage grew only form 3,300 to 3,700. The canal, which could not be used in winter, which frequently broke its banks, or lacked water during seasons of drouth, could not compete with the all-year-round, fast-scheduled railroad.

A number of things happened to the railroads during the 20 years before the Civil War. The earliest tracks had been hastily laid, with short curves and flimsy trestles across the ravines. Strap-iron rails, imperfectly bolted to their wooden sills, frequently worked loose, curled upward, and thrust themselves through the floors of the coaches. As speeds increased, accidents became more and more frequent.

So the roads began improving their tracks. Curves became wider. Stone and iron bridges replaced wooden trestles. Heavy T-rails replaced strap iron. Where cables and stationary engines had hauled cars over inclined planes, tunnels were now driven through the hills.

In 1844 a startling invention was introduced to the world, an invention that was to have a profound effect on railway operation. Samuel Finley Breese Morse, a portrait painter and inventor, had spent his spare time tinkering with wires and coils and metal keys until he had evolved a device that he called the "telegraph."

This train closely resembles the first to run west from the Missouri on the Union Pacific. It is composed of a locomotive, built in 1870; a combination mail,

At that time, on all single-track railroads, it was necessary to have some agreement by which certain trains would wait at sidings for other trains to pass them. On the Erie Line, eastbound trains had the right of way and westbound trains took the siding. But if by chance one train was delayed, the other train was compelled to wait in ignorance until the missing train made its appearance.

Out of the telegraph came the modern system of train dispatching. Today, by the use of both telephone and telegraph, the location of every train is known and traffic is intelligently directed over immense networks of lines.

Ever since the beginning of the railroads, men had tried to get aid from the federal government for the building of the roads. The government had refused, with the result that the roads had been built by private corporations with some help from state and city governments.

Soon, however, through the efforts of Stephen A. Douglas, the government was to give away between 150,000,000 and 160,000,000 acres of land to railroads during a 22-year period which began in 1850. These land grants made possible the construction of railroads to the Pacific Coast long before there were enough people in western states to justify a railroad from a strictly economic standpoint.

Another important event in the history of railroading also occurred before 1860. In 1858 George M. Pullman got permission to convert two Chicago and Alton coaches into sleepers.

From these first crude sleepers Pullman developed the famous "Pioneer," the first real Pullman car. This car was 54 feet long and 10 feet wide, with more headroom than the converted coaches. It was finished in handsome woods and luxurious upholstery, with larger washrooms and every comfort, including sheets and towels. The cost was $20,000.

By 1870 the upper berth had become hinged so that it could be swung up out of the way, all made up and ready for use.

The General Haupt, *Orange and Alexandria locomotive, was named for the first chief of the Military Railway Service.*

baggage and passenger car, built in 1865; a passenger coach of the times; an old emigrant sleeper of the 70's; and a business car, built in 1883.

Interior of early Pullman car.

The Pioneer's *first trip was the solemn one of bearing the Emancipator to his final resting place.*

Progress viewed with alarm.

The car, however, was too wide to enter station platforms and too high to go under bridges of that day. Pullman's car might have rusted in the yards had not an historic tragedy occurred on April 14, 1865. The assassination of Abraham Lincoln forced the acceptance of the new car. Lincoln's body was to be transported in state to Springfield, Ill., and the "Pioneer" was commandeered for the funeral train between Chicago and Springfield. Platforms and bridges which could not be altered for an oversized sleeping car could certainly be cut down for a martyred President. So the "Pioneer's" first trip was the solemn one of bearing the Emancipator to his final resting place.

An important change in the organization of railroads also occurred in the period up to and including the Civil War. Short lines began to unite into end-to-end combinations. Between Albany and Buffalo, for instance, 11 short roads combined to form the New York Central, and the resulting road was able to operate more cheaply and offer continuous service.

So the period up to and including the Civil War saw radical changes in railroad operation and operation and construction. The telegraph for railroad operation, the land grant, the Pullman coach, end-to-end combinations—these were four of the outstanding developments of the period. By the end of the Civil War the country had largely solved its transportation problem east of the Mississippi. The important centers of trade were linked by railroads, steamship lines and canals; of the three methods of transportation railroads were rapidly becoming the most important.

But by that time many things had been happening to turn the eyes of America westward. War with Mexico, the discovery of gold in California, and the settlement of important boundaries—all these occurred in the middle of the century. The Pacific Coast regions began to fill up and as the population grew, the need for better transportation became greater.

The gold rush did most to spur the era of railroad building. California was separated from the Mississippi Valley by the Rockies and a thousand miles of rolling Indian country. It was a month away by water. In time, a highway like the National Road would undoubtedly have been built, but even after it was finished, the Mississippi and California still would have been weeks away from each other.

But the '50's were the years of the railroad fever. East of the Mississippi, wherever a new railroad threw out its shining twin tracks, new towns sprang up, new farms

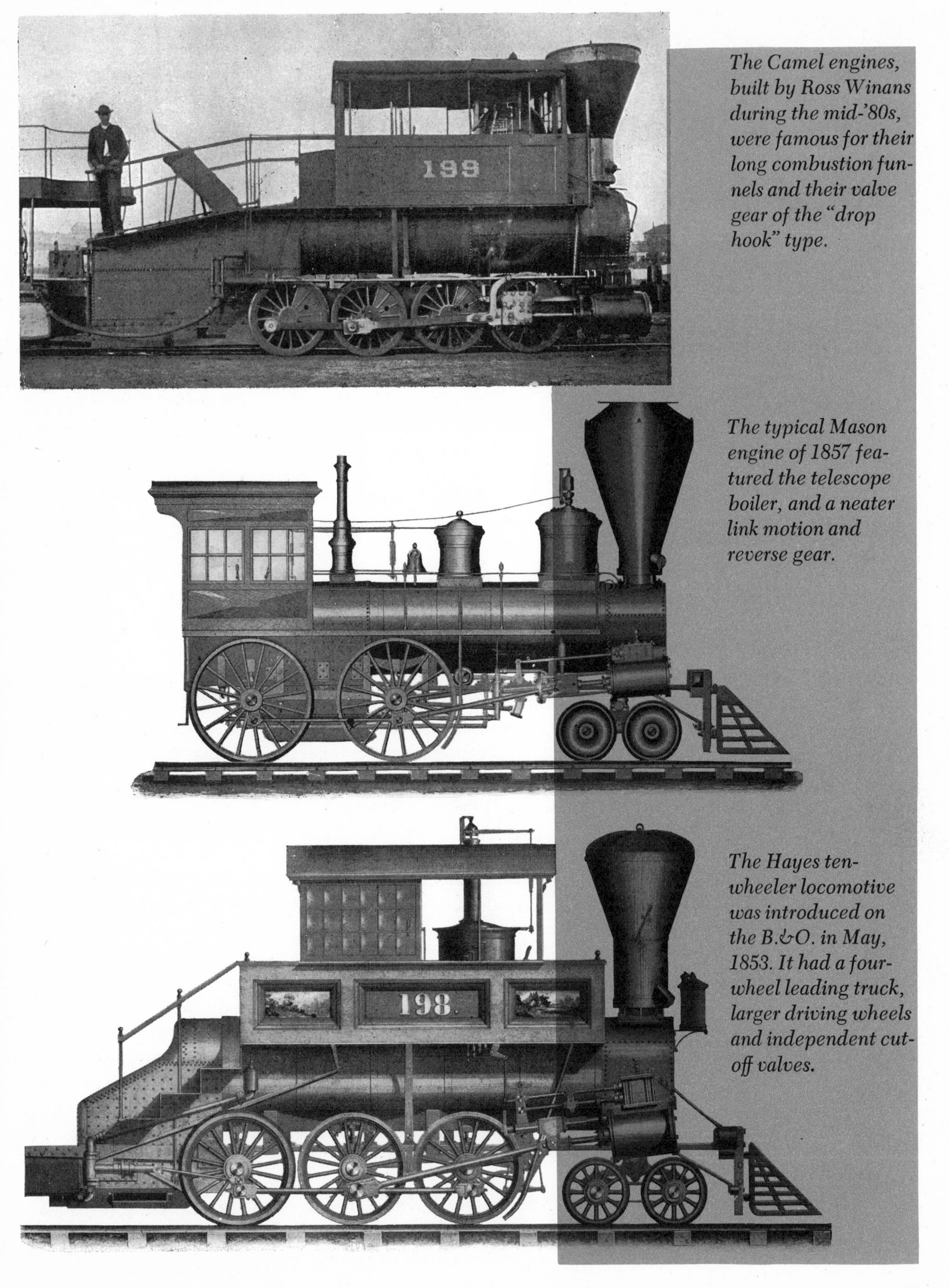

The Camel engines, built by Ross Winans during the mid-'80s, were famous for their long combustion funnels and their valve gear of the "drop hook" type.

The typical Mason engine of 1857 featured the telescope boiler, and a neater link motion and reverse gear.

The Hayes ten-wheeler locomotive was introduced on the B.&O. in May, 1853. It had a four-wheel leading truck, larger driving wheels and independent cut-off valves.

Indians, the Sioux especially, fiercely fought the expanding railroads. Even track-workers had to be handy with a rifle.

An 1853 Amoskeag locomotive had neat lines and simple trim.

Richard Norris' Western model of 1856 had lavish brass trim.

checkered the map, land prices boomed, and factories worked overtime to supply the new communities with lumber, furniture, farm machinery, and everything else that people needed. The railroads were another name for prosperity.

So, when visionaries suggested a transcontinental railroad, many of those who laughed at first came to like the idea. Why not? Suppose it did cost a lot of money! It would pay for itself, the argument ran. Towns held railroad conventions. Congress considered the matter of Federal aid to railroad-construction companies. The idea of a railroad to the Pacific Coast grew. In 1861 the idea became more than a dream; paper work was begun on two lines, the Central Pacific and the Union Pacific.

If the financial aspect was difficult, the physical problems of building the two roads were staggering. The Central Pacific had difficulty in obtaining materials and supplies. Rails, tie plates, spikes, and tools had to come by ship from the East; the lighter materials by way of the Isthmus of Panama, and the heavier materials, such as rolling stock, all the way around South America. Rails that cost $91.70 per ton in the East mounted to $143.67 when shipped via Panama.

The labor supply was just as serious a problem. Few men wished to work on a railroad when there were opportunities for wealth in mining, farming, and storekeeping. In 1864 the Central Pacific was able to find only 1,200 men willing to work for it. Finally Chinese coolies were imported who were willing to work for $35 a month and board themselves. The white laborers received $35 and were boarded by the railroad. In 1867 the railroad was employing 14,500 laborers, and work was moving swiftly.

Meanwhile, from the East, the Union Pacific was unroll-

Early Chicago lake front scene shows the Illinois Central and the passenger station at South Wabash Street.

ing across the plains. It had been chartered by Congress on July 1, 1862, about a year after the chartering of the Central Pacific and ground was broken at Omaha in December, 1863. It received the same financial aid as the Central Pacific. It was using the same gauge track, 4 feet 8½ inches, a width that was to become standard all over the country, so that eventually the cars of one road could ride on the tracks of all roads.

It had as much difficulty getting money and material as the Central Pacific. Most of the supplies were carried by boat up the Missouri and hauled out to the line on wagons. Here also was a labor shortage, because most able-bodied men were fighting in the Civil War, and the Union Pacific didn't go so far as to import Chinese labor. As a result, during 1864 and 1865 only 40 miles of track were laid.

After Lee's surrender at Appomattox on April 9, 1865, the picture changed swiftly. Civil War veterans were released for peacetime jobs. Thousands of ex-soldiers, mostly Irish, drifted west in 1866 and went to work for the Union Pacific. Also, men of the highest type became available to lead the mobilization of Union Pacific workers.

But as the line stretched farther out into Indian country, the tracklayers' troubles increased. There were 15,000 Indian braves to dispute the right-of-way.

One statistician of the period calculated with eloquent regret that it cost approximately $100,000 a head for the Indians actually killed. Even so and notwithstanding the hundreds of white scalps they took, the red men reluctantly realized that their occasional triumphs were hollow victories. In spite of their utmost efforts, the railroad still worked its way into the West.

By July, 1866, the Union Pacific was completed to Kearney, Neb., 305 miles west of Omaha, and the young

Eight-wheel coal car in use by the Pennsylvania (1860's).

Iron boxcar of 1863 used as a powder car during the war.

One of the first freights on the Central Pacific with brakemen – head, swing, and parlor – ready to "tie them down" if necessary.

Laying track and stringing telegraph line on the first transcontinental in 1868.

The Reuben Wells *surmounted a record-breaking incline of 7,012 feet in 1868.*

line was opened for business with a fare of 10 cents per mile.

In the winter of 1867-68 the U. P. reached Cheyenne and began racing the C. P. Congress had specified no particular meeting place. It had only guaranteed to lend money ranging from $16,000 to $48,000 per mile for each mile completed. Both roads realized that each mile built meant that much more money in the coffers, and each road meant to take as much of the premium as it could.

They whipped the track gangs into frenzied efforts, and their road building became heroic for its feverish pace if not for its excellence. Observers marveled at the way in which track was laid.

First went the graders, working with scrapers, picks, and shovels, cutting through hills and filling in hollows, laying a smooth, narrow bed of earth and gravel.

Then came the ties, cut by gangs in the forests of the Black Hills and on the slopes of the Rockies. The ties

Champagne christened the locomotives as the Union Pacific met the Central Pacific on May 10, 1896. The crowd, in the words of one who was there, was "yelling fit to bust."

then were hauled by team to the roadbed, where they were swiftly set in place.

After that the rails were laid, and this part amazed all watchers. Back at the supply depot the rails were loaded on horse-drawn trucks, with wheels flanged to fit the track. These truckloads of rails, with tie plates and spikes, were driven at a gallop down to the end of the track.

There gangs pulled the rails off the wagons, carried them forward, and at a signal lowered them to the track. Rail after rail was carried forward and put in place until the truck was unloaded.

The empty truck was then dumped over on its side, off the track, to allow the next loaded truck to pass it at a gallop, on down the new sections of track already bolted in place. When the loaded truck had passed, the empty one was lifted onto the rails again and driven back to the supply depot.

Using these methods, the U. P. laid from four to seven

The famous "Last Spike," fashioned from about $400 worth of gold, was ceremoniously driven, then replaced by one of steel. Now in the Wells Fargo Bank, San Francisco.

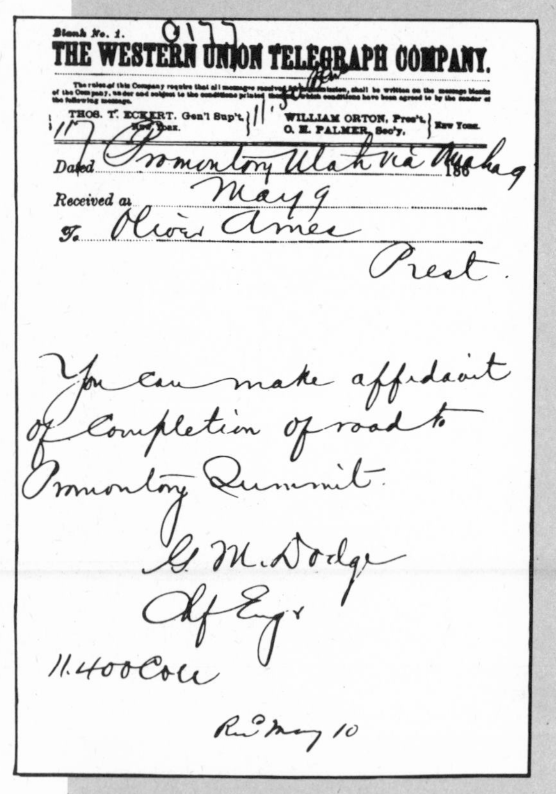
Blank No. 1. 0177

THE WESTERN UNION TELEGRAPH COMPANY.

THOS. T. ECKERT, Gen'l Sup't, New York. WILLIAM ORTON, Pres't, O. H. PALMER, Sec'y, New York.

117

Dated Promontory Utah via Omaha 9

Received at May 9

To Oliver Ames Prest.

You can make affidavit of completion of road to Promontory Summit.

G M Dodge
Chf Engr

11.400 Coll

Recd May 10

Telegraph announcing completion of the road, signed by G. M. Dodge, U.P. chief engineer, and sent to Oliver Ames, president of the Union Pacific.

Last spike monument, authorized by Congress at Promontory, Utah.

miles of track per day, and on record-breaking days as much as 10 miles. Into the winter of 1868-69, without calling a halt for cold weather, the gangs worked at breakneck speed.

By the spring of 1869 both companies were working in western Utah—Chinese coolies laying track eastward on the C. P., Irish laborers and ex-soldiers sweating westward on the U. P. Day by day they came closer until they were within hailing distance, and finally, on parallel roadbeds within a stone's throw, they began passing each other, the C. P. blithely laying track eastward and the U. P. as unconcernedly laying track toward the West. In their eagerness to dig into the federal treasury both roads apparently intended to keep on building until stopped by the oceans.

To remedy the oversight, Congress designated Promontory Point, Utah, as the meeting place and there, on May 10, 1869, the two roads performed the ceremony of completing the first transcontinental railroad. The C. P. had laid 689 miles of track eastward from Sacramento over the Sierra Nevada, and the U. P. had laid 1,086 miles westward from Omaha through Indian country and over the Rockies.

The telegraph had kept pace with the roads and now, on that historic spring day, the singing wires were to carry to the world the story of the placing of the last tie and the driving of the last few spikes.

The tie was a piece of laurel wood from California. It was placed on the roadbed, and the last two rails were laid down.

Seventeen spikes would be needed to hold the two rails in place—10 spikes for one rail, seven for the other. Three of these spikes were unusual. Nevada contributed a spike of silver, Arizona a spike of iron, silver, and gold, and California a spike of pure gold.

Over the tapping telegraph keys the message sped to cities and villages throughout the United States where citizens had gathered in the squares in honor of the event:

"Almost ready . . . Hats off . . . Prayer is being offered." Then, in dot-dash: "The spike is about to be presented." A little later: "All is ready now."

Finally, as the spikes of silver and gold were driven home, the telegrapher signaled each blow of the sledge, and these selfsame blows were recorded in every city by the ringing of a bell.

Had there been radio and television then, the entire ceremony would have been broadcast to the world by swift-talking announcers. But the telegraph was marvel enough and people must have felt, as they listened to the tolling bells, that they were themselves out in Utah watching the welding of the last link in America's most daring, romantic epoch of railroad building.

A scene on Broadway in the 1840's. On the upper level are omnibuses — the huge, lumbering "boxes on wheels" that provided the chief public transportation of the day.

·III·

Period of Settlement and Immigration

NOT EVERYONE went west, of course, and in the growing cities of America local transportation became a problem. In 1825 New York City had a population of 200,000 and Brooklyn was a village of 15,000 hardy souls. There was one ferry, operating across the East River to Brooklyn, and stagecoach lines connected New York with such towns as Greenwich Village, Yorkville, and Harlem. Within the city the few that could afford it rode in private coaches and carriages; the rest walked.

Ten years later there were 100 public passenger vehicles operating in New York City. A certain Abraham Brower started it all in 1829 with a vehicle he called the "Accommodation." It was like a stagecoach, but large enough to

A "bob-tailed" horse car, typical during the 1850's. The cars were about 12 feet long, seated 18 passengers, and had no rear platforms.

The opening of a new route in the horse-car days was an occasion for civic celebration. Here Chicagoans gathered for the extension of the Division Street line from Milwaukee to Western Avenue.

Horse-drawn buses were experimented with in the early 1850's, but they provided neither the speed nor the comfort of cars running on rails.

Even during the heyday of horse cars, other motive power was tried. This car ran on Brooklyn's Broadway behind a steam dummy engine.

accommodate 12 passengers. For a shilling fare, the "Accommodation" rolled over Broadway from the heart of the city to Bleecker Street. Brower added other vehicles, all of them called omnibuses, and made each model larger, until they were like nothing more than huge, lumbering boxes on wheels.

By 1835 you could ride from the Battery to Bond Street for 12½ cents. At first fares were collected by a boy who rode on the rear steps, but he soon gave way to a fare box which was pulled up through a hole in the roof by the driver atop the vehicle. Any change was supposed to be returned in the same way. But the driver, safely outside the coach, was impervious to any sounds within, and it became well known that a passenger had to count his change carefully.

Not only could the driver not hear, but there was no way for him to see the inside of the omnibus. His signal to stop came from a strap attached to his leg and running to the back door. A tug at the strap meant the door in the back was open and the driver was to stop. If the strap was loose, he knew the door was closed and he could proceed.

The drivers were a reckless lot and inspired many impassioned newspaper editorials. Sometimes they would race or try to see how closely they could cut around a rival driver, rattling the wooden wheels over cobblestones while the passengers bounced inside.

Modern critics of the subway and other forms of local transportation may reflect on the *New York Herald* editorial of Oct. 2, 1864:

"Modern martyrdom may be succinctly defined as riding in a New York omnibus. The discomforts, inconveniences and annoyances of a trip on one of these vehicles are almost intolerable. From the beginning to the end of

The train terminal at Madison Square, Fourth Avenue and 26th Street in 1856. One of the street cars shown is drawn by four horses, a relative rarity.

the journey a constant quarrel is progressing. The driver quarrels with the passengers, and the passengers quarrel with the driver. There are quarrels about getting out and quarrels about the ticket swindle. The driver swears at the passengers and the passengers harangue the driver through the strap hole—a position in which even Demosthenes could not be eloquent. Respectable clergymen in white chokers are obliged to listen to loud oaths. Ladies are disgusted, frightened and insulted. Children are alarmed and lift up their voices and weep. Indignant gentlemen rise to remonstrate with the irate Jehu and are suddenly bumped back into their seats twice as indignant as before, besides being involved in supplementary quarrels with those other passengers upon whose corns they have accidentally trodden. Thus, the omnibus rolls along, a perfect Bedlam on wheels."

But it was transportation of a sort and omnibus lines appeared in Philadelphia in 1831, in Boston in 1835, and in Baltimore in 1844. By 1855 there were 593 of these vehicles in operation over 27 routes in New York City.

The first street railway was started in 1832 by the New York and Harlaem Railroad Company, whose trains from

The open car was a delight in summer. Conductors moved agilely along the running boards to collect fares and become the heroes of small boys.

Chicagoans thrilled to this double-end horse car in 1870. It marked a step in local transportation from the 12-foot bobtails. There were two horses instead of one, and a conductor to collect the fares.

The interior of a bobtail car offered few comforts and no heat.

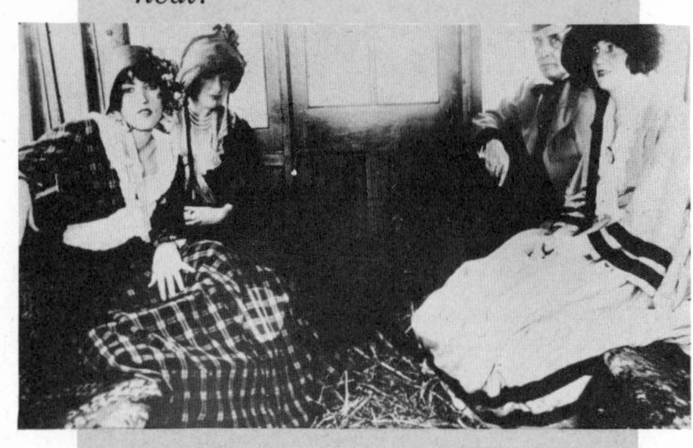

The single-horse streetcar averaged three miles an hour.

Albany stopped at the Harlem River. The double tracks, flat strips laid on blocks of stone, ran one mile between Prince and Fourteenth streets. Over these, on wheels of steel, ran the horse-drawn coaches, each accommodating 30 passengers in the gliding comfort that could be provided only by rails. In 1833 another mile of track was added, and by the next year the route was four miles long. Cars ran every 15 minutes and the fare was 12½ cents.

Beyond this line and another which operated in New Orleans only a few months, no other street railways appeared in America until the early 1850's. Then another line began in New York and still another in Brooklyn. Boston followed suit in 1856 and soon the citizens of many cities were talking pro and con about a "tramway."

There was a great deal of opposition. In Philadelphia the Sunday *Dispatch* sneered, "It is perhaps scarcely worth while to allude to the fact that in New York City they kill one person each week on city railroads and mangle three or four on an average in the same space of time. Human life is really of little value nowadays."

In Baltimore they tried to prevent construction with an injunction. When this failed a drugstore owner, near whose store the track would run, staged a sit-down in an armchair in the middle of the street until the company overcame his opposition with $300. Thus another street railway was laid and by 1859 they were in operation in Cincinnati, Pittsburgh, and Chicago.

There were many operating problems. Some of the larger railways required as many as a thousand horses, costing about $125 each. These had to be stabled, fed, and shod—and all this well, since animal lovers of the era spent a great deal of time inspecting stables. There was the manure problem. It was valuable—in one year the Third Avenue Railroad sold $13,750 worth of this by-product—but the companies had trouble persuading the public that storing it outdoors was beneficial to the general health.

Then, as now, winter was the worst time for the street-railway man. Because sleighs were in general use, it was against all custom to remove snow from the streets. Boston's mayor forbade the removal of snow from car tracks until it was worn too much to be any good for sleighing. Some companies tried to melt the snow with salt, but it was the consensus that this would lower the temperature of the air sharply and endanger public health.

Another winter problem was the heating of cars. Some early cars were built with a box furnace underneath the floor, but these were abandoned because of frequent fires. A large segment of the public believed that heated cars were bad for the health, and most companies just threw straw on the floor for cold feet and let it go at that.

The large two-horse cars had a conductor and the responsibility of collecting fares was his. But the little one-horse cars called "bobtails" had only a driver. In these were fare conveyors—metal tubes running along each side of the car and mounted slightly higher in the back than in the front. Coins placed in the tubes would slide down into a fare box beside the driver.

The companies ran into bad times during the Civil War when the government requisitioned horses for the cavalry, and again in 1872 when a kind of horse influenza broke out in New York, Baltimore, Philadelphia, and other cities. Horses died by the hundreds and some companies had to suspend service. In other places, the driver and conductors pulled the cars for limited trips.

By 1880 there were more than 100,000 horses and mules pulling 18,000 streetcars over 3,000 miles of track in U.S. cities. But here and there the cable car and the electric railway already were installed, and the days of the horse car were numbered. By the turn of the century, only a few were left. One line, on New York's Bleecker Street, kept running until July 26, 1917. During its last year it collected only about 30 cents a day from passengers.

"Carettes," a Chicago vogue of the 1890's, were like streetcars on wagon wheels. This one ran from the old post office at State and Quincy north on State and Rush to Lincoln Park.

This horse-drawn bus, with lines reminiscent of the old Concord stagecoaches, operated in Chicago as late as 1900.

The four-in-hand coach, named for the way its quartet of horses was harnessed. This one was built by Studebaker in the 1890's.

In the western towns, the single-seated, flat-bedded buckboard was a favorite vehicle. This model is more finely built than most.

Carriage makers styled their best coach designs as smartly as the demand for ruggedness of construction would permit.

"Have you heard of the wonderful one-hoss shay,
That was built in such a logical way
It ran a hundred years to a day? . . ."
—OLIVER WENDELL HOLMES, *The Deacon's Masterpiece*

IN 1841 an act of Congress announced to the world that from here on in one of America's dreams would be the private family vehicle—a dream that started with a horse and buggy in every barn and changed later to a car for every garage. The act that Congress passed required licenses for all wheeled vehicles. Prior to that there were state licenses. One of the first, issued in 1817 in Indiana, permitted a private citizen to use a chaise for the payment of $2 a year. If the chaise—a light one-horse carriage with folding top—were sold without notice, the payment was forfeit.

The American family's gleaming carriage evolved from English styles and methods of construction after years of experiment by local builders in the United States. Until 1830, the American vehicle was usually heavy, without roof or doors. The thick wheels were made of oak, and the springs ran parallel to the body. The body was set high on these springs, so high that a person had to climb a step or two to get to the seat.

In 1830 a builder by the name of Carter, from Newark, N. J., designed a new type of buggy that became extremely popular. The most important change he made was to fashion the wheels and parts of the body out of hickory wood, thus making it much lighter and stronger. The buggy looked better, too. Carter set steel springs of an elliptical form in several sections so that they were parallel to the axles. The body had only one seat, and was suspended on heavy steel wires along the top of the springs. There was a folding top and a decorated dashboard with pockets in which the driver could keep his rain curtains.

Carter's carriage was soon copied by other buggy builders. Some of them built square bodies instead of rectangular ones. Others set the body higher so that the wheels were completely under the main part of the carriage. There was also the "side-bar" buggy in which the body was set directly on top of the springs.

There were many other types of carriages. There was the two-seated surrey for the family. And then the American woman liked to ride to church in a brightly gleaming carriage of her own, joined by her husband. She would settle herself importantly, gather her rustling skirts about her, and perhaps allow a child to squeeze onto the seat, watching so that he would not wrinkle his Sunday best. There wasn't too much room and with Father at the reins the ride was apt to be bumpy and certainly crowded.

In the West the stagecoach, adapted from the Concord coach of New England, provided the principal means of transportation for many years. The roads between communities were generally too rough for light buggies and road wagons.

The spring suspension of a coach would be described by auto engineers today as "highly sensitive." The coaches were hung by leather from steel springs.

This American-made victoria was awarded a gold medal at the London Exposition of 1862.

It was in this typically rural buggy that Lincoln campaigned in 1860 when he did not travel on horseback.

Then there was the phaeton, lower than the other buggies, which was used mostly by older people. It had broad seats set in a roomy body.

Henry James in his book, *An International Episode*, described the horse and buggy in Newport in the '70's when the smart set used the carriage for display as well as for transportation. Ladies of fashion shopped in basket phaetons, stopping to greet their friends every few yards and piling their purchases in the small space around the footboards.

On opera nights and on Sunday mornings the rich rode in victorias. Footmen, standing on the boxes in back, wore white breeches, blue or pink shirts, black stovepipe hats and boots.

But it was late on a weekday afternoon that the most spectacular displays were held. A newspaper writer in 1876 described the Newport of that day.

"On every fine day," he wrote, "between four in the afternoon and dusk, Bellevue Avenue is thronged with equipages, equestrians and promenaders. Nowhere in America can so many elegant turnouts be seen as here;

General Ulysses S. Grant used this beautiful carriage during his final term as president, 1873-1877.

every specie of vehicle known to the wheeled vocabulary is in requisition. The cortege is not, as might be supposed, a racing mob, but a decorous-paced, well-reined procession—a sort of reunion on wheels of all that is brilliant and fascinating in Newport society. The quiet though elegant carriages with crests on them are Bostonian; the most stylish horse-furniture and mettled horses are at home in Central Park; Philadelphia is self-contained and of substantial elegance. Imagine this pageant of beautiful women and cultivated men passing and repassing, mingling and separating, smiling, saluting, admiring and admired; the steady beat of hoofs on the hard gravel and continuous roll of wheels proceeding without intermission, until the whole becomes bewildering, confused, and indistinct, as if the whirl of wheels were indeed in your brain."

A familiar sight in Canton, Ohio, was the carriage of President McKinley when he visited home.

THE TRAP was used by the young sportsman of the day. It had one, or sometimes two, seats; the second often facing backward. The Klondike, or storm buggy, was a closed vehicle used by people, such as doctors, mail carriers, and farmers, who needed their carriages for serious business.

Women here had a special name for the "sulky," a one-man cart. They called it a "selfish." It was originally made in the 1800's by an English physician who wanted to ride alone when he was in a hurry to make his rounds. Often delayed by self-invited passengers, he finally had a new cart made with only a single seat. His neighbors called him sulky and his carriage also took the name.

Many American men, wanting no back-seat drivers, also had single-seaters made much like the doctor's and the sulky became well known on the roads in this country.

The demand for all kinds of buggies grew, and by the 1850's there were more than 1,000 buggy factories in the United States. Each plant, however, had workers who labored by hand, slowly. Because of this buggies cost about $500 each.

A brougham built for President Benjamin Harrison and used by the Harrison family until 1911.

A forerunner of the horse-drawn bus, but still reminiscent of the lines of the stagecoach from which it obviously evolved.

Then the picture suddenly changed. Jacob R. Huntington of Massachusetts decided to try making buggies by mass-production methods. He made a model carriage and had its parts duplicated by machines. He set up a factory in Cincinnati and made buggies which sold for between $50 and $100. Soon factories began producing in mass quantities all over the Middle West.

The old carriage makers claimed that the new buggies were poorly constructed, but the lure of an inexpensive private vehicle made the public ask for more.

There was still a demand for the custom-made carriage, however. One advertisement in the 1850's listed the types of carriages one maker would build to order.

The list included:

BAROUCHES
BROUGHAMS
CABRIOLETS
COACHES
COUPE ROCKAWAYS
COUPES
DEPOT WAGONS
DOG CARTS
BUGGIES
LADIES' PHAETONS
LANDAULETS
LANDAUS
LIGHT ROCKAWAYS
ONE-MAN WAGONS
CANOPY-TOP PHAETONS
PHYSICIANS' PHAETONS
PONY PHAETONS
ROAD WAGONS
ROCKAWAYS
ROCKELETS
RUMBLE PHAETONS
SKELETON WAGONS
SULKIES
SURREYS
T CARTS
VILLAGE CARTS
VIS-A-VIS
VICTORIAS
WAGONETTES
EXTENSION-TOP PHAETONS

Between 1890 and 1900 there were over 8,000 factories in the United States producing about 2,000,000 carriages.

The famous "surrey with the fringe on top." This was a popular family vehicle throughout the horse-and-buggy days.

About 75,000 people worked in the industry. International exhibits were held.

Besides the men directly connected with making the carriages, there were other trades closely related to the industry and employing thousands more.

There were the harnessmakers and saddlers. What became the largest harness shop in the world, the Smith-Worthington Saddlery Company of Hartford, was begun by a certain Normand Smith in 1794. At that time Hartford was a town with fewer than 50 shops and a population of about 5,000. Smith's enterprises began modestly, but business was so good that in 1818 a branch was opened in New Orleans. Export trade grew and, a hundred years later, the firm was still in operation. During World War I an order from the Russian government came, requesting 10,000 saddles from Smith.

But most of the business was done in the small retail harness shops all over the country. These small shops were typical of every phase of industry in those days. Wares were many. One advertisement in a New England city directory in 1860 listed the following pieces:

HARNESSES, TRUNKS, SADDLES AND COLLARS
Our Stock Consists of the Following Goods.

HARNESS
Buggy, Phaeton, Tandem, Trotting, Droskie, Coach, Hack, Draft

TRUNKS
Sole Leather, Ladies' Dress, Ladies' Hat, Ladies' French, Single-Double Folio and Valises

SADDLES
Ladies' Quilted, Ladies' Plain, Gents' Somerset, Gents'

The trap, with its forerunner of the rumble seat. In the South, this was for the inevitable manservant.

Velour, heavy silk, and fine cabinet woods went into the park phaeton, most luxurious product of the carriage-maker's art.

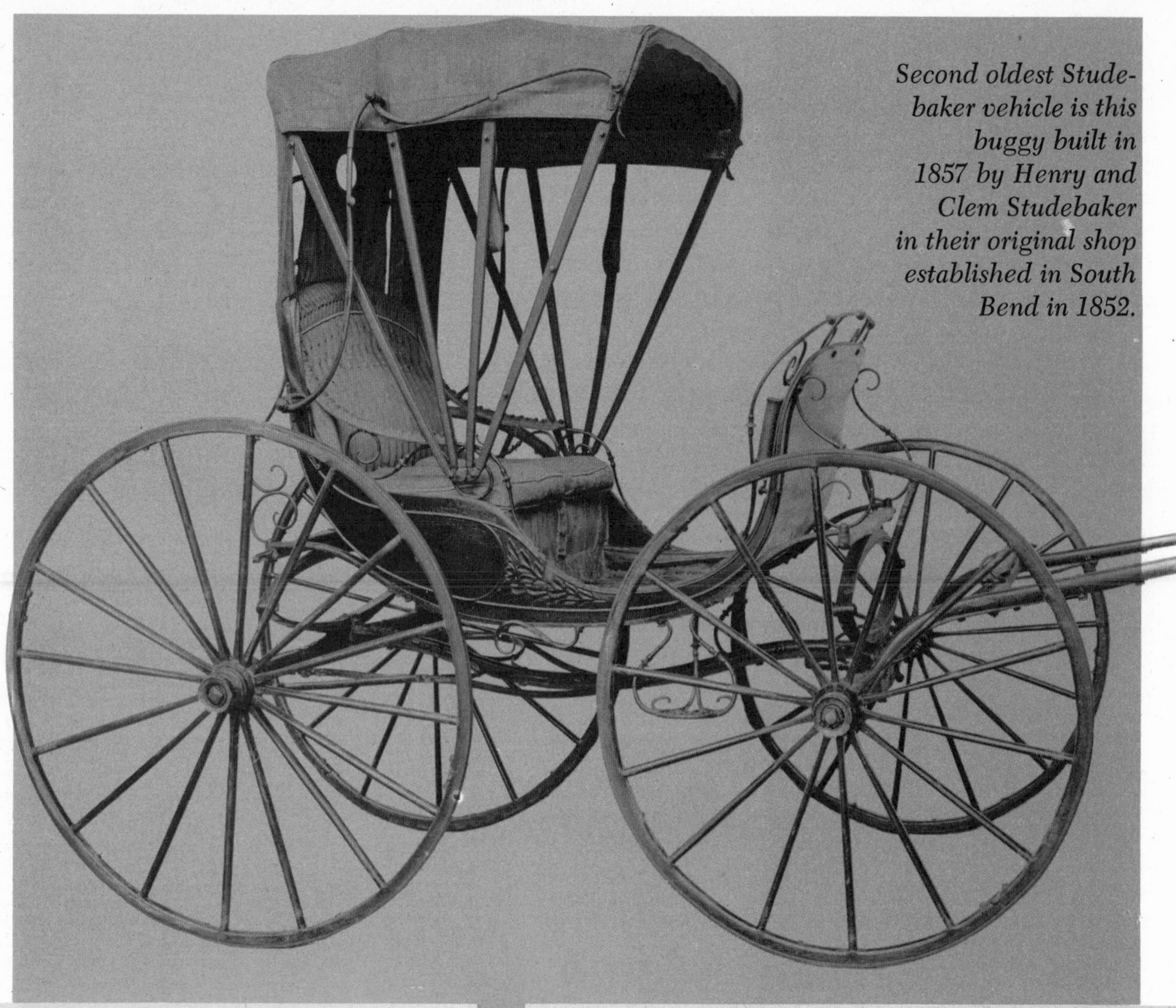

Second oldest Studebaker vehicle is this buggy built in 1857 by Henry and Clem Studebaker in their original shop established in South Bend in 1852.

The last horse-drawn pleasure vehicle built by Studebaker in December, 1919.

Plain, Boys' Pilchs, Girls' Pilchs, English Saddles, Mexican Saddles

WHIPS

Buggy, Phaeton, Hack, Ladies' and Gents' Riding Whips

BITS

Pelham, Buxton, Single Snaffles, Double Snaffles, Arch and Port, Military, Embossed, Steel Curb

HORSE CLOTHING

Summer, various patterns; Winter, various patterns; Knee Caps, Ear Nets, Neck, Flank and Body Nets, Rollers, Surcingles

Also Brushes, Combs and Curry Combs.

Russet Round and Flat Riding and Driving Bridles.

Fancy Leather Riding Bridles, Plated Martingales.

Hand Pieces, Holders, Buttons, Children's Chaises, Dusters, Mats.

Pole Straps, Rubber, Clothing, Sleigh Bells, Halters.

COLLARS AND INTERFERING BOOTS made to fit the most difficult leg or neck. REPAIRING, OILING, &c.

No Stitching Machines used in this Establishment.

THEN there was the blacksmith. One of the most famous was Elihu Burritt of New Britain, Conn. He became known throughout this country and in Europe as "The Learned Blacksmith." A self-taught scholar, he shod horses in numerous towns in the U.S. as he went about on lecture tours.

George J. Capewell, another Connecticut blacksmith, invented an automatic machine for making horseshoe nails. These nails were soon used in more than half of the horseshoes in that era. They did not split while being driven into even the toughest hoof and they were said to be much more flexible.

Boys in those days found another use for the horseshoe nail. A boy would visit the smithy, waiting until the blacksmith had a little free time. If he was in a good mood, the blacksmith would fashion a ring for the boy. Some lads' hands were covered with these nails, which, with the head of the nail on the outside of the ring, could make a pretty powerful weapon in a fist fight.

The manufacture of buggy whips also grew into quite an industry. Ninety per cent of the world's supply of whips was made in Westfield, Mass. One year, 20,000,000 whips were turned out. By 1900, 40 firms, employing hundreds of men, were going strong in New England. By 1912, only three were still in existence.

There were various kinds of whips: the twisted whip, the plaited whip, and the style whip. The handles of the

Wagon Studebaker built for the U. S. Army during and after the Civil War.

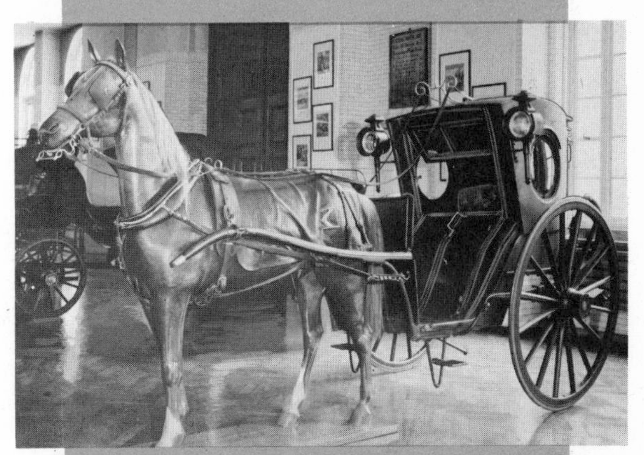

This hansom cab (about 1880) is typical of thousands used in large cities until about 1900.

Rattan was attractive material for vehicles like this trap.

This carriage-maker offered 170 styles of vehicles and 65 styles of harness. A canopy-top surrey was $115, "complete with curtains, storm apron, sun-shade and fine lamps."

SEND ONE DOLLAR Cut this ad out and send to us and if you live east of the Rocky Mountains we will send this **HIGH GRADE TOP BUGGY** to you by freight C.O.D., subject to examination, you can examine it at your freight depot and if you find it equal to any $100.00 top buggy you ever saw, perfectly satisfactory and the **GRANDEST BARGAIN YOU HAVE EVER SEEN OR** heard of, pay the railroad agent **OUR SPECIAL OFFER PRICE, $55.00** and freight charges, less the $1.00 sent with order.

$16.50 ..TO.. $90.00 BUGGIES ..AND.. SURREYS

BUILT IN OUR OWN FACTORY in Chicago, on honor, from the best material money can buy. While in our Free Buggy Catalogue we show top buggies, made by other makers at **$21.50, $28.75** and **$34.75,** the exact same buggies that are being sold by machinery dealers at $45.00 to $75.00 and are being widely advertised by many at $35.00 to $60.00.

OUR ACME QUEEN at $55.00 Is the most wonderful value ever offered. The lowest price ever quoted on the best buggy that can be built. We maintain our own five story buggy factory for the sole purpose of building and selling a better buggy than we can buy elsewhere, and to save our customers manufacturers' profit. The material and labor in our **ACME QUEEN** costs more than double that in the ordinary factory buggy. We use a $2.50 cushion cloth, some use 90 cent; we use a $1.50 head lining, some use 40 cent; we use a 23-cent leather, some use 9 cent; we use $3.50 colors and varnishes, some use 75 cent and $1.00. We pay almost double the price most makers pay for Wheels, Axles, Springs, Dashes and Sockets because we want the best. Our wheels, gears and bodies are water rubbed and the material and labor in painting our Acme Queen would paint 3 cheap buggies. **$55.00 BARELY COVERS COST** of material and labor, leaving us the smallest profit imaginable, but we are building 70 buggies a day and to advertise our buggy factory we are willing to sell them on $1.00 profit each. We know $70.00 daily profit on 70 buggies will satisfy us, advertise us everywhere and build up the LARGEST buggy business in the world.

Every buggy we make is....... **GUARANTEED TWO YEARS....** and they will outwear........... **Five Ordinary Factory Rigs.**

THE ACME QUEEN we build in narrow or wide track, cl th or leather trimmed, end springs, buffed leather quarter top, solid panel back, springs in back, leather covered bows and nuts, rubber steps, velvet carpet, body 24x54 inches, No. 1 Sarven's patent screwed rim wheels, painted in 16 coats, body black, gear dark green with very delicate modest striping, complete with shafts, side and back curtains, boot, storm apron and anti-rattlers and shafts. Pole, neckyoke and Whiffletrees in place of shafts, $1.75 extra. Buggy weighs 400 lbs. and the freight will average for 200 miles, $2.00; 300 miles, $2.75; 400 miles, $3.25; 500 miles, $3.60; and 1000 miles, $6.00.

SEND ONE DOLLAR with your order, we guarantee the buggy to reach you safely, and if satisfactory, pay the railroad agent balance, $54.00 and freight charges, otherwise pay nothing and the agent will return buggy at our expense and we will return your $1.00. **DON'T BUY A CHEAP FACTORY BUGGY** now sold almost exclusively by all machinery dealers and catalogue houses. Buy the best buggy money can build direct from the maker at the lowest price ever known. ORDER TO-DAY. DON'T DELAY. Write for our Free Buggy, Carriage and Harness Catalogue. Address

SEARS, ROEBUCK & CO., (Inc.) CHICAGO, ILL.

Underselling practically everyone was Sears, Roebuck & Co., who claimed to be satisfied with a profit of $1 each on their buggy factory's daily output of 70 vehicles.

The storm buggy, with sliding, glass-windowed doors, was a favorite with doctors and mailmen.

twisted whips, which were sometimes covered with sheepskin, were usually made of hickory or white oak. The plaited whip was made of 15 or 20 strands of silk or cotton, wound around a center of whalebone. The style whip was for the ladies. It was a bough of holly with a lash that could be detached and replaced when worn. Still other whips were made of mixtures of rawhide and rattan. To give the whip a proper balance, most makers put a piece of iron in the butt. Fancy whips, naturally, were made for the young man's rig. Some of the handles had silver mountings, buttons, or carved figures.

The cheaper whips sold for 25 cents, and there were some as low as 10 cents. Most of them cost a dollar or two. But a fancy whip could cost $25.

It was not uncommon to see whip sellers standing on street corners calling their wares. Usually, they carried bouquets of flowers to dress up the whips. Sometimes they

A stretch of the National Road in Fayette Co., Pa., in pre-automobile days.

went around watering the parked horses while trying to sell whips to the drivers.

One of the worst insults that could be offered to a person was a lash of the horse whip. Men sometimes tried it as a public form of revenge, and offended women occasionally took the whip to men. One actress horsewhipped a newspaper drama critic because she thought he had insulted her.

The livery stable keepers were another important part of the horse-and-buggy industry. The liverymen took care of transient horses, boarded horses for private owners, and ran stables in connection with hotels and inns. Ralph Waldo Emerson, when he lectured near Boston, used to ask for a $10 fee and feed for his horse. People who came in from the country left their horses at livery stables for the day, and the care for such a transient would cost about 25 cents. Saturday was a busy day at these stables, because

The Moline wagon was a sturdy and practical all-purpose farm vehicle.

The whalebone road wagon, light and strong (top), was ideal for long distances. Whereas Bailey concentrated on a single line of quality, other manufacturers offered an almost unlimited variety of styles, and liberal free trial inducements to secure a competitive advantage.

that was the day on which most of the country folk would come in to shop and trade. Another busy day was Sunday, when the young swain wanted a horse and buggy to take his girl out for a ride.

If a person owned his own horse, it would cost him $4 a week to have it boarded at a convenient place. For this price the horse was fed, groomed, and stabled, and the carriage was washed. Sleighs would be kept for little or no fee.

For the rider coming in to stay overnight at an inn, there was always some place near by where he could stable his horse for about a dollar. All over the country, small inns carried signs, "Food and Shelter for Man and Beast." The sign over the livery stable was nearly always the picture of a horse's head. But the sign was not needed. The odor and the noise of the stable would direct you to the place.

Private coachmen, too, had a part in the horse-and-buggy industry. The private coachman had a distinct place in society. His appearance was, of course, of primary importance to the society lady who could afford to hire one or even two coachmen. His uniform was brightly colored, sometimes matching the fine upholstery and damask coverings of the carriage itself.

It was an ordinary sight, on a theatre night in New York or Boston, to see lines of carriages with their erect coachmen, waiting for their employers after the show. There was always a carriage crier, who would go up and down the lines calling for the coachman.

Firemen and policemen depended on the horse to carry out their duties. Fire horses were very well cared for; a fire engine with crew weighed as much as four tons.

Mounted police are still proud of their horses, but the patrol wagon drawn by a spanking pair of mares is now hardly remembered.

Public carriages and express wagons made up another important segment of the horse-and-buggy industry. From the beginning, licenses and laws were in effect in this country to regulate hackmen and fixed passenger fares and baggage rates were set early by municipal ordinances. Usually, it cost 25 cents for a ride in the first zone, one or two miles away. Small baggage was carried without extra charge. Children under four, if with an adult, rode free. Youngsters between four and twelve years of age paid half fare. Fares would be doubled between midnight and six A.M. There were also public carriages and sleighs for rent. The fee for these was $1.50 or $2 for the first hour and about $1 for each hour after that. Some young men used to pool their money and rent carriages together for dates.

Hansom cabs were used mostly in New York and Boston. They were lighter and very much smarter looking than an ordinary cab. They also were more likely to tilt over, and a passenger had to be careful when climbing into them.

Local expresses, which were wagons for light transfer hauling, were regulated in the same way as public carriages. There were public express stands at railway depots and business centers, especially along the East Coast. Near such a stand you could see the expressman, a bright umbrella open to shade him from the sun, dozing off while waiting for a customer.

There were also expresses between cities by 1840. An important one carried passengers and packages between New York and Boston. Before that, post riders carried the bundles, often stopping off to make purchases for a small fee. When the post rider came with a package for you, he

Cleveland's "rolling road' was an oddity of the horse-and-wagon days. This moving platform carried wagons up a steep incline of Factory Street, rising 65 feet within the 420-foot length of the mechanical roadway.

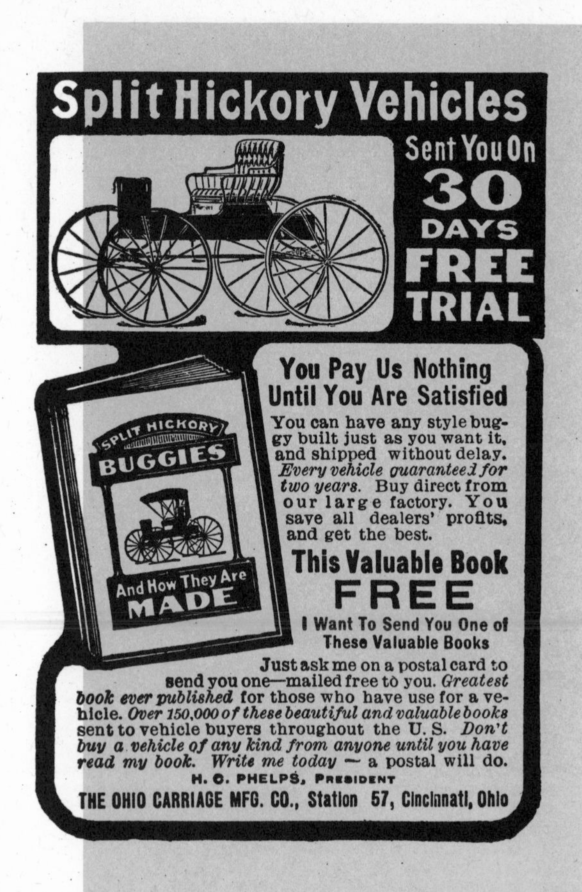

announced his arrival with a loud toot on his tin horn. The Adams Express Company, made up of a merger of several small companies, was organized in 1845. Their wagons, often seen in pictures of those times, had large, distinctive square tops.

ANOTHER IMPROVEMENT was on its way. In 1876, in England, the rubber tire was invented. But it wasn't used in that country because people were afraid that, since you couldn't hear them coming along on the road, quiet buggies were dangerous. The first set of rubber tires was brought to the U.S. in 1886. They were sold for $150. Other experiments were conducted with pneumatic tires, which were mounted on wire wheels, much like those on bicycles. But these were never really very popular.

In 1900 one tire advertiser claimed:

"No jolt. No jar. All vibration, which is so spine-racking and debilitating to nervous people, is taken away. They (the tires) make the vehicle run absolutely noiselessly, permitting conversation in a low tone of voice; make the roughest roads smooth; prevent slewing on street car and railroad tracks."

Five years later the carriage industry hit a sudden slump. There were a few who laid the blame to the increasing number of automobiles on the road. Most experts, however, refused to believe that the age of the horse and buggy was over. The automobile was considered a passing fancy. Thirty years later, however, there were fewer than 3,000 buggies being manufactured during an entire year. They were used in rural sections where roads were bad.

Some of the buggy men tried desperately to keep the carriage in the limelight. They painted the bodies and gears in bright red, green, and yellow. Gadgets of all kinds were added, including electric lights run by batteries.

But nothing helped. Carriage makers followed the trend to automobiles. Many of the old names—Brewster, Studebaker, Durant, Timken, Gardner, and Fisher—became known again in the automobile industry.

Horse-drawn vehicles were more sparing of life than either trains or street cars in Chicago in 1906.

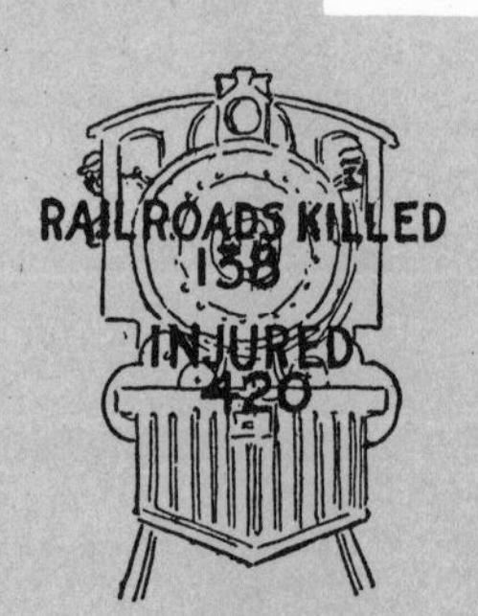

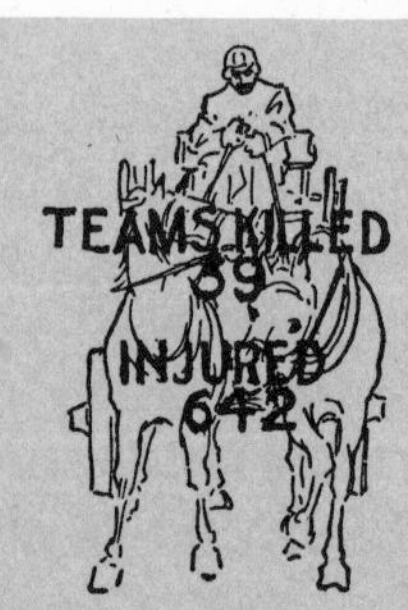

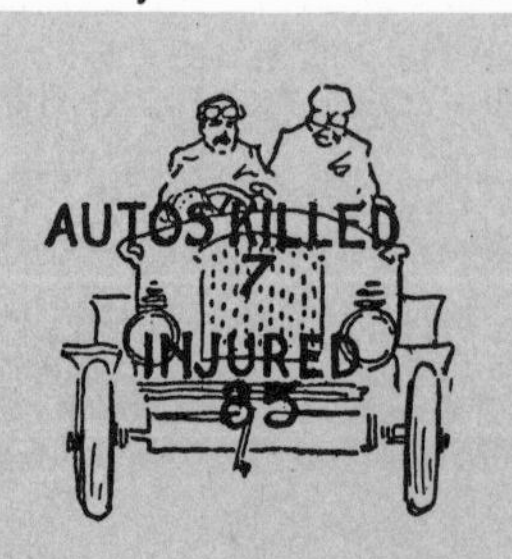

The Chicago cable-car system was the model for similar systems throughout the U. S. in the 90's. Even in cable-car days, riders were subjected to advertising placards.

IT WAS OBVIOUS even during the heyday of the horse cars that something better was needed. That something better came on Aug. 1, 1873, when the first cable car was drawn to the top of Clay Street hill in San Francisco.

The inventor, Andrew S. Halliday, a manufacturer of wire rope, had studied the English railways that ran down into coal collieries on cables. He saw that this system could be adapted to San Francisco, where horse-drawn vehicles could not manage many of the steep streets. And he knew the American penchant for riding unless a walk was unavoidable.

Halliday's cable, operated by a stationary steam engine, ran on rollers under the street level. The car had a long fork hanging from its middle which reached the cable through a slot in the pavement. The fork had a gripping clamp which engaged the moving cable and allowed the car to be carried along. The car was stopped by releasing the cable grip and using the brakes.

Although San Francisco was first with the cable car and is now famous for the ones still used there, Chicago actually had the most extensive cable car lines. The first line was laid on State Street from Madison to Twenty-first and opened on Jan. 22, 1882. Twelve years later there were 86 miles of track in the city and 469 grip cars, each usually drawing two trailer cars. The Chicago lines became so famous that street railway men came from throughout the country to examine them.

One of the earliest cable cars, photographed in the early 1880's.

Cars operated by compressed air were tried out.

Storage - battery street cars were unsatisfactory.

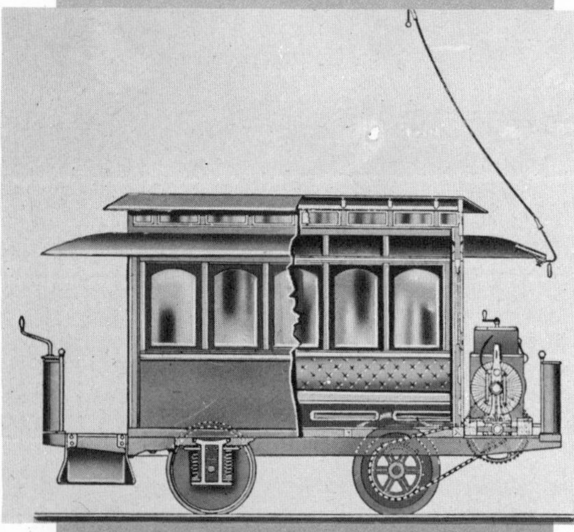

A chain-drive electric car had a brief trial in Chicago.

The grip cars ranged from small ones 12 feet long to some as long as 33 feet. Twenty passengers could crowd into the small cars and the larger ones, with eight wheels, took in 38 passengers. The cable cars sped through town at speeds of 12 to 14 miles in outlying areas and slowed to six or eight miles an hour in the downtown section.

To those who fought the introduction of cable cars because they would be dangerous, H. H. Windsor, Sr., then secretary of the Chicago City Railway and later founder of *Popular Mechanics Magazine,* had this to say:

"The wheels . . . of all cable cars operated by this company are guarded with wooden fenders coming to a point at each end of the car, the lower edge being lined with strips of rubber. These fenders are suspended from the running gear so as to barely clear the street surface, rending it impossible for anyone to get beneath the wheels. The determined attempt of an insane lady, who one night threw herself directly across the track of a cable train approaching at full speed and only a few feet distant, was frustrated and the would-be victim pushed uninjured to one side."

Arguments like this usually won. By 1890 there were some 5,000 cable cars running over more than 500 miles of track in the United States. They carried about four million passengers a year. A famous cable line contractor was Edmund Saxton, who did much of the work on the New York, Washington, and Kansas City lines.

But cable lines were expensive and intricate, demanding constant care and inspection. The relentless search of inventors for better and cheaper transportation went on. The State Street Line in Chicago, which opened so auspiciously twenty-odd years before, was closed in 1906. The *Chicago Tribune* was unsentimental about its passing:

"Groaning and wobbling, as one decrepit and having earned a long rest, the final cable train rattled and bumped around the Loop for its last performance . . . Just behind it came the first State Street trolley car, forerunner of a faster means of transportation."

The public saw it at state fairs all over the country, but it was just a curiosity . . . a little car running back and forth on a short line of railway track, with nothing to pull it but a small wire overhead. It was the life's work and dream of Charles J. Van Depoele, a young Belgian sculptor. His little electric car was on display at the Toronto Agricultural Fair in 1885 when it drew the attention of James A. Gaboury, an engineer and promoter who had built several horse-drawn and cable street railways in U.S. cities. Gaboury took Van Depoele to Montgomery, Ala., where they established the first electric street railway in the world.

An early trolley car operated by the Lynn and Boston R.R. as a feeder to the terminal.

These first cars had a small, two-wheeled carriage, called a "monkey," which ran on the overhead power line and was connected to the car by a flexible cable. Because streetcar men often received severe electrical shocks in replacing the monkeys when they came off the power wire, they were soon replaced by a trolley pole which maintained a rolling contact with the wire.

Depoele's successful experiments had been preceded by years of less happy experiments. Moses G. Farmer ran some battery-powered cars at Dover, N.H., as early as 1847, and there were other experiments with battery and dynamo-operated cars, but none proved practical. Third-rail devices were too dangerous for public streets. In East Cleveland, however, a third rail was run underground, reached through a slot like those used for cable cars. But weather conditions affected the rail and the line lasted only one year.

In the 1880's a young former assistant to Thomas Edison, Frank J. Sprague, became interested in electric railways and organized the Sprague Electric Railway and Motor Company. In 1888 he opened his first line, in

Dummy electric engines were used to pull old horse cars on some early street railways.

The Pullman vestibule was a double-decked monstrosity built by Pullman-Standard Car Manufacturing Co. during the 1890's.

The "picnic special," a gay way for members of political clubs, lodges and marching societies to go to an outing in the 1890's.

Richmond, Va. It was an immediate success, and in the summer of that same year Sprague was invited to install an electrified system in Boston, Mass. Within a few weeks trolley wires hung over Beacon Street and moved Oliver Wendell Holmes, then 80 years old, to write:

"Look here! There are crowds of people whirled through our streets on these new-fashioned cars, with their witch-broomsticks overhead – if they don't come from Salem they ought to!—and not more than one in a dozen of these fish-eyed bipeds thinks or cares a nickel's worth about the miracle which is wrought for their convenience. We ought to go down on our knees when one of these mighty caravans, car after car, spins by us under the mystic impulse which seems to know not whether its train is loaded or empty."

By the 1890's cities all over America followed the example of Montgomery, Richmond, and Boston. Hundreds of electric cars ran in Minneapolis, St. Paul, Cleveland, St. Louis, Pittsburgh, and Tacoma.

In Chicago, for instance, the first electric route appeared on the south side of the city in 1890, and during the next

15 years there was a steady change-over from horse car to electric operation. But because overhead trolleys were not permitted in the downtown Loop district until 1906, cars had to be changed from electric to horse or cable power when coming into the downtown area. When the ordinance banning overhead trolleys was repealed in 1906, the last cable line, operated on State Street, was dismantled and the last horse car line, operating on Dearborn from Randolph to Polk streets, was changed to trolleys.

For years a motorman and a conductor were a traditional streetcar crew. In the early 1920's, however, "pay as you enter" cars were introduced which eliminated the conductor in many cities.

During the 1930's a new kind of trolley vehicle appeared, the trackless trolley, combining the economy of electric operation with some of the mobility of a trackless bus.

If the idea of an elevated railway was popular with the passengers that would be using them, it was not so with one section of the public. Unlike other means of transportation that often helped to raise the price of the real estate near where they ran, elevated lines usually meant that some property was going to lose value. The dirt and the noise furthered the public's antagonism to the elevated.

But through the untiring efforts of Charles T. Harvey, organizer of the West Side & Yonkers Patent Railway, America was soon forced to swallow the bitter pill of elevated traffic. The old West Side Railway, later reorganized as the New York Elevated Railway, kept working and expanding its line and it slowly took its place as an important link in New York's transportation system.

By 1876, 40 trains a day ran on this line. The fare was 10 cents, but a special nickel rate was established for the rush hours. Steam dummies hurried along the tracks trailing boxlike cars. People would line up just before the rush hour, waiting for the change in price. The crowds became so large that the company had to hire guards to see that the doors were closed and that there were no passengers left hanging outside.

Boston had rumblings about the elevated as early as 1879, but actual construction, because of public apathy, was delayed until 1898.

In 1897, Chicago designed its elevated to circle its central business district. Later, this section became known as that city's famous Loop, getting its name from the almost continuous lines of cars that moved around it.

Opposition to the elevated never completely ceased, and in some cities the structures have been taken down. But for about 30 years the elevated was the principal means of "rapid transit" in the cities.

Crewmen took pride in their cars and their uniforms, and small boys dreamed of becoming motormen.

In the 90's, street cars became longer and better proportioned.

Pay-as-you-enter cars with enclosed platforms began to appear in the early 1900's.

An early elevated locomotive.

Steam locomotives were used over certain routes of the Chicago elevated system until the turn of the century.

Meanwhile in 1864, Hugh B. Willson, after viewing London's new subway, returned to the States full of enthusiasm and proposed that New York also build a subway along the lines of the one he had seen in England. The idea fell into a bog of financial and legal difficulties and actual construction didn't materialize until a full 40 years later.

It was Boston that took the lead and, despite opposition, opened the first real subway in the United States in 1897. The building of Boston's Tremont Subway cost four million dollars, but it more than made up the city's investment, carrying 50 million passengers during its first year of operation.

Chicago was the latest of the big cities to build a subway. With new and more efficient tools at its disposal, it began its digging in 1938 and completed part of the system six years later.

Wooden-car elevated train purchased for Chicago system in 1892.

Pneumatic engine tried on New York City's elevated system.

The elevated tracks along The Bowery in New York during the 1890's.

Electric cars on elevated tracks over the Chicago World's Fair of 1893.

Wood-burning engines stored in Washington, D. C., during the Civil War to prevent their falling into rebel hands in the event of a raid on Alexandria, Va. The Capitol can be seen in the background.

IN 1870, the year after the completion of the Union Pacific-Central Pacific, the United States had 52,922 miles of railroad, enough to go twice around the world. That was a tremendous growth when compared to the 9,000 miles of track in 1850. But it was the merest beginning of the building that was to take place in the next 20 years.

By 1880, in spite of the fact that the country had just emerged from six years of depression, railway mileage had increased to 93,262. During the next decade, the United States went into a fever of grading and track-laying such as the world had never seen. No fewer than 70,000 miles of railroad were added, bringing the total mileage in 1890 to 163,597.

The Union Pacific-Central Pacific had been the first transcontinental line, but others followed. In 1881 the Atchison, Topeka, and Santa Fe was completed from Kansas City to Deming, N.M. Here it connected with the Southern Pacific, then being constructed from San Francisco via El Paso, Texas, to New Orleans. In 1883 the Northern Pacific from St. Paul to Portland was opened. In 1884 the Union Pacific secured a second connection with the Pacific Coast through the Oregon Short Line and the Oregon Railway and Navigation Company, the route extending from a point on the Union Pacific east of Ogden to Portland.

Most of these new roads were being built in the West and were an important part of the mass movement that was changing the West from a frontier to a settled country. Wherever the railroads went, they opened up new

The four-wheeled Atlas was used a great deal for moving cars at stations, and for other "workhorse" purposes.

Old Roundhouse at Norwalk, Ohio, where locomotives were repaired. Performance sheets of all locomotives, showing miles run, cars hauled, coal and oil consumed and other details, were kept even then.

sources of wealth. The wheat of the Dakotas, the cattle of Texas and Wyoming, the gold, copper, silver, and lead of the Rocky Mountain regions had a new way of getting to market.

And, as new farms were settled and new mines opened, town after town sprang up on the railroads. Hamlets and sleepy cow towns grew into bustling cities. The number of people west of the Mississippi in 1870 was only seven million; in 1890 it was 17 million.

And the cities! Kansas City leaped from 3,000 population in 1870 to 37,000 in 1890! Denver grew from 5,000 in 1870 to 107,000 in 1890! Omaha went from 16,000 in 1870 to 140,000 in 1890, and Salt Lake City's 13,000 boomed to 45,000 in the same 20 years.

Only four states were still to be admitted after 1890—Utah, Arizona, New Mexico, and Oklahoma. The country was settled to the whistle and smoke of railroad locomotives. In 1887, the banner year for the railroads during that decade, transportation of 540,000,000 tons of freight and 472,000,000 passengers was recorded.

But while railroads were performing the great service of settling the West, some of their activities aroused great indignation. Most of this indignation was due to the way in which freight rates were charged.

For example, if you were a manufacturer and wished to ship a certain kind of cloth from New York to San Francisco, the cost was $1 per 100 pounds, but if you wished to ship the same amount to Salt Lake City, the cost was $2.30 per 100 pounds!

There was a reason for the railroads to practice what is

The Denver and Rio Grande Mountaineer, *the 101, built in England in 1873. She was equipped with three throttles and screw-type reverse gear.*

The famous Mount Washington incline railway, with the locomotive whose boiler could be kept vertical at any angle.

known as "local discrimination." Between New York and San Francisco there was water competition. If the railroads charged too much, the manufacturer could send his goods by boat by way of Panama. But there was no boat service to Salt Lake City.

There was another practice called "personal discrimination," and this was less excusable. In 1885, an Ohio railroad charged the Standard Oil Company 10 cents per barrel to ship oil from Macksburgh, Ohio, to Marietta, Ohio. The same railroad charged smaller independents 35 cents per barrel and actually turned over to the Standard Oil Company the extra 25 cents. To many critics, this meant that the railroad was co-operating with one company to drive other companies out of business.

These matters caused so much protest that in 1887 Congress passed the Act to Regulate Commerce and created the Interstate Commerce Commission to administer it. The object of the Act and of the amendments that have increased its power since 1887, is to regulate rates and guarantee equal treatment to various shippers and localities.

So the period of the railroads' greatest growth also saw them come under the regulation of the United States government. And the same period saw the introduction of

Central Pacific locomotive No. 82, and a typical 4-wheel, 15-foot "dinky" caboose. These were in operation on the Central Pacific and Southern Pacific in 1890.

Some "old-timers" may remember when the small-town railway agent's office looked something like this.

two of the greatest contributions to railroad safety, the automatic coupler and the automatic air brake.

The automatic coupler, an invention of Eli Hamilton Janney, was first patented in 1868 and then improved in 1873. Before Janney's device—and on many a railroad for 30 and more years after—cars were connected with links and pins, a crude affair that did hold the cars together but also accounted for the majority of maimed trainmen, who had to stand between the cars in order to steer the link into the socket, then drop the pin that held them in place.

This link-and-pin coupling was the dread of all brakemen, and there are old railroaders living today who can recall when a comrade lost a finger or a hand, or even his life, in that instant when two cars came together. Amputated fingers or hands told railroad men that a man so maimed, no matter what his present job, was likely once to have been a brakeman on a link-and-pin road.

Janney whittled out of wood his first model for an automatic coupler. Six years later he managed to get the Pennsylvania to test it. The Pennsylvania found it good and in 1876-77 made the coupler standard equipment for its cars. But not until 1882, when the Master Car-Builders Association at last adopted the device, did Janney and the company he had formed begin to prosper. Even then, and for

Shops of the Baltimore and Ohio at Martinsburg, W. Va. Shown are a group of Camelback locomotives and a train of iron-pot coal cars.

Locomotive No. 11, built by Brooks Locomotive Works, ran from 1883 to 1918, when it was scrapped.

Pennsylvania Railroad mail car, 1863. Post Office Department clerks began the practice of "working" the mails for early dispatch.

The Hannibal & St. Joseph Railroad (now part of the Burlington) in 1862 began converting stubby little baggage cars into traveling post offices.

another decade, there were far more link-and-pins than automatics on American railroads, and the maiming and the slaughter of trainmen continued.

Shortly after the Civil War, two trains collided head-on between Troy and Schenectady in New York State. Although the damage in battered and crushed rolling stock was heavy, this was one of the most fortunate accidents that could have befallen the railroad because one of the observers at the scene was restless, mechanically-minded George Westinghouse.

On this day when he gazed at the overturned cars, all his professional curiosity was aroused. He could see little excuse for a collision. The day was clear and the track level. Somebody must have been extremely careless.

"What was the matter?" he asked a trainman. "Wouldn't the brakes work?"

"Sure, but there wasn't time," was the reply. "You can't stop a train in a moment."

The Southern Pacific main line through the San Joaquin Valley between San Francisco and Los Angeles was made possible by completion of the famous Tehachapi Loop in the mountains south of Bakersfield, Calif. The Southern Pacific builders accomplished a climb of 2,734 feet in 28 miles of twisting track which wound up the mountainside through 18 tunnels and around gradual curves on a 2.2 grade. This ingenious "loop" permitted a gain of 77 feet in elevation in a short distance. The route was opened Sept. 5, 1876.

When an engineer wished to stop his train with the brake system then in use, he signaled with his whistle. The brakeman, standing on the platform of a car, frantically turned a hand wheel, thereby drawing a chain taut and setting the brake. At other points in the train other brakemen did the same thing.

The engineers of the wrecked trains had undoubtedly whistled "brakes down" as soon as they saw each other, but before the necessary braking could be done the trains had come together with enough force to cause a bad wreck.

"If an engineer had some way of setting the brakes from the cab instead of depending on a crew of men," Westinghouse thought, "wrecks like this could be avoided."

Why wouldn't it be possible, he mused, to have a single chain running from the locomotive down the length of the train? Then if the engineer had some way of taking up the slack on the chain, he could set all the brakes at once.

Old link and pin coupler (top) caused one fourth of the 391 rail accidents in Massachusetts in 1880. Automatic coupler (below) can be set by a rod extending from the side of the car. When the cars come together the coupler locks automatically in the manner of a Chinese handshake.

One day, while he was eating lunch, a woman sold Westinghouse a subscription to a magazine called *Living Age*. Glancing idly through the copy she left with him, he became interested in a story describing the boring of the Mont Cenis tunnel in Switzerland. Compressed air had been used to drive the rock drills, the compressed air traveling through long pipes from a machine at the tunnel mouth.

Here then was the answer to the brake puzzle! If compressed air could be conveyed through long pipes without losing its power to do work, then it could be used to set brakes on a train.

Finally, with borrowed money, Westinghouse equipped a four-car train belonging to the Panhandle Railroad and invited railroad men to watch the demonstration.

Judged by present-day standards, his device was primitive. On the engine he had an air pump and a compressed air reservoir. Pipes led from this to cylinders on the four cars. By opening a valve the engineer could send air to the cylinders, thus operating pistons and setting the brakes.

The train pulled out of the station with Westinghouse and the observers aboard. Suddenly, a drayman drove his horse and wagon in front of the train. The horses took fright and lunged. The drayman toppled from his seat, fell to the ground, and lay unconscious across the tracks.

The Commodore Vanderbilt, *built in 1870, was a 4-4-0 type locomotive. It had cylinders of 16-inch bore and 24-inch stroke, and 66-inch drivers. It was one of the most ornate engines of its time, with matched wood and brass trimming and a portrait of the Commodore himself on the headlight.*

The engineer of the test train applied the air brakes and the train screeched to a stop so abruptly that the passengers inside the coaches were thrown out of their seats. At first they were irritated at the rough treatment, but when they discovered that a tragedy had been averted, they looked at young Westinghouse with new respect. A more severe test could scarcely have been planned. The new brake had stood up.

Today's safety air brake works just the opposite from this early model. Air pressure holds the brakes open. When the air is exhausted from the lines the shoes are set by springs. Thus if a line breaks or a car becomes uncoupled the brakes are automatically applied.

In the 1870's the worst food served in the United States was unquestionably that put before travelers in the quick-lunch restaurants of depots. For the most part these dismal places operated on the theory that speed and not food was what counted. Dining cars were still rather esoteric things, especially in the West. Many western lines did not possess a single diner. The practice on long trips was to stop the train for 10 minutes at some station, at or near noon and again around supper time. The passengers would be told they had time for a meal, while a fellow stood on the depot platform and rang a bell, shouting what he thought were enticements to "come and get it." Like a herd of buffaloes,

Ball-type signal formerly in service on the Boston and Maine Railroad, and a three-position signal, installed in 1887 in Louisville, Ky.

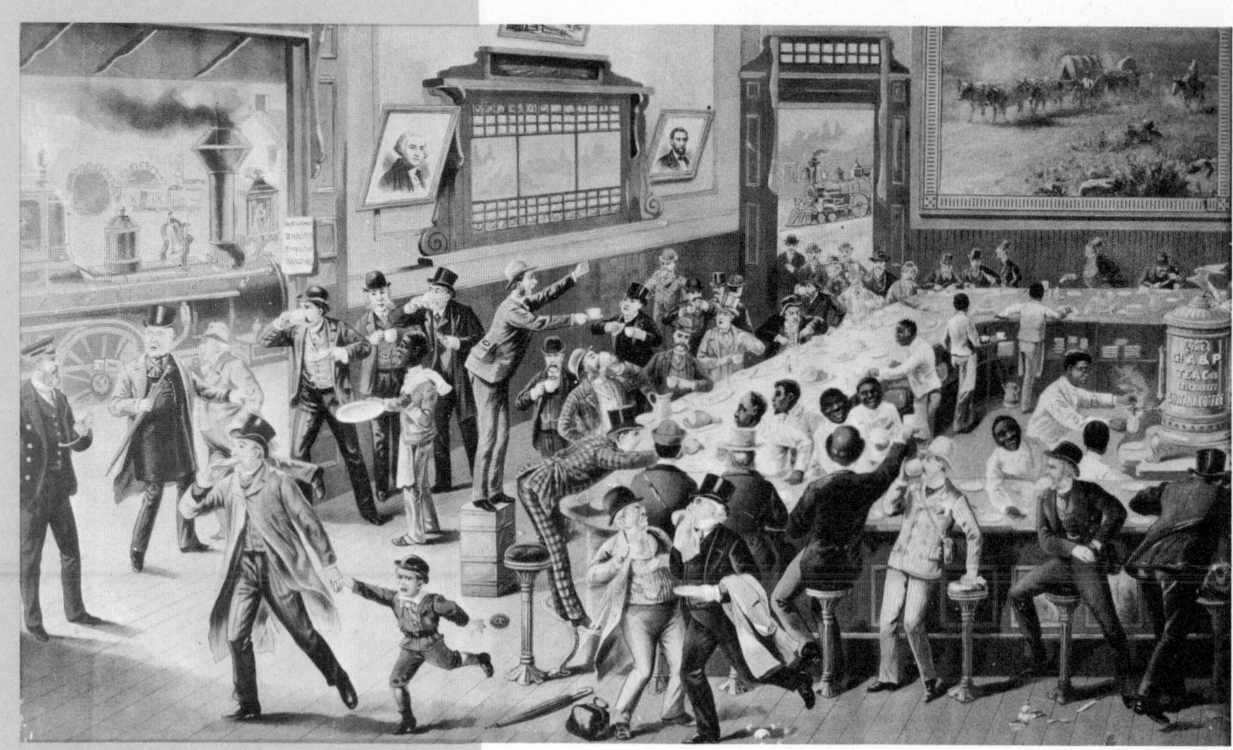

Overworked countermen tried to serve coffee and sandwiches to coachloads of hungry travelers in 10 minutes.

A railway station of the 1880's. Through Pullman service — sleeping, lounging and eating cars — was initiated in 1875.

Before the checking system and the use of special baggage cars, passengers were required to handle and keep track of their own baggage as best they could.

the travelers then stampeded into the quick-lunch, and there greasy, strident viragos, called waitresses, shoved soggy doughnuts and muddy coffee at them across the counter.

In 1876, Frederick Henry Harvey came to Charles F. Morse, superintendent of the Santa Fe, with an idea. Harvey had been operating eating houses in small Kansas towns and had done very well. He told Morse that if the Santa Fe would help him with space and supplies, he would open a depot eating house that would amaze everybody and be a credit to the railroad. Morse agreed to let Harvey try. Harvey took over a room in the Topeka station, scrubbed it thoroughly, painted it, got brand new tablecloths, napkins, and silver, and stocked up with good food. The place quickly caught on. Both the Santa Fe and Fred Harvey knew that they had something worth while.

Fred Harvey and his waitresses, known as "the Harvey Girls," have been credited by more than one observer with civilizing the Southwest at least in the matter of decent food. The Harvey Girls made such a record, both in the business of serving food and of attracting matrimony, that they became the subject of a movie, the true accolade of success in the United States.

But during the years 1890-96, construction fell to about 46 per cent of that of preceding years. In miles, the gain was 33,669—making the total mileage of the country 193,000. Besides this gain in line mileage, however, more

Two pairs of drivers and a truck became so generally adopted in this country that it was known as the "American type" locomotive.

The locomotive engineer is still the popular "hero of the rails." He must run a fast express through midnight darkness with as much confidence as in broad daylight.

The first train into Santa Barbara on Aug. 19, 1887, was the occasion for a big civic celebration. Most of the population of the little California city was at the station to greet the train.

than 66,000 miles of track had been laid as auxiliary trackage, yard track, and sidings, and between $300,000,000 and $400,000,000 had been spent in equipping the trains with air brakes and automatic couplers. The panic of 1893 showed on the railroad records as a tremendous loss in comparison to the preceding year's business. In spite of the enormous crowds which railroads carried to the World's Fair in Chicago, there was a loss of over $16,000,000 in passenger receipts.

By 1896, however, a new period of construction had begun, marked by the larger (relative) expansion in the southern, central, and western sections. The South had pretty well recovered from the long-drawn effects of the Civil War, and the central and western sections were experiencing an immense growth in population, particularly in the agricultural regions.

By this time the New York Central had learned a good deal about public relations since the second Vanderbilt had uttered his famous cry: "The public be damned."

A really swift locomotive, a special job, was built just for the purpose of publicizing the Central's Empire State Express. This was built in the West Albany shops of the company under the direction of the remarkable designer, William Buchanan. The Empire State locomotive was a high-wheeled Atlantic-type engine. On Sept. 14, 1891, she performed the feat that has been reported in print thousands of times: she ran from New York to East Buffalo at the unprecedented rate of 61.4 miles an hour. This record

In 1890 the coaches were heated by circulating hot water from the boiler of the locomotive through pipes along the floors of the cars.

Flint and Père Marquette locomotive No. 3 and two-car passenger train, 1890.

The 1892 Pennsylvania Limited, *first completely electric-lighted train, crossing the Susquehanna River.*

wasn't enough for the directors of the New York Central. They ordered work on another famous locomotive, No. 999, which was designed to be a feature at the coming World's Fair in Chicago, set for 1893.

On May 10 of that year, with Charles Hogan at the throttle, 999 picked up the Empire State Express at Syracuse for the last lap of the run to Buffalo and on a straight, level piece of track west of Batavia, he reputedly drove her for one mile at the rate of 112.5 miles an hour. Nothing that rolled, all railroad historians agree, had ever gone so fast.

The "father" of modern high-speed trains was Dr. Plimmon H. Dudely (1843-1924), who for 43 years was the New York Central's consulting track engineer. Dudely was the first engineer to realize the need for radical improvement in track to permit the railroad industry to develop still further. His best known invention, the track indicator to record track retarding and often dangerous irregularities in track, was the ancestor of the Sperry Rail Detector Car, without which present-day railroad operation as we know it would not be possible.

Railmaster Dudely also designed a new type of rail that increased strength 66 per cent while adding only 23 per cent to the weight. As a result, heavier rolling stock was built; and the world's first heavy, high-speed train, the Empire State Express, in 1891 began blazing the trail for today's fleets of passenger rail liners and hotshot freights. Dudely's rail design became the basis for rails now in use

Locomotive 723 of the Milwaukee Road in the year 1890.

A caboose of about 1885, when emigrant trains (mixed trains of freight and tourist passenger cars) were common.

Parlor cars were first introduced for day runs. They added greatly to the luxury of travel, providing comforts not found in ordinary cars.

Northern Pacific's first North Coast Limited.

all over the country. That, combined with Dudely's other work, is largely credited with reducing the number of broken rails on the New York Central from one in 600 to one in 142,000 over a 13-year period. The fruits of his inventions and research were made available not only to the New York Central but to all American railroads.

America's greatest era of railroad expansion also was a period of great names and men. Especially well known during this period were the financiers, the "Railroad Kings" of the East: Gould, Fisk, Hill, Harriman, J. P. Morgan, the Vanderbilts, and numerous others. There were other men famous for bravery and courage. Among these the name of Casey Jones still remains deeply set into the hearts of the American people in legend and song. You might gather from the song, "Casey Jones," with its fantastic disregard for geography and other known facts, that Mr. Jones belongs to the fabulous realm of Santa Claus, the stork, Paul Bunyan, Little Red Riding Hood and Rip Van Winkle. Such is not the case. The engineer in the song was a real man.

Even during his lifetime Casey built up a sort of legendary reputation for himself. Dispatchers regarded him as a "fast roller," a runner who could be depended upon to get his train over the road "on the card," to take advantage of every break they could give him at passing points. They knew he never dawdled at coal chutes, water cranes, or cinder-pit tracks, or wasted time along the pike.

There was no standard whistle on trains then as there is now; the engineman put on a whistle of his own with a tone that suited him and then practiced a technique of blowing it in a way that would be distinctive.

Casey soon "went on the air" with a long, plaintive wail that advertised to the world that "the man at the throttle was Casey Jones."

It was just three o'clock on the morning of April 30, 1900, when Casey, with his hand on the throttle of No. 638, decided he wouldn't slow down for the sharp curve ahead. A long freight, taking the siding to get out of his way, was not quite in the clear. The caboose and two or three heavy boxcars were still short of the switch when 638's headlight bored through the darkness. Jones choked her, threw the air, let his sand pour over the rails, gave her the "big hole," and told his fireman to jump. The fireman accepted this advice and escaped with his life, but "Casey" stuck to his post. He had both hands on the heavy Johnson bar and his drivers were dancing a mad race in reverse when he took that farewell journey to the "promised land."

As the railroad legends grew, so did the track and rolling stock of the roads. By 1896 nearly all our leading railroad systems were established, and thereafter new construction consisted chiefly of branch lines needed to round out the existing systems and to enable them better to serve the region traversed by the main lines. A few new systems were laid down in the West. Railroad expansion by no means had stopped. Mile after mile was still to be added to America's network of rails.

An electric-lighted parlor car used by the New York Central in 1896.

THE INTERURBAN RAILWAY, a brief but vital development in the evolution of American transportation, made its appearance in 1890. A vast network of interurban railroads sprang up throughout the country almost simultaneously. The interurban fever was particularly fast-spreading in the Middle West, Indiana and Ohio. The lines prospered briefly by carrying millions of passengers each year and died suddenly in the '30's under the accumulated impact of the motor bus, the automobile, and paved highways.

The typical interurban was a single car, although trailers were added on many runs. Parlor cars and diners even appeared on some lines. Fancy 10-section sleepers, with windows in the upper berths, rolled nightly between some cities.

An 1896 N.Y.C. dining-car.

Clockwork banner signal warned approaching trains if another train was standing at the station.

But the great attraction of the interurban was the convenience of door-to-door transportation, not in the glamorous limited service. A farmer could flag a car at a highway crossing, which probably was less than a half mile from his farm, and a city passenger might alight in front of his residence.

This superservice slowed the schedules, of course, and so a few limited trains operated between the larger centers, stopping only at designated points.

Famous old 999, designed by William Buchanan, scooping water from a New York Central track pan. In 1893 Number 999 pulled the Empire State Express at a rate of 112 miles an hour for a short stretch between Syracuse and Buffalo.

Early wooden car used by the Union Traction Company. This car operated between Indianapolis and Tipton and was the type used in through service between Indianapolis and South Bend.

The first cars were of wood construction, usually on steel underframes. Steel sheathing, later used extensively, improved the appearance but added little to the strength. Consequently, the death toll in collisions was appalling, until all-steel cars were adopted.

Most early cars ranged from 45 to 60 feet in length and carried about 55 passengers, usually one-third in the smoker. A baggage compartment was considered important, since many of the traction's best customers were traveling men loaded with sample cases.

Cars operated at a maximum speed of 60 m.p.h., but overall schedules were much slower because of the long, slow trips through city streets and the frequent stops. However, in all cases schedules were comparable to those of the present-day bus services that replaced them, and on some runs the traction car of 35 years ago was faster than the motor bus of today.

The interurban day began around 5 A.M. and stopped when the last car reached its terminal about midnight. Except for the earliest and latest portions of the day, the cars usually departed principal stations hourly on main lines and at one-and-one-half or two-hour intervals on lines of lighter traffic. During afternoon rush hours, cars sometimes were operated oftener.

Indiana's interurban story is typical of the story elsewhere. For more than a decade after the first car entered Indianapolis on New Year's Day, 1900, new lines pushed from the capital at the average rate of one a year until by 1911, like spokes from a hub, they extended in all directions.

The Winona Flyer, *a double-truck, single-end "wind-splitter" used from 1910 to 1926 between Indianapolis and South Bend.*

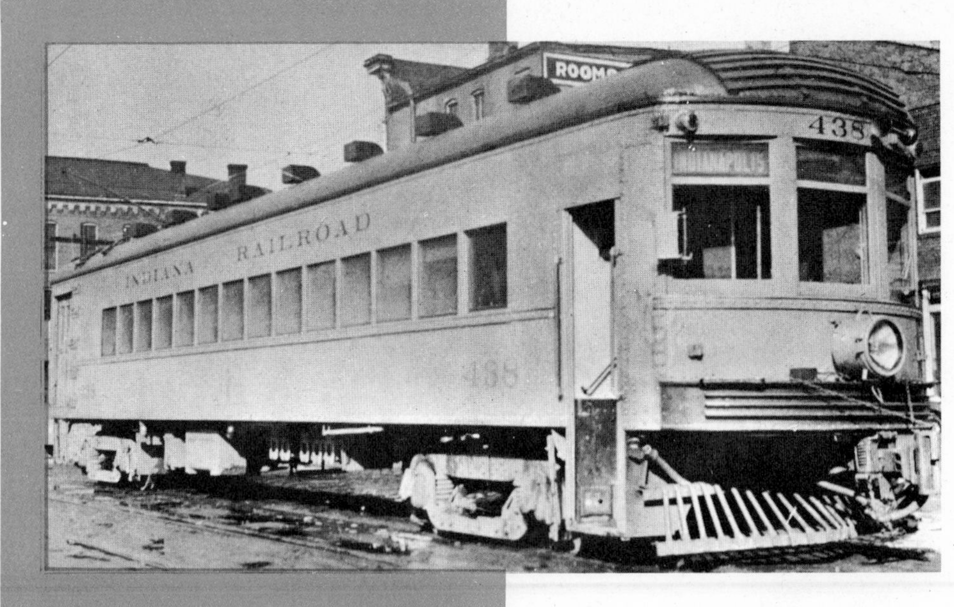

Heavyweight car built in 1925 by the St. Louis Car Company for Union Traction, and taken over by the Indiana Railroad. The car weighed 45 tons and carried 44 passengers. It was retired in 1940.

In 1911, Seattle, Wash., installed cars that provided for 70 passengers—this being obtained by placing cross seats at each end of the car and a long side seat on the blind side of the car facing the side entrance.

Early interurban train that crossed the Ohio River over a bridge at Wheeling, W. Va., to the Ohio towns of Martins Ferry, Bridgeport and Bellaire.

Indianapolis terminal as it appeared during the early days. Its nine tracks are now gone and the space is used by bus lines.

The coverage by this network was so complete that the lines served two-thirds of Indiana's 92 counties, and if the additional projected lines had been built the system would have touched all but about a half-dozen counties.

There is convincing proof of the interurban's immediate popularity. More than 377,000 passengers paid fares the first year, when only two short lines served the city of Indianapolis. The following year the number jumped to 955,000 and in another year to 1,500,000.

In 1904, more than 3,000,000 riders traveled the lines radiating from the city. In 1906 the number of passengers exceeded 4,000,000, a year later it passed 5,000,000 and by 1913 it had reached 7,000,000. Cars were installed at a proportional rate.

The Indiana Railroad revamped three former Indiana Service coaches into coach-railway post offices. The cars, built in 1926 by the St. Louis Car Company, weighed 50 tons and carried 28 passengers.

Double-truck, single-end combine built in 1926. This light-weight steel car was converted eventually from two-man to one-man operation.

Familiar sights were highway-crossing station and cattle guards.

The reasons for this tremendous growth were the large number of manufacturing cities and towns and the unusual density of rural population in the midwestern states at that time. In Indiana, for example, there were 170 towns and cities with a combined population of more than 1,000,000 that lay on the interurban lines converging on Indianapolis.

The mounting pitch of interurban fever sent dozens of other lines reaching across states—but on paper only. Nearly every city and town dreamed of getting into the act. At least 124 companies were organized that never operated although many of them started construction. This figure does not include defunct companies whose lines were constructed by succeeding corporations.

Box-cab locomotive used in freight service by the Interstate Public Service Company. It was built in 1926.

In the very shops in which the first Pullman car was built, the first interurban sleeper came into existence.

Many projects duplicated each other as rival companies vied for investors' money and suitable rights-of-way. Usually the traction companies were locally inspired and financed, built on the hopes of small businessmen who sought to attract trade from surrounding towns or to link their cities with larger centers.

A few, however, had their eyes on something bigger. The most stupendous project was the Chicago-New York Electric Airline Railroad Company, which chose a route it claimed was nearly 200 miles shorter than any steam line. The road, which never was built, promised to carry passengers between the terminals for a $10 fare.

As passenger traffic began to dwindle in the mid-'20's, traction men increased their efforts to develop freight

Day arrangement of a convertible sleeper.

When the night's ride was over all compartments were rolled into the walls and into the floors. The beds were rolled up into parlor-car chairs and the car was nothing more nor less than a parlor car itself.

Steel sleeper which operated nightly. Cars were 10-section sleepers with windows in upper berths. They were built to carry trailers.

Interior of wooden car used by the Terre Haute, Indianapolis and Eastern Traction Company. Beyond glass partition is the smoking compartment.

business. Indianapolis built a new freight depot in 1926, which was described as the world's largest interurban less-than-carload terminal. Fast freights departed nightly for distant cities in that state and way freights from nearer communities arrived in Indianapolis about midnight, departing with new loads about 3 A.M.

The interurban lines withstood frequent receiverships until the early '30's when they began to fold at an alarming rate. By this time rapidly-improving highway travel had beaten the traction system to its knees and, despite a gallant last stand, the interurban was doomed.

Larger lines began buying out smaller ones, thus cutting operating expenses and increasing the efficiency of service. Improvement programs were launched. Lightweight, high-speed cars capable of traveling at 70 m.p.h. were installed.

For a short time, the invigorated interurban system seemed to be making money. Then, as suddenly as they had appeared, interurban lines began to disappear. The automobile and the motor bus and truck had become firmly entrenched in the transportation system of the country, and the last tentacles of the mighty interurban octopus were cut in 1941.

Lounge section at rear of an Indiana Railroad lightweight. Seats were upholstered and floor carpeted. Rear end had all-around observation effect.

Two Indiana Railroad lightweights, purchased in 1931 when the road made a last effort to attract business. Front car is a coach-lounge seating 38 passengers.

A smash song hit of the Nineties—"A New Thing under the Sun."

The second stage in the development of the bicycle was the velocipede, or boneshaker.

The hobby-horse was a crude affair which the rider straddled and propelled with his feet.

The high point in a cyclist's year was the American Wheelmen's annual affair. On Friday excursions from 25 to 40 miles were held, followed by a Saturday parade, another outing and banquet.

General Committee League of Am. Wheelmen.

Eighth Annual Meet May 20 & 21, 1887.

Saint Louis, Mo.

COMMITTEE CHAIRMEN:

W. M. BREWSTER, Chairman, 309 Olive Street. BADGE: PURPLE.

L. J. BERGER, Secretary, 1901 Oregon Ave., St. Louis.

TRANSPORTATION: BADGE: RED. B. B. AYERS, 212 Clark St., Chicago, Ills.

PARADE: BADGE: PURPLE AND WHITE. Prof. C. H. STONE, 310 N. 11th St., St. Louis.

FINANCE: BADGE: GOLD. J. E. SMITH, Simmons Hd'e. Co. St. Louis.

RECEPTION: BADGE: WHITE. EDW. SELLS, 105 N. 2d St., St. Louis.

RUNS AND TOURS: BADGE: GREEN. L. J. BERGER, 1901 Oregon Ave., St. Louis.

PROGRAMME: BADGE: BLUE AND WHITE. A. K. STEWART, Care "Spectator" St. Louis.

ENTERTAINMENT: BADGE: BLUE. G. W. BOSWELL, 416 N. 2d St., St. Louis.

BANQUET: BADGE: GOLD AND WHITE. Dr. H. H. KEITH, 2248 Wash'n Ave. St. Louis.

PRESS: BADGE: RED AND WHITE. W. E. HICKS, Care "Post-Dispatch" St. Louis.

In the 1890's, bicycling became something more than the reigning fad of the nation. In an age known for its isolationism because of lacking transportation means, the bicycle enabled people to make more meaningful face-to-face associations. In hosteling, the cyclist met people from all kinds of life as he couldn't before. On the road he saw the intimate structures of communities: the particular homes, stores, streets, and industries. The farmer, general storekeeper, the villager all became real people, especially for the city rider.

It might be hard for us now to believe what an important place the bicycle had in the Gay Nineties. But manufacturers were selling 1,000,000 bikes a year in spite of the high price—from $100 to $150—which was a lot of money for times when a gentleman could buy a good suit for $15 and a dozen eggs cost 14 cents.

By 1899 there were 312 bicycle factories in the United States and still the supply could not meet the demand. Old timers remember the excitement every year on Washington's Birthday, the day the cycling season officially opened and the bike industry showed off its handsome new models.

People were spending so much money on bicycles that other businesses suffered a sharp recession. Shoemakers sat idle. They said it was because "hardly anyone walks anymore." By 1896 the piano business was off 50 per cent, jewelry stores were empty, and a prominent hat manufacturer, in desperation, demanded that Congress pass a law requiring every cyclist to buy two felt hats a year.

Barbers complained bitterly that their customers were cycling every evening instead of getting a shave and sprucing up. "When a man skips a shave," the barbers pointed out sadly, "we can't sell him two shaves tomorrow. The shave is gone forever."

The wheel size of the boneshaker required the rider to pedal fast without attaining much speed.

The velocipede had pedals attached to the front hub and a larger front wheel.

Two styles of the ordinary, or high-wheel, bicycle — circa 1872–1892.

Diamond Jim Brady, fabulous figure of the times, had his stock of "luxurious" bicycles, a dozen with gold-plated frames and silver-plated spokes, and studded with diamonds and rubies. Brady's triple tandem was one of the first three-seaters ever made.

People built their leisure time and much of their social activities around the bicycle. Special clubs for biking spread throughout the country. Every small city and town had its cycle club, many socially important. In a large city there would be hundreds of cycling clubs, some of them housed luxuriously and boasting an elite membership.

There were mottos, songs and poems that grew up along with the bicycle. "For men may come and men may go, but we roll on forever" was one club's way of putting the new sensation into words.

Special wardrobes were designed for cyclists. Men wore short woolen jackets, slim woolen knickers, and small round caps with visors. The woman rider gave up her long rustling skirt with its voluminous petticoats. For her bicycle costume she wore tight fitted jackets with huge puffed sleeves and cut her skirts so that they almost revealed her ankles. Her gloves matched the color of her straw hat, which was attached firmly to her pompadour with huge hat pins.

Newspaper editors, preachers, and, of course, chaperones, did a lot of worrying about the spirited young ladies who were riding the rear seat of tandem bikes. After all, until the bicycle outdistanced her, the chaperone had always made it a threesome when a girl stepped out with her beau. And besides, until then, women never played anything more strenuous than a mild game of croquet.

But there was no stopping these lady free-wheelers. And the biggest scandal, the greatest head-shaking of all, was still to come. Mrs. Amelia Bloomer, an intrepid lady cyclist, decided that an ankle-length skirt cut down your speed on the road. She designed herself a more suitable garment, a pair of trousers with a buttoned waist band and neat two-inch cuffs just below the knee.

Other girls on the road quickly took to wearing bloomers, and for the first time women were wearing pants and were showing their shapely legs.

It was no wonder that a New Haven clergyman in 1896 told the few people in his congregation who were not out cycling that the Sunday cyclists were rolling downhill to a place "where there is no mud on the streets because of its high temperature."

Few listened to the barbers or the clergymen or the chaperones. A prominent physician defended the bicycle. He said that not in 200 years had any one thing "so benefited the human race."

A bicycle club of Oakland, Calif., during the Nineties. Members used to spend their Sundays and holidays on all-day jaunts over the countryside.

The tandem soon gave rise to the "triplet" tandem, followed by the "quartet" and then the "quadruplet."

Ignatz Schwinn, his son Frank, and Mrs. Schwinn made a cozy trio on this family tandem bicycle of 1896. The Schwinn factory was one of about 300 then manufacturing bicycles in United States.

The Columbia Bicycle Club of Chicago.

Robert D. Garden cut a natty figure on his Columbia Light Roadster safety, one of the first to have a spring fork.

In 1896, *Forum* magazine admitted: "Putting all other social and economic influences of the bicycle aside, its influence as a missionary for scientific road building is alone sufficient to entitle it to the lasting gratitude of the American people."

Any Sunday the streets were filled with cyclists. The young couple on a date or the group of young women out for an airing were usually members of the local cycling club. Many clubs ventured on all-day trips to the country. Families on machines built for three or four mounted their bicycles early on a holiday, with their lunch baskets swinging from their handlebars, bound for the picnic grounds. Weaving in and out of every crowd that moved along at a comfortable rate of 10 to 12 m.p.h. were one or two gay young men on racers, determined to show how fast they could dart in and out of traffic.

But bicycling was not only just a sport for pleasure. Laborers and office workers used them as a means of getting to work. There were long bicycle racks set in back of some of the factories and even the larger office buildings in many cities.

One of the organizations of this era which agitated successfully for better roads was the League of American Wheelmen. In 1881, one year after its start, a thousand wheelmen from all parts of the country rode in the league's parade. The organization's membership grew rapidly after this and for the first time the United States had an organized group of voters who wanted good roads.

The league was interested in speed and endurance records as well as roads. It issued official medals to any

The girl cycling on a Sunday in billowing bloomers was a most darling young lady in the Nineties.

cyclist who could do a "Century." The requirements were simple but vigorous. All the cyclist had to do was to ride his bike in any chosen direction straight out for 50 miles, then turn around and ride back the same 50 miles. The trip was expected to take around 10 hours.

When did bicycles really get their start and how did they reach the peak of popularity in the Nineties?

Bicycle manufacturers like to remind us that the bicycle is probably the oldest article still being manufactured in which the basic principles were the least changed. Forerunners of the bicycle go back at least to 1816.

The earliest bicycles had two wheels connected by a plain wooden bar which the rider mounted. He propelled himself forward by pushing his feet against the ground. This curiosity, invented in 1816, was called the Hobbyhorse. The vehicle cost so much money, however, that only the very rich could afford to buy one and it soon became known as the Dandyhorse.

About 1840 Kirkpatrick MacMillan added cranks, driving rods, pedals, handlebars, a seat and fancy armrests to a Dandyhorse. He rode the machine himself, and once he was arrested and subsequently fined for "furious driving."

The first bicycles manufactured on any sort of commercial scale were sold in Paris in the 1860's. They were the invention of a Frenchman, Pierre Lallement, who added rotary cranks to the machine. Lallement sold his patent and came to the United States, where he also went into the bicycle business.

Lallement's bicycles (he called them velocipedes) soon became known to the public as "boneshakers." By this

Thirty-five dollars was a lot of money for a bicycle in 1899, and for one without mudguards, at that.

A bicycle without fork allowed tire changes in a few seconds.

To dismantle or set up a folding bike: five minutes.

Freakish delights—bicycle balloon ascensions, the cycloplane, and (opposite page) the bicycle fitted to run on a railroad track.

time the machine looked somewhat like the modern bicycle; the two wheels were almost the same size. The pedals and driving cranks, though, were attached to the center of the front wheel. These wheels were of wood and the tires were made of heavy iron. The entire frame of the vehicle was fashioned from thick metal. These machines shook so on the roads that the driver was quickly tired out, and after a short trip, could easily appreciate the vehicle's nickname.

The first American manufacturer was Colonel Albert A. Pope of Boston. He had visited London and Coventry, and after studying the construction of the bicycle, brought back samples of English wheels. About 1878, Pope bought a sewing machine factory at Hartford and turned it into a factory known as the Pope Manufacturing Company. The famous *Columbia* bicycle was turned out in this pioneer factory. The ball bearing and coaster brake were improvements added at this time. The weight of the average bicycle was reduced to 25 pounds. But it still cost from $75 to $125.

By this time a bicycle known for many years as the "high wheel" or "ordinary" had been developed. The heavy wooden wheels had been gradually replaced with metal ones with thin wire spokes. Solid rubber tires were cemented to the rims. The most famous trademark of the

An early advertisement of the Pope Manufacturing Company—the first bicycle factory in the country.

ordinary was the high front wheel. On a seat over this a man sat sometimes five feet above ground. Here he could pedal away at great speed—if he could keep his balance. If he couldn't, and this was not too infrequent, a fall from his high mount could result in broken bones.

The front wheel, which drove the vehicle, was made larger than the rear wheel so that greater speed could be attained. The largest wheels were 65 inches high. As the front wheel was made larger, the size of the back one was reduced and on some models was only 12 inches in diameter. But the tall front wheels made it difficult for a short man to ride comfortably and various other designs were tried for greater comfort. One early bicycle had cranks and pedals set above the front axle and a chain was attached so that short riders could manipulate the machine easier. Three-wheelers, like large tricycles, also became popular. But the high wheeled ordinary was the bicycle in most common use for a good 20 years.

Later, experiments with wheels of equal size and a set of sprockets developed what was to be the basic design for the modern bicycle. This model was called the "safety." The sprockets in a safety bicycle made it unnecessary to have the large front wheels. The sprockets were designed so that the driver exerted little effort and the speed would still be great. This was done by setting a toothed disk in

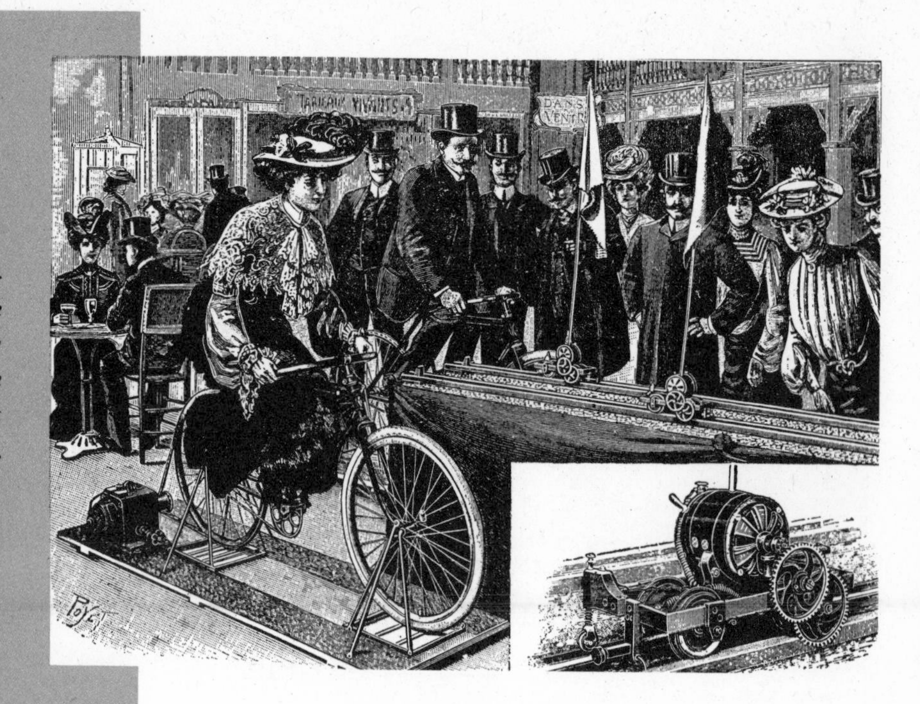

Penny arcades once featured the stationary bike race to their eager Gay Nineties clientele. In the picture the woman is about two miles ahead.

In 1904, a daring stunt man jumped a 56-foot gap on a bicycle.

between the two wheels. The pedals were attached to the disk and a chain running around it also circled a smaller toothed disk set in the hub of the rear wheels.

The transition from the ordinary to the safety bicycle was rapid. In 1889, nearly five times as many people rode the safety as the ordinary. The next year only one person in about 25 still rode the ordinary.

As the bicycle industry flourished it did much to encourage other business—the rubber and steel industries, primarily. Better roads were demanded by cyclists and some of their demands were met. Among some of the early bicycle men were those who later went into the automobile business and others who were to play such a large part in the development of the airplane – such as Glenn Curtiss and the Wright brothers.

Some early multi-cycles could carry as many as 13 passengers, and with 26 feet working the pedals, they actually ran very easily and smoothly.

The first U.S. bike race was held in New York City in 1891. These bicycle marathons became very popular. The two-man teams rode in relays for 142 hours, taking turns at resting, eating, and sleeping.

In 1899 a complicated system of variable gears improved the driving mechanism still further. These gears made it possible to obtain three speeds on a bicycle and gave the rider his choice of high speeds or smoother and easier pedaling on hills and over rough roadways.

Special bicycles were designed for women and girls. The center bar was dropped on these models, making it possible for a woman to ride a bike in a skirt. The tandem, which had two seats, two sets of handlebars, and two pairs of pedals, became one of the most popular models and is still used to some extent today by couples who wish to ride together. A modification of the tandem carried a small seat between the two riders in which a child could be placed for a family ride. Some bicycles, following the same principle as the tandem, were designed to carry five riders.

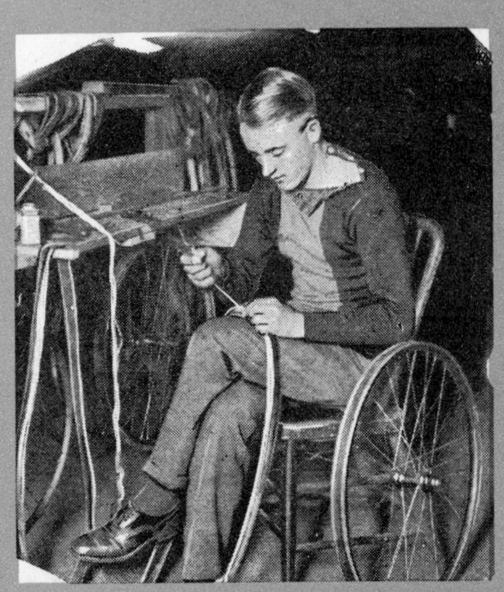

Racing tires were made from a special linen, woven from selected thread and cut and sewed together to form a thin but tough tube. A race with a dozen riders would require an average of six repairs or replacements of tires each hour during ordinary racing, and from 15 to 20 per hour during sprints and jams.

On June 30, 1899, Charles M. Murphy startled the world when he rode a mile behind a Long Island R.R. train in 57 4/5 seconds.

Paced racing, in which a single rider was paced by a three, four or five-seated machine, was popular.

Manufacturers worked to make the bicycle more comfortable and the frame was constructed so that bumps on the road could be absorbed before the rider was jarred. This was accomplished to some extent by curving the fork, the bar of steel extending from the steering column to the center of the front wheel. The steering column itself was set in ball bearings. A simple system of brakes was also added for the driver's safety.

Professional bike racing became the nation's favorite spectator sport during the Nineties. The sports sections of newspapers were crowded with stories of current cycle-racing events, and the breaking of a record for any distance was front-page news. Track racing drew tremendous crowds, and streets were lined for blocks with spectators watching the finish of road races. Almost every young cyclist had racing aspirations.

There are people who still remember the racing stars of those years, men like Buddie Munger, Arthur Zimmerman, and Eddie Bald. Major Taylor was a pint-sized cyclist who outdistanced every racer in the world from 1899 to 1902.

In 1893, Johnny Johnston became the first cyclist to ride a mile in less than two minutes. He was paced by a sulky towing a large canvas wind screen. A still more sensational ride was turned in in 1899 by "Mile-a-Minute" Murphy, who pedaled a mile in 57 4/5 seconds behind a special vestibuled railroad car built by the Long Island Railroad.

At the turn of the century, with other forms of transportation growing rapidly, the demand for bicycles collapsed almost overnight. Between 1900 and 1905 more than three-fifths of the manufacturers went out of business.

Three decades later, however, the bicycle underwent a revival of popularity. A generation that grew up with the motor car discovered all over again that it's fun to pedal your own wheels. By 1940, manufacturers again were turning out more than one million shiny new bikes a year. The modern machine was lighter and faster than the popular safety bike of the Nineties. Its weight was reduced one-third in 1930 when manufacturers started to use Duralumin, an aluminum alloy, in the frames.

Ten years later the sale of bicycles reached 2,800,000 units a year, or more than twice the number produced at the height of the Gay Nineties.

Bicycles today, with their mudguards, bright colors, and leather seats set on springs, are cheaper than in the days when they were an important means of transportation. Most of the 18,000,000 American bicycle riders are now riding them for pleasure.

The present-day stage of bicycle evolution. Balloon tires have been common since 1933.

An 1895 racer featured rat-trap metal pedals, light wooden rims and severe frame design.

The present American racing bike, with slight modifications, was developed in the mid-Thirty's. A strong lightweight metal, duralumin, is used for present-day frames, decreasing the racer's weight to 15 lbs.

The Island Queen, *completed in 1896, was one of the first river boats exclusively for excursions. She carried passengers from Cincinnati to Ohio's Coney Island.*

·IV·

Horseless Carriages and Piano Wire Crates

The Queen City *managed to operate into the 20th century due to a freight agreement between her owners and the rail lines at Cincinnati.*

ALTHOUGH THE STEAMBOATS fought a losing battle against the railroads after the Civil War, they were able to stave off extinction for another few decades. From

The Delta Queen, *last of the overnight passenger-carrying packets on the Mississippi, on a regular schedule between Cincinnati and New Orleans.*

about 1870 until the end of the century, steamboating was able to get its second wind and do a fairly prosperous business. The cotton trade revived, providing both freight and wealthy passengers. A planter and his family might live aboard a luxurious steamboat for weeks at a time.

There was a struggle, however, before the packets regained some of their prewar form. The Atlantic and Mississippi Steamship Corporation started out in a big way in 1866 when the owners of several large, swift side-wheelers pooled their resources to form the biggest steamboat combination the West was to see. Organized as a joint-stock corporation, this company had capital stock with an estimated value of $2,240,000. But the corporation was short-lived and had to discontinue operations in 1867.

The Liberty *was the last commercial packet to ply the Ohio River. When she abandoned her trade in 1936, the "good old steamboating days" ended.*

Nakomis operated on the Mississippi in the government-sponsored freight service, 1918.

The upper Mississippi bordered lumber regions, and vast rafts of logs were floated to the sawmills, from the 1860's until 1915.

The St. Paul and Sidney are pictured going through the lock which by-passed the Keokuk Dam across the Mississippi.

An association of Ohio steamboat owners was more successful. These steamboat men pooled their interests in 1870 to form the "O" Line. Most of the vessels in the line were long, slender stern-wheelers. The individual owners maintained certain dates for sailing and agreed not to engage in any rate-cutting. As a result, the "O" Line steamboats did a profitable business for several years.

From the bankrupt remains of the Atlantic and Mississippi Steamship Corporation, the St. Louis and New Orleans Packet Company was formed in the 1870's. Under this name and later that of the Merchant's Southern Line Packet Company, the reorganized company prospered for almost a decade. Another reorganization took place in 1879, and the Anchor Line emerged to operate into the next century.

The Anchor Line stressed prompt and reliable service and became a respected name in the Mississippi Valley. The company discarded all the old boats left over from before the Civil War and developed a new kind of vessel, about 250 feet long and quite fast, which was built by the Howards of Jeffersonville, Ind. They were equipped with spacious, luxurious cabins and were all named after cities and towns along the Mississippi, the *City of Baton Rouge* being one of the largest and most popular.

By the 1880's the steamboats may have started to decline but they were still doing a healthy business. No railroads yet paralleled the Mississippi between New Orleans and Memphis in the early 1880's, so the people along the river still depended upon the water transportation. Even where there was a choice, most of the New Orleans and Memphis people preferred traveling by water. To go by trains still meant making many changes and tolerating many delays. The steamboats, on the other hand, provided through passage with comfortable accommodations and good food.

However, the railroads encroached further and further into steamboat territory each year and did all they could to kill off the competitor. By 1887, almost all the towns on the lower Mississippi with a population of more than 1,000 inhabitants had railroad connections.

The number of steamboats on long runs began to decrease as it became easier for the railroads to get the trade away from the river. Only one regular steamboat line from Cincinnati to New Orleans remained by 1887. The regular Louisville boats were no longer operating. Then, when the Interstate Commerce Commission ruled that the Louisville and Nashville Railroad did not have to observe the long- and short-haul clause where water competition was present, the steamboats all but gave up.

The towboat John J. Rowe, *towing 18 barges of coal and an empty gasoline barge on the Ohio River.*

The barges shown below contain pipe, steel, paper, sugar, sulphur and gasoline. The total cargo weighs some 8100 tons.

The Wheeling Steel Corporation has its own towboats and barges.

Standard Oil's towboat, the Stranolind A, *is capable of pushing six barges loaded with 2,400,000 gallons of petroleum products against strong river currents.*

Another view of the Ductillite *(above, center), a fine example of a modern screw-propelled towboat.*

As early as 1918 some 200 motorcars were shipped from Cincinnati to Memphis aboard river barges.

Comprised of three 175-foot units, this tow of barges can hold 600 cars. Bow and stern sections have four cargo-carrying levels.

Flat-deck barges of the type shown here are used to carry automobiles and trucks down the river.

To compensate for the loss of business on the through trade, the boats increased activity in the port-to-port trade, and they managed to hang onto the cotton and sugar trades which they had brought into being and fostered for so many years.

During the 1880's Frederick A. Laidley gathered several small steamboat lines together and combined them with the old United States Mail Line. The new organization was called the White Collar Line. Laidley's line managed to do an extensive business among the better class of travelers until as late as 1890.

By 1894 the river traffic had visibly declined, so Laidley tried once again to revive it. He proceeded to build and put into the Louisville trade three fine steamers: *City of Louisville, City of Cincinnati,* and *Indiana.* They were completed by 1898. Each ship was equipped with large, airy staterooms. Although the general design of these vessels was restrained as compared with the ornate old-time boats, they were the finest steamers built within the previous two decades on the Ohio.

Both the *Louisville* and *Cincinnati* were destroyed in

The 800-horsepower M/V Mary Ellen *has a retractable pilot house. She is shown here with six grain barges in tow. The total capacity of this group of barges is 162,000 bushels.*

the ice during the winters of 1918 and 1919. This put an end to the steamboating career of Frederick A. Laidley. The romantic age of the steamboat had come to an end.

The opening of the twentieth century found the steamboating slump growing progressively worse. The railroads had done a thorough job of practically exterminating freight shipping on the rivers.

However, the time soon came when the railroads were unable to handle all the nation's freight and had to call for help. Actually, it was the federal government rather than the railroads that sought the help. During World War I, the government took over the operation of the railroads and found that wartime shipping demands were beyond the normal capacities of the rail lines. Long-haul

This barge was specially built to transport chemicals on inland waterways. It measures 195 x 35 x 8 feet and has a capacity of 1100 tons.

Special combinations, built to carry a single cargo, are sometimes built to work as a single unit, with adjoining ends fitted flush to eliminate dead water between barges.

motor truck routes were set up, but at the same time it was realized that still more freight facilities would be needed.

Therefore, a special committee was appointed to investigate the possibilities of putting the western rivers back into use. The result was the birth of the Mississippi Warrior Service — also known as the Federal Barge Line — which was sponsored by the War Department. All available equipment was brought together and the construction of a new fleet was begun.

A rather unimpressive fleet (as far as looks were concerned) was put together and placed in operation in September, 1918. Once again the western rivers served the nation well. This experiment proved so successful that

This special barge is for moving paper from Bucksport, Me., to Chicago. The trip is made via the Atlantic Coast to New York City, up the Hudson River and through the New York State Canal and the Great Lakes.

The diesel-powered towboat Winchester *is shown here with two of its four barges. This equipment is the latest development in safe, efficient bulk-petroleum transportation.*

Here is a view of the bow rake of a modern tank barge with a 21,000-barrel capacity. The bow steering propeller unit is in lowered position for use when the barge is empty.

Congress decided it was too good a thing to give up after the war was over.

At the urging of shippers along the western rivers, Congress voted to continue to furnish money for the operation of the Mississippi fleet in peacetime. The idea was to stimulate the establishment of privately owned lines of river craft. As soon as the Federal Barge Line could operate on a paying basis, the government intended to turn it over to private interests. As could be expected, the railroads protested long and loudly.

A new era on the rivers was begun as the emphasis shifted from passengers to freight. The traffic in passengers continued to decline until not a single packet line remained on the Mississippi. Today a traveler cannot get river passage, even by a series of changes, from New Orleans to Louisville, or even to Cairo or Memphis. There is not even a packet to take passengers from New Orleans to St. Louis.

Before passenger packets sounded their last death rattle, there was one last gasp of activity in 1929 between Cincinnati and Louisville. The Louisville and Cincinnati Packet Company, which had grown out of the old United States Mail Line, operated a few boats between the two cities. This was a particularly convenient service for businessmen commuting between the two cities on the Ohio. Such passengers boarded the *Queen City, Cincinnati,* or one of the other packets in the evening, had a good supper and breakfast aboard ship, a good night's rest, and arrived

The towboat Mount Vernon, *powered by three Cooper-Bessemer, FV-8, diesel engines, is owned by the Cooper-Bessemer Corporation and the Jeffersonville Boat and Machinery Co.*

Modern, screw-propelled, diesel-powered vessels like the W. S. Rhea *maintain regular schedules over the 4,000-mile inland-water network. The* Rhea *was built by the Dravo Corporation of Pittsburgh.*

The M/V Celeste *is powered by twin-screw, Cooper-Bessemer diesel engines with 1350 horsepower.*

The tugboat Stemwinder *is the type which operates on the Gulf intracoastal waterways.*

Although pipelines provide the main means of transporting crude oil and products, many companies such as the Ashland Oil and Refining Company make extensive use of the inland waterways.

in the neighbor city early enough the next morning to transact business. All this cost no more than a railroad ticket alone.

Although the number of steamboats now operating on the Mississippi system is but a fraction of the total which plied the rivers during the 1800's, there are a few modern versions operating in the excursion trade. Among the most well-known of the river excursion steamers is the luxury liner S.S. *Admiral,* the flagship of the Streckfus Line, which operates out of St. Louis.

The *Admiral* is a descendant of a famous line of excursion packets. Streckfus Steamers, Inc. was begun by John Streckfus in 1884 when he bought the small steamboat *Freddie.* The Streckfus Line then ran the eight miles from Rock Island to Andalusia. Captain Streckfus served as a virtual errand boy for the farmers, taking their produce and grain to town, marketing the cargo, and even shopping for the farmers and their wives.

In four years Streckfus bought a second steamboat, the double-deck *Verne Swaine,* and opened a run between

The Dravo 42 *isn't the biggest or the most powerful or the newest towboat on the rivers, but she is nevertheless a handsome boat with excellent proportions.*

Rock Island and Clinton. As business expanded, another boat was added to the line—the *City of Winona,* a raft towboat converted into a packet. These early boats were used exclusively for the traffic in freight.

Then, in 1901, Streckfus built the *J. S.*, designed exclusively for pleasure excursions. The four-deck *J. S.* was 175 feet long and 45 feet across the beam. There were often as many as 2,000 passengers aboard this ship, which went from town to town between New Orleans to St. Paul. In 1903 the *J. S.* began winter excursions from the harbor of New Orleans, a practice which has been continued by the line every year since.

In 1911 the Streckfus family bought the remaining four boats of the Diamond Jo Line, which formed the nucleus of the present fleet. Two of the boats were used in the excursion business, one ran a passenger and freight service between St. Paul and St. Louis, and the fourth ran between St. Louis and Burlington. The Streckfus Line then put on an aggressive advertising campaign to rebuild regular passenger service. As a result, the Streckfus boats kept the

The integrated tug-and-barge Rampant *is operated by 1200-horsepower twin engines. It can handle a load equal to 26 tank cars.*

Queen of the Columbia and Willamette Rivers is the new Portland, *modern and efficient, yet patterned after stern-wheelers built at the turn of the century.*

With brass band playing, the Harvest Queen *did a lively excursion trade on the Columbia River in the 1890's.*

river from being entirely forgotten as a highway of travel. But after 1917, the country went Model T crazy and forgot the rivers once again.

The Streckfus Line managed to hang on until business began to boom again on the rivers. Today it operates the largest excursion fleet in the world, with the S. S. *Admiral* as its proud flagship. The *Admiral* is 374 feet long and 90 feet wide. She accommodates 4,000 passengers, who are provided with a vast ballroom, several dining rooms, a promenade, terrace garden, and other luxuries usually associated with an ocean liner.

The Streckfus steamers operate on 3,000 miles of waterways in 14 states. In addition to the *Admiral* there is the steamer *President*, an all-steel ship which completely revolutionized inland marine design a few years back.

The Mississippi has indeed changed since the 1800's. The old-time captains and pilots would probably frown upon the contemporary modern steamboats with steel hulls, condensing machinery, twin-screw propellers and Diesel engines.

However, the old-time stern-wheelers are not altogether extinct. Over on the Columbia River this type of craft has been put to excellent use. One of the heroines of this river was the steamboat *Harvest Queen*, which in 1890 was clocked at four minutes over a distance of four miles. The *Harvest Queen* was a fast boat to be sure, but even she could not do better than 23 to 25 miles an hour under ordinary conditions. The mile-a-minute pace was made possible by the help of rapids at flood stage, a stern wind and a skillful pilot. But it also took a highly maneuverable ship to challenge those rapids. And that's exactly what the *Harvest Queen* was—an able craft.

The *Harvest Queen* and all the other old packets on the

The Cascades *guides tow barge loads of wheat through Columbia rapids.*

The old Portland *noses a tanker up the river. The tug is lashed alongside the steamer for berthing.*

Operating in the 1890's, the stern-wheeler Regulator *is shown carrying covered wagons. Note the similarity to today's river tugs.*

This shallow-draft, motor-driven, homemade ferryboat was in operation between Poplar and the Fort Peck Indian Reservation on the Missouri River around 1912.

The fixed-level canal for ocean shipping was built at New Orleans in 1919.

Columbia were specialized ships—slender, fast boats with huge engines and great maneuverability. They carried fewer passengers and less cargo than the famous stern-wheelers of the Mississippi. They also had to be maneuverable to run those narrow, treacherous channels.

These stern-wheelers are still making themselves useful on the Columbia and Willamette rivers. The clumsy ocean liners which come into the deep-water sections are helpless in these rivers and must be towed. One stern-wheeler on the Willamette, the *Henderson,* handled more than 5,000 ships by herself during World War II, even though she was built in 1912 and was being run with engines taken from a still older ship.

In the fall of 1947, the old stern-wheel design proved itself again on the West Coast. The City of Portland decided to replace an old municipal-owned stern-wheeler, the *Portland,* which had been berthing ships on the rivers for 30 years. A modern Diesel tug was recommended, but experienced river pilots asked if anyone had looked at the stern-wheelers lately. The pilots admitted that Diesel tugboats were cheaper to build but argued for stern-wheelers because of the greater maneuverability that was needed in fast currents. They proved it takes only one of even the oldest stern-wheelers to handle a ship, instead of the two to four Diesel tugs that are required. They proved from the records that the stern-wheeler requires much less maintenance. After long testing and planning, a modern stern-wheeler, the second *Portland,* was built.

Perhaps the most interesting feature about this new ship is that neither its builders nor its designers could find any major improvements to make over the ships built at the turn of the century. They will frankly admit that the greatest change is in the price, the new *Portland* costing $500,000 while the most elegant packet of the 1800's cost only $45,000. The designers of those old-time ships can receive no better praise.

The new *Portland* has an all-steel welded hull instead of a wooden one and she has double the horsepower of the older stern-wheelers. The gingerbread decorations that the early skippers cherished are gone and the deck space is much less congested. But the basic design is the same; little improvement has been found for the shape of the hull, superstructure, huge paddle wheel, rudders, and design of the engines.

The new *Portland*'s pilothouse contains some of today's aids to navigation. Loran and radar have not been installed, as this ship operates only along the waterfront of a busy port. But the power steering is improved with the latest in steam-operated rudder engines that enable the

The Robert Fulton *was completed in 1909 in time to participate in the centenary of Robert Fulton's successful trip on the Hudson River. The vessel was 348 feet long, 75 feet wide, had four decks and a carrying capacity of 4000 people.*

Far removed from traditonal river boats is this streamlined, five-deck, Mississippi River vessel completed in 1938.

The Harry Truman, *a powerful Mississippi towboat, holds a record for the New Orleans-to-St. Louis run.*

Aerial view of the Harry Truman *pushing her integrated barges with total length of 1200 feet.*

The first J. S., *a Streckfus line vessel built exclusively for excursions.*

pilot to turn the ship by moving a small lever. Throughout the craft, intercommunication systems carry the skipper's instructions to his crew.

With its great flexibility and power, the new stern-wheeler now is handling steamers easily by itself. No fleet of tugboats is needed as in eastern ports. Capt. Robert Williamson, skipper of the new *Portland,* pays the following tribute to his ship.

"She just handles a liner better. We call it rudder power because her power of maneuver is obtained from the thrust of the wide paddle wheel on several rudders.

"Say you turn a ship with an ordinary tugboat. The only turning force or rudder power you have is the water moving against one rudder. If you must stop your tug and then turn, the only rudder power you get is the little bit of water that's pushed by the propeller against the one rudder. It's not enough out here. You'll have to get help from other tugs to swing a big ship in these currents. But a stern-wheeler's different. With her seven rudders she'll twist a liner around in a bathtub. Even if she's dead in the water (fully stopped), you still have rudder power because the paddles still push water against some of the rudders—even in reverse!"

When we get back to the Mississippi, however, we find that towboats and barges have pushed steamboats into the background. As a matter of fact, the barges on inland waterways are carrying more freight today than the packets ever did. The best year the old steamboats had in freight traffic was in 1888 when they transported 28,000,000 tons of cargo. Compare this with the 127,000,000 tons of freight hauled on waterways in 1943. In 1945 the freight traffic on the Mississippi alone totaled 2,278,047 tons.

Why this marked rise in freight tonnage? The answer lies in the huge barges, with their remarkable loading

The President, *first all-steel passenger steamer on the Mississippi, runs between New Orleans and St. Paul.*

capacity, and the numbers which can be linked together and towed by a single boat. Although towing actually means pulling, drawing, or hauling, such is not the case where Mississippi towing is concerned. Pulling a barge down the ever-winding Mississippi would be an impossibility. Instead, the barges have to be pushed down the river by the towboats.

In order to push such heavy loads down the river, the towboats have to be sturdily built. The St. Louis Shipbuilding Company recently launched the *Havana Zephyr*, a 2000-horsepower twin-screw towboat. The *Zephyr* can push ten 10,000-barrel oil barges, a load equal to 4,000,000 gallons of gasoline, or about 450 railway tank cars.

The Jordan River Line, Inc., of New Orleans, operates the 2000-horsepower twin-screw *M/V Winchester*. With its complement of three integrated tank barges, the *Winchester* can transport as much as 55,000 barrels of gasoline. The boat is equipped with modern navigational instruments such as a gyro compass, a transmitter-receiver and a Fathometer. To further facilitate navigation, the barge itself is equipped with a bow steering unit. A 275-horsepower engine turns a three-blade propeller, which in turn deflects the front end of the tow to the desired course. This bow-steering unit is operated by remote control, from the pilothouse of the towboat, and makes possible the handling of longer tows with greater safety. The river docks are also equipped with electric-powered cranes which load and unload barges, hoisting five tons of freight in one bite.

On the Mississippi, the bulk of freight consists of oil, gasoline, grain, coal; sand, gravel, and cement. But traffic is forever changing. The transportation of automobiles by river barges is rapidly developing, with St. Louis as the center of the traffic. The St. Louis Shipbuilding and Steel

The steamer Capitol, *the Mississippi's largest stern-wheel passenger vessel, operates between St. Paul and New Orleans.*

The steamer, Senator *operates on the Ohio River and spends the summer excursion season at Pittsburgh.*

On her trial trip on May 28, 1940, the Admiral *passed every test of the rigid safety code of the Bureau of Marine Inspection and Navigation.*

Contrasting sharply with the gingerbread work on the traditional pilot houses are the sleek lines of this one, located well forward on the ship.

The S. S. Admiral *is streamlined and air-conditioned, the latest model in a long line of Streckfus steamers.*

Company has constructed long, three-deck barges for an Evansville, Ind., firm for the express purpose of shipping cars by water.

One of the large items of upstream traffic on the river is sulphur from Louisiana and Texas to the steel mills in St. Louis. Other products transported up the Mississippi from New Orleans are sisal from Africa, rubber and tin from the East Indies, nitrates from Chile, coffee from Central and South America, spices and coconut oil, bananas, and other fruit from Central America and the West Indies.

There is a regular movement of grain along the rivers from St. Louis to Chattanooga, Tenn., on the Moccasin bend of the Tennessee River. These 2000-ton bargeloads of wheat and corn are frequently seen on the Mississippi. One tow can pull as much as the equivalent of 300 freight cars of wheat.

One of the most familiar sights on the western rivers is a huge caravan of coal barges from the Pennsylvania and western Kentucky coal fields. Many of the coal, oil, and steel companies maintain their own fleets of powerful towboats and barges on the Mississippi and Ohio.

Engineering improvements, such as the removal of sand bars, the digging of canals, and building of dams, have further facilitated navigation on the western rivers. The Ohio River has been canalized with locks and dams from head to mouth to provide ample channel all the year around. The series of canals on the Mississippi River from the mouth of the Missouri River to Minneapolis represents one of the world's greatest river-navigation projects. Dredging and contraction works have also improved the navigability of the lower Mississippi. With these developments, the outlook for inland water transportation is brighter than it has been in many a day.

The S. S. Admiral's *main deck boasts an area of 33,550 square feet. Here excursionists spend much of their time in fun and relaxation.*

A good idea of the immensity and sweep of the Admiral's *ballroom is given here. Nautically known as the "cabin," the ballroom extends the full length of the steamer.*

The terrace-garden tea patio is a cool spot from which to enjoy the passing scenery.

The first steam carriage was built in France in 1769. Above is a Roper machine of 1863.

The earliest practical self-propelled vehicles were huge, lumbering, steam road engines.

DURING the last five years of the nineteenth century a new phenomena—the snorting, bucking, and for the moment undependable automobile—burst on the American scene like the first slow rupture of a mighty and unending chain reaction. Twenty-five years later the whole transportation system of the United States had been changed almost unrecognizably; the automobile had affected every aspect of American life. A vast and sprawling continent was transformed into a cohesive and efficient free-trade area. The free movement of people and goods was many times more efficient than in many European nations only one-fiftieth the size of the U.S. Thirty years after the Sioux warriors cut down Custer on the Little Big Horn, in a battle then almost as remote from the settled East as Timbuctoo, eager American tourists were roaming the battle site in "touring cars." Frontier marshals and peace officers like Wyatt Earp, isolated by miles of prairie badlands and Indian country, lived to see state troopers in high powered, radio-equipped patrol cars give chase to outlaws over miles of smooth macadam highway.

So eagerly did Americans seize on the automobile to end their isolation from each other—which from the first had been one of the prices Americans paid for the free land as they moved west—that the gigantic growth of American automobile production was literally forced upon the industry. In 1895 there were four automobiles in the U.S. The following year there were 16. In 1897 this number was increased to 90; in 1898, 800; in 1899, 2,300. By 1900, when we had 8,000 automobiles, things really started to roll. Five years later 78,000 licensed motor vehicles roamed America. Ten years after that, in 1915, the figure had jumped into the millions—3,500,000. In another 10 years that total was just short of 20,000,000. In 1935, despite the depression, the number had risen to 26,000,000. Ten years later, at the close of World War II, there were 35,000,000 registered motor vehicles, and today over 40,000,000 vehicles knit the U.S. into an ever more homogeneous community.

Nobody was more surprised than the very Americans who made it all possible. Their first reactions to the automobile were negative. The cry, "Get a horse!" became a national joke. Most of the skepticism was due to the isolation of American villages from each other and from the rest of the world. For the automobile really wasn't as startling as it appeared to most citizens who first set eyes on one around the turn of the century. In fact, horseless carriages already had quite a history. The final step in its development, which made the automobile seem to erupt suddenly into our whole national life, was simply the substitution of a gasoline engine in something that had existed for about a hundred years—the steam road carriage.

When James Watt invented his engine to work the pumps in England's coal mines, he also foresaw its use in transportation and tried to make a steam carriage himself. He was unsuccessful but only a few years later, in 1769,

Every village had what was claimed to be "the first auto in the United States."

This traction engine was the largest known in 1903. Average speed —about 8 m.p.h.

The 1907 traction engine at left drew a train of 14 loaded wagons eight miles on a half ton of coal.

Cars of the 1890's: (top to bottom) Serpollet steam carriage, Electrobat, Duryea motor wagon, which won the Times Herald *race in 1895, Daimler—speed 15 m.p.h.*

the Frenchman Cugnot took the new engine and made the first really self-propelled vehicle. It moved at the rate of two miles an hour, and exhausted its steam in about 10 minutes, but it *was* self-propelled.

From then on there was a scramble by inventors to make a really serviceable steam vehicle. Not until 1820 was the steam engine good enough to be practical for this use. Steam carriages were built and used for the next hundred years in England, and now and then in America. Both the automobile and the railroad locomotive are descended from them, parting company in the early 1800's when the locomotives were put on rails.

In America, Oliver Evans of Philadelphia patented a steam carriage in 1789 and got around to building it in 1805. He made it for one specific job: to drag a 40,000-pound steam-operated harbor dredge from his shops to the harbor. All he did was connect a walking beam between the dredge engine and the axle of wheels he installed under the dredge. Having delivered his dredge, he forgot about it.

Nathan Read of Salem, Mass. in 1790 built a small working model of a steam carriage powered by two cylinders, but he never built a larger one.

These efforts more or less ended the matter in America for about half a century. Then, in 1869, Richard Dugeon of New York built a steam-powered carriage for city use. Steam-driven pistons on either side of a horizontal boiler were connected to the rear wheels. The front axle was mounted on a pivot for steering.

From that time on, a sprinkling of steam road engines began to appear around the country, most of which were used for heavy hauling and for farm work. At that moment most Americans had their hands full of other things, and had no time to do much tinkering. Yet, these steam road engines stimulated the first American efforts toward the automobile. It is said that Henry Ford, for example, first became fascinated with the possibilities of an automobile in about 1875, when he was a boy of 12, at which time he saw a steam road engine on a farm. Ford is said to have built a steam car while in his twenties, which would be the following decade, and most of America's pioneer auto men tinkered with steam cars before they concentrated on the gasoline engine.

So the transition from the horse and buggy was far smoother and more inevitable than you could have persuaded any irate citizen whose horses had just reared and bolted at sight and sound of a "gas buggy" around 1900.

The first electric automobile in the U.S. was made by William Morrison of Des Moines, Iowa, in 1891. By the turn of the century these stately machines were second

Then, as now, the foibles of motorists provided inspiration for cartoonists.

From " Auto-Fun."]
" How quickly could you stop, if necessary?"

"About like that."

One of the first Duryea cars built. Its one-cylinder, four-cycle engine rated about four hp.

The Benz "Vis-A-Vis" was imported to the U. S. around 1891 to 1892.

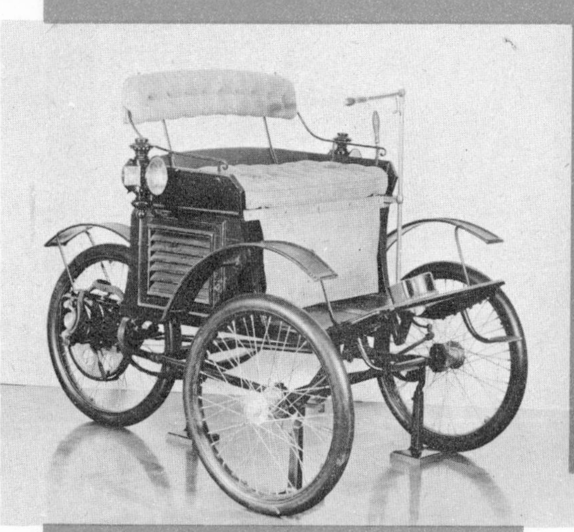

Ricker – 1896.

Benz phaeton – 1892–1896.

Two ads of 1899–1900.

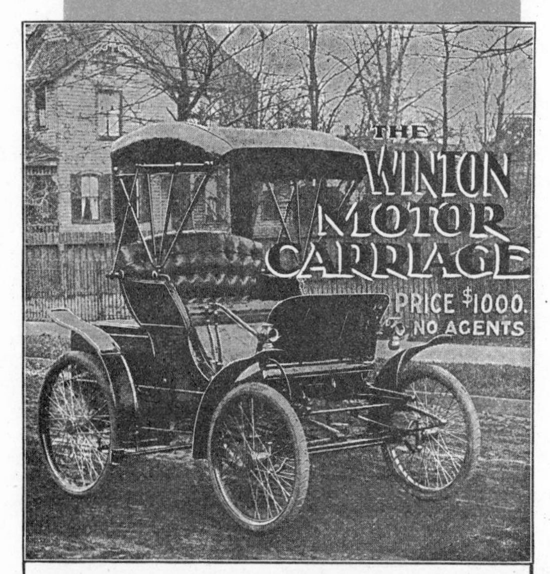

THE WINTON MOTOR CARRIAGE is a demonstrated success. A full year's service in the hands of the public proves its complete practicability. ***Safe, simple, durable and easy to operate.***

Hydro-carbon Motor - - ½ Cent per mile.

Variable speed up to **18 miles an hour** and under perfect control. Write for Catalogue.

THE WINTON MOTOR CARRIAGE CO.,
472-478 Belden St., Cleveland, Ohio.

only to the steamers in popularity and well ahead of the gas buggies. They had a range of 25 to 40 miles on the usual battery charge, although one Rauch and Lange electric could travel 100 miles by carrying one-cell storage batteries. Speeds were around 15 miles per hour. The electric was most popular among society women who liked its quiet dignity, simple operation, and cleanliness. The medical profession also preferred electrics while the gas buggy was still in its unpredictable infancy.

Although the electric "showcase on wheels" lingered on for several decades in Chicago's northern suburbs, San Franciscoo's Nob Hill, Newport, and similar localities, it was doomed from the first by its hobbled travel range and slow speed: There was talk for awhile of setting up a nationwide system of battery-changing and charging stations, but nothing came of it.

America owed Europe also for the gasoline engine. In 1863 Jean Joseph Lenois built a one-cylinder internal combustion engine mounted on a carriage-type of vehicle and drove it for six miles before it broke down. This and one built a year later in Vienna by Siegfried Marcus were two-cycle engines using alcohol for fuel. A further development took place in 1883. Two Germans, Gottlieb Daimler and Karl Benz, simultaneously invented four-cycle engines that ran on gasoline. Within a few years, primitive automobiles were running every day through the streets of Paris and Berlin.

In the United States, George B. Selden, a patent lawyer of Rochester, N. Y., read about the Benz and Daimler automobiles and made a rough sketch of a horseless carriage which he filed with the U. S. Patent Office. Thereafter Selden kept filing amendments to his patent applica-

1899 hand-built steam car.

The famous Winton of 1900.

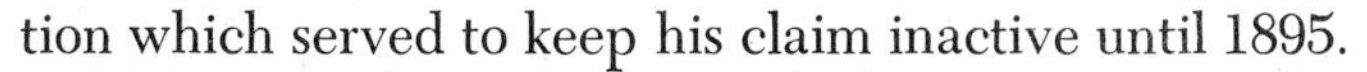

tion which served to keep his claim inactive until 1895.

Selden showed astute judgment in letting his patent come through in 1895. That year, America was seething with back-yard engineers inflamed by but one idea: to make a horseless carriage.

J. Frank Duryea and his brother Charles E. Duryea made the first gasoline-propelled automobile in the U. S. The year 1891 found them living in Chicopee Falls, Mass., where Frank worked as a toolmaker and Charles was employed by a bicycle company. That same year Charles read about the horseless carriages running around Paris, and the following year in Springfield, Mass. the two brothers began working on their own version. Charles made the designs and ordered the engine parts from a machine shop and Frank made the actual assembly.

Choosing a starlit night, to avoid frightening horses, Frank took the assembled car and made a test. The machine barely moved, but it did and it did not stall. This was the first successful operation of a gasoline automobile in the U. S.

The following year the two brothers built another horseless carriage, which they drove through Springfield on Sept. 22, 1893. The results were better, but still disappointing. In 1894, the brothers hit upon the idea of a bevel-gear transmission and in March, 1895 they produced their third motor buggy. It had two cylinders instead of one, three forward speeds instead of two and boasted besides electric ignition, a water pump and pneumatic tires. This model brought fame to the brothers when Frank drove it in America's first motor-car race in Chicago on Thanksgiving Day, 1895. He beat two electric wagons and three other gasoline powered cars, two of them fitted

The sleek 1900 Gladiator.

Ford's second car – 1898.

1900 Packard.

The 1901 Crestmobile.

with imported Benz motors. The brothers had already formed the Duryea Motor Wagon Company and during the winter of 1895-96 they built 13 cars, the first automobiles regularly manufactured for sale in the United States.

Meanwhile, Elwood G. Haynes of Kokomo, Ind., a graduate engineer in metallurgy, ex-schoolteacher and field superintendent of the Indiana Natural Gas and Oil Company, had become fascinated by the same idea. He too got his ideas from reading about the French automobiles. He drew some sketches in 1892 and the following year bought a one-cylinder engine and a light buggy body. He then hired Elmer Apperson and his brother Edgar to put the engine and buggy together. On July 4, 1894, the Haynes motor buggy was towed by horse well outside of Kokomo and tried out. It was a sterling success. Haynes and Apperson drove about a mile and a half at the rate of seven miles an hour, then turned around and went all the way back to Kokomo without mishap.

Haynes' motor was a standard Stinz one-horsepower, two-cycle gasoline engine, connected by chains to a jackshaft and thence to wheel sprockets, much like the Duryea automobile.

Stephen M. Balzer, a New York maker of gasoline engines, brought out the third horseless carriage in America in 1894. Balzer's machine had a three-cylinder air-cooled engine which revolved around a stationary crankshaft. There were three forward speeds, but no reverse. Balzer was the first to use pneumatic tires on an automobile.

The following year, in 1895, a number of companies were formed to make automobiles of one kind or another. Haynes and Apperson formed a company named for

The 1900 Mobile was actually higher than it was long!

"THE HOTEL ESSEX, BOSTON, MASS., Sept. 13, 1900.
"'MOBILE' CO. OF AMERICA.

"GENTLEMEN:—Thinking you would be interested in an account of the performance of one of your carriages, I will state that my wife and I left Philadelphia and came to New York City; then north to Hudson, N. Y.; from Hudson across through Great Barrington and Lenox; through the Berkshire Hills to Pittsfield, Mass.; from Pittsfield to Springfield, Worcester and Boston—a distance of five hundred and ten miles. The road from Pittsfield to Springfield was very bad—steep hills, sand and dust. In fact, I don't think in the last three hundred miles there were over seventy-five decent roads. Time not being an object, we made the trip in eight days, an average of over sixty miles a day, and did not have a breakdown of any kind, and arrived in Boston with a good opinion of what your carriage could do under the most severe tests.

"Yours truly, M. M. YOUNG."

themselves, and the Duryeas formed the Duryea Motor Wagon Company. Among the autos making an appearance that year were: the Electric Wagon; Electrobat; Morris and Salom Electric Wagon; Hertel; Hill's Locomotor; Hall Gasoline Trap; Howard Gasoline Wagon; and J. B. West's Gasoline Vehicle. Two motor magazines, *The Horseless Age* and *The Motorcycle,* appeared in November of 1895.

No one knew just what to call the new contraption at first. While names such as "autopher," "autovic," "molectro," "trundler," "autobat," and "self-motor" were being tried out, the number of motoring enthusiasts began to grow, limited principally at this stage either to wealthy sportsmen or to monkey-wrench engineers who made their own cars.

In 1892 Hiram P. Maxim had begun experimenting with a self-propelled road vehicle, and in 1895 he entered the field with a motorized tricycle. It really was a large, old-fashioned tricycle simply equipped with a motor. Louis S. Clarke finished a gasoline tricycle in 1897, building his frame of bicycle parts. The one-cylinder motor had a mechanically operated exhaust and an automatic intake valve.

The first of this early group to achieve lasting success in the new industry was Ransom E. Olds, whose name lives on with the Oldsmobile. Like Ford, Olds had built a steam road vehicle about 1887 and in 1893 he made another. He finished a gasoline-driven vehicle in 1895, but it was a failure. Success came in 1897 with an automobile far ahead of the other primitive machines.

This first Oldsmobile carried four passengers and could

1902 Studebaker electric.

Model T, Haynes Limousine

The makers of the Haynes have been developing their car for *13 years*. They know their car through and through. Year after year they have seen their old cars come back after varied use and have spotted here and there chances for improvements.

Their experience has developed for 1907 a car that can be safely advertised for *reliability*—a car that can be *trusted*. It contains no parts *not made in the Haynes Factory*, no principles that are unfamiliar to the Haynes designers.

In these days, when every blacksmith is buying parts and assembling cars under a private trademark, the fact that the Haynes factories really make *everything* in their car is a guarantee of Haynes *reliability*.

From an ad of 1907.

Two curved-dash Oldsmobiles, manufactured from 1901 until 1906, at the start of an overland race.

First Studebaker electric – 1902.

A 1902 Packard speedster.

1903 Packard.

Strong backed companions were always welcome.

outrun any other car in the field at a snappy 10 miles an hour. A one-cylinder, six-horsepower, water-cooled engine was mounted horizontally beneath the body. The transverse crankshaft was midway between front and rear axles and a vertical flywheel was located near the center of the car. Three friction clutches were controlled by a system of cams and levers on a post at the right of the driver. Two clutches engaged a chain sprocket on the crankshaft and provided two forward speeds. The third clutch engaged a planetary gear to provide the reverse. Power was transmitted by chains to sprockets on a sleeve mounted on the rear axle. A pedal-operated brake band was mounted on the differential. The car was steered by a tiller, like all the early automobiles, and had high wooden wagon wheels.

Another pioneer, Alexander Winton, owned a bicycle shop in Cleveland, Ohio. In 1895 he built not a car, but a motorcycle. The following year he made a horseless carriage, and in 1897 Winton produced two phaeton-type machines. Winton tried to get into production quickly with his machines but was stymied for awhile by the fact that his customers kept returning the machines and demanding their money back. Such incidents made prospective buyers dubious so, to show what his car could do, Winton drove one from Cleveland to New York, some 800 miles, in 10 days. He then entered countless track and road races, which were becoming crowd-attracting features of fairs and expositions everywhere, and by 1901 Winton was recognized as national track champion.

Last of the real trail blazers in the auto industry but destined for bigger things than any of the others, was Henry Ford. He turned out a homemade car in 1896 while he was working for the Detroit Electric Company. He then formed two auto companies that failed before, in 1903, he launched the Ford Motor Company with $28,000 borrowed from 13 different men, an average of slightly more than $2,000 apiece.

In 1900, by far the most popular automobiles were the steamers. They were far faster than any gasoline car, were smooth and silent in operation, and of course much more efficient than the gas engines. A steamer could run on almost any kind of cheap fuel: kerosene, light furnace oil, or banana oil. But it had several drawbacks. Foremost were the necessity to wait until you got steam up at least for the first operation of the day and the necessity for cleaning the boiler, burner, and operating parts each and every week. For years, however, the steamers were favorites of a good section of the motoring public. The most famous was the Stanley Steamer, whose tremendous speed gave rise to the legend that one of them would be given

A 1902–1903 Stanley steamer.

free to anyone who could hold it wide open for one minute. Even if this hopeful yarn had not been apocryphal, the Stanleys would have had little to fear from takers. As early as 1907, the famous race driver Fred Mariott cracked one of them up on Daytona Beach when he hit a bad spot in the sands while traveling 180 miles an hour! Few prospective buyers then, or now for that matter, wanted any part of that.

The two Stanley twins, F. E. and F. O., built their first steamer in 1897. By spring of the next year they had three of them. They sold one of them and then when F. O. set a world record in 1898—a mile in 2:11—they received orders for 200. They bought a bicycle factory and converted it to the making of Stanley Steamers. Early in 1899 they sold out for $250,000 to the Locomobile Company. But without the brothers the steamer sales sagged, and the twins bought back their company for $20,000 in 1901. From then until after World War I, they sold all the steamers they wanted to make. Neither of them seemed to care for devoting every working minute to business. F. E. in particular liked to race around the country roads in his own steamer. This fondness for speed led to his death in 1917 when he left the road to avoid hitting a horse and wagon. His brother sold the company and it lasted only two more years.

1904 Pope-Hartford.

Studebaker's first gas car—1904.

A 1905 two-cylinder Maxwell and four luckless passengers.

A. B. C. AUTOMOBILE Simple Name— Simple Machine

A fine hill climber. Speeds up to 25 miles an hour. Most practical, powerful and durable automobile of its class. Is made easy to operate—no complicated parts—no tires to puncture—no repairs. Safest machine made. Built for 2, 3 or 4 passengers. 10 to 12 h. p. Price $600.

Write today for particulars.

A. B. C. MOTOR VEHICLE CO., 3932 Morgan St, ST. LOUIS, MO.

AUTOMOBILISTS

and men in all walks of life should know the merits of

LITHOLIN WATERPROOFED LINEN COLLARS and CUFFS

No matter how soiled, they are cleaned instantly with a damp cloth, and made white as new. Absolutely waterproof, they hold their shape under all conditions. Being linen they look it. NOT celluloid. Wear indefinitely, and don't wilt, fray or crack. Every fashionable style in all sizes.

COLLARS 25c   CUFFS 50c

If not at your dealer's, send, giving styles, size, number wanted, with remittance, and we will mail, postpaid Booklet of styles free on request.

THE FIBERLOID CO., Dept. 25, 7 Waverly Place, N.Y.

The keenest rival of the Stanley was the White Steamer, boasting a flash boiler which required less time to get warmed up in the morning. But the flash boiler could not store steam, and the White Steamer therefore lacked reserve power for steep hills or emergency bursts of speed. There were other steamers, some of which continued to be made until the late '20's.

The bicycle smoothed the transition from horse and buggy to automobile. Many of the same people who were among the 10,000,000 owners of bicycles in the U. S. by 1900 were soon changing their cycling clubs into automobile clubs. Caravans of automobiles began making their way into the country for week-end outings. In those days, the automobile was primarily used for sport and amusement. The American Automobile Association was formed and slowly displaced the cyclists' League of American Wheelmen. Colonel Albert A. Pope, maker of one of the best bicycles offered during the cycling craze, himself had entered the automobile industry in 1897.

The motorist in those days had to be prepared for many emergencies. No car was complete without a kit of tools tied to the running board or fender, and this kit itself had better be complete indeed. Among the articles required were an almost infinite number of wrenches of different sizes, pliers of assorted design, light and heavy hammers, hacksaw and blades, wrecking bars, pins, nuts, bolts, gas tips for headlights, files, blowtorch, solder and flux, oil cans, chamois for straining gasoline and, of course, gloves, overalls, and soap for the driver himself.

Even when mechanical troubles didn't develop, a motoring trip was a rugged adventure. Until the '20's about 90 per cent of all automobiles were either open or touring models. Leather clothing was considered a must for trips of any distance. Even on short Sunday drives, at least a linen duster was required if the driver and passengers wanted to save their clothing from the clouds of dust.

Motoring was strictly a fair weather sport for several years, because of the dirt roads and the exposure of the passengers. Fifty miles was a taxing day's drive and the car might break a spring or axle any minute on some mudhole, rock, or stump, leaving the driver stranded. Yet the automobile clubs continued to replace the bicycling clubs. Usually the groups took a repair car with them on their trips and outings to help in such emergencies. All went well unless the repair car itself broke down, which happened more than a few times.

Except for a few relatively inexpensive runabouts, automobiles were luxury possessions so far as the average citi-

A Stevens-Duryea of 1904.

A Benz Mannheim – 1905 to 1909.

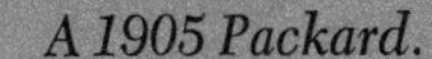

A 1905 Packard.

A 1907 Studebaker touring car.

A 1907 Studebaker limousine.

zen was concerned. The Mitchell six-cylinder two-seated touring model sold for $1,895 in 1911, a lot of money in those days. Moreover, the automobile met with a great deal of resistance from horse owners because of the effect it produced on the animals. It was not uncommon for motorists to be cursed by farmers as the machines chugged past the farms. In many places village ordinances were enacted to hamper automobilists in one way or another. All these things—price, roads and public animosity—conspired for a time to keep the automobile a luxury device.

In 1906 wealthy Long Islanders built their own exclusive road.

The First Model T Ford was sold in 1908. It had four cylinders, 100-inch wheelbase, 20 horsepower, and lots of room. It would go 40 miles an hour, ran 22 miles on a gallon of gas.

An airship built by Capt. Thomas S. Baldwin in 1904. The 54-foot-long dirigible was driven by a seven-horsepower gasoline motor. The pilot balanced his ship by moving about on a flimsy catwalk.

THE BALLOONING CRAZE that swept Europe during the 1790's was not long in being carried across the Atlantic to America. President George Washington was one of the interested spectators at a balloon ascension in Philadelphia in 1793. The balloonist was John Pierre Blanchard, making a barnstorming tour of America exploiting the fame he gained in crossing the English Channel in a balloon in 1785.

Since directional control of a balloon was impossible, there was no possibility that transportation would be affected by the balloon itself. But the experiments with balloons provided data for other kinds of flight, and the hero worship to which the balloonists were subjected at fairs and exhibitions helped prepare the public for aviation.

The balloon led directly to dirigible airships, and while most of the early experiments with these were conducted in England, France, and Germany, there were controlled flights of this sort in the United States. These strange-looking craft—cigar-shaped lighter-than-air bags supporting a long catwalk for the aviator—were sometimes pedal powered and sometimes propelled by a one-cylinder gasoline engine. Prof. Carl Myers was noted in the 1890's for the manufacture of pedal-operated aircraft he called "sky cycles," and he later made engine-operated airships.

Public interest in such ships was stimulated at the St. Louis World Fair of 1903 when Alberto Santos-Dumont, the charming, 96-pound daredevil Brazilian who

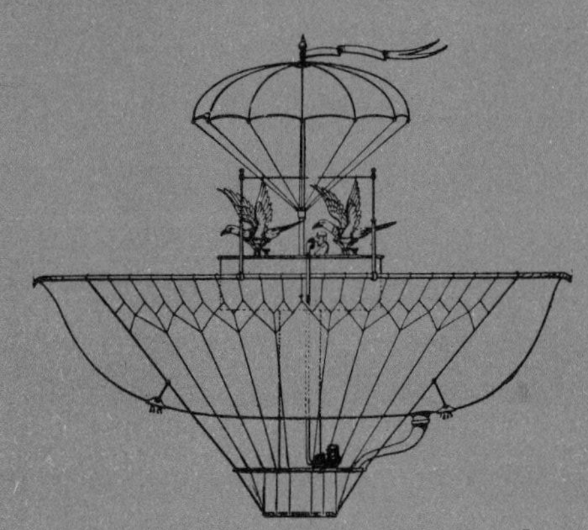

1887 patent on a scheme to hitch a team of eagles to a balloon.

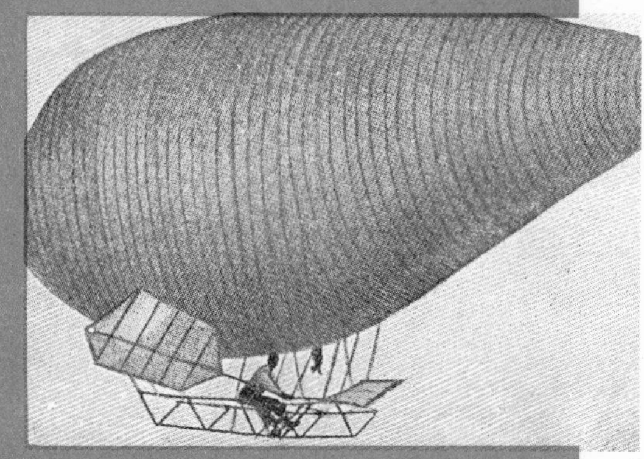

Alva Reynolds at the oars of his "aerial rowboat" in 1906.

Seen more often than airships at the turn of the century were balloons – ascensions featured every county fair.

made his ships in Paris, came to the United States to perform for the fair. Afterward he made a series of exhibition flights throughout the country and the name Santos-Dumont, hardly recognized now, became for some years a household word in the U. S.

Some idea of what it meant to be aloft in an airship of this period is gained from an interview with Prof. Myers, published in *Popular Mechanics* of March 7, 1903:

> "That careful aerial navigation is not essentially dangerous is proven by the fact that I am before you today, alive and unharmed—after a quarter century spent in aerial travels ranging over thousands of miles, 21 of these United States, the District of Columbia, and the Canadas.
>
> "During all this time the only real danger that I seem to have run was from a single possible collision between my airship and a railroad locomotive. I had made a flight with my skycycle from Pittsburgh, Pa., in the presence of 300,000 spectators, gathered at one Fourth of July celebration when the temperature was 105 degrees in the shade on the ground. It was a great relief to get up in the cooler air and the scene below me was the most

Santos-Dumont's No. 10, which the Brazilian flew at the St. Louis Exposition in 1904.

This motor skycycle was the nineteenth airship to be built by Prof. Carl E. Myers in a 24-year period.

Samuel Langley's flying machine shown on the launching ramp built on a houseboat anchored in the Potomac River.

wonderful of my experience for three great rivers united beneath me dividing a labyrinth of winding roads encircling the hillsides making the whole territory visible as an enchanted landscape garden, flat as any map or mosaic.

"After I had strolled about in the air half an hour tracing the paths below me, I sought a safe place for a landing, away from the mob, which would have destroyed me in their excitement had I landed in their midst. The only space clear from trees or people in my vicinity was the railroad track. I hovered close over it while two long trains met and passed, and then dropped just behind on the clear rails and began emptying my gas, when along came a wild cat locomotive with a terrible racket of bell and whistle and I almost lost my life

Hoisting the Langley machine to its launching stage for an attempted flight.

Wreck of the Langley plane after it crashed into the Potomac in October of 1903.

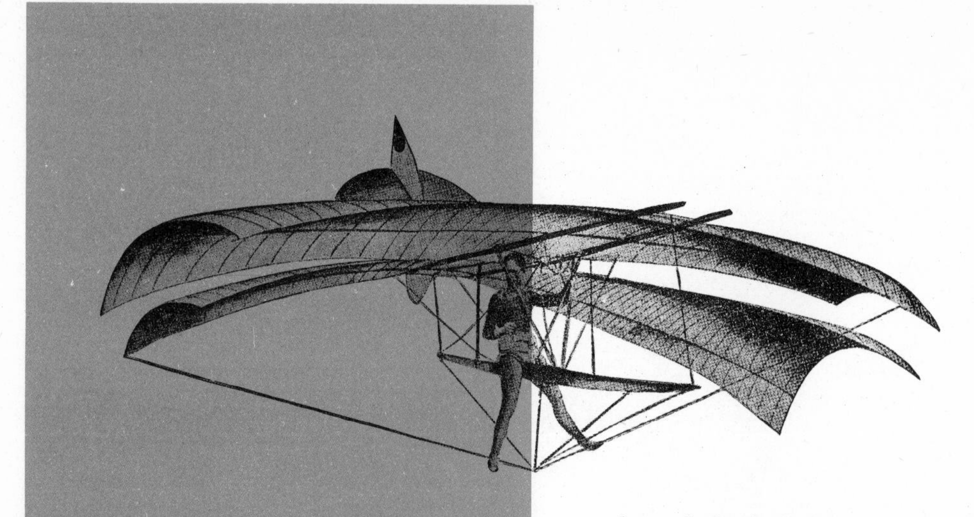

Balanced in this birdlike glider, Prof. John J. Montgomery of Santa Clara College cut loose from a balloon at 4,000 feet and made a successful descent in 1905.

through fright before I could hustle my half empty gas spindle off the track. What would have happened to that careless locomotive had my wasting gas exploded I can't think.

"This is the only time in my high career that I have been 'real scared,' but at another time I nearly frightened to death a young Cannuck farm hand near Lewiston, Maine, one November day when I landed in freezing weather and a 30-mile wind and the only person in sight ran away screaming when I called for help to check my skycycle. He ran into the farm house yelling, 'Oh Lord, come quick, the devil is after me big as a house and talks like a man.' "

The "Aeriator," built by George A. Lawrence of Sayre, Pa., flew for 200 feet in 1908.

Another witness to the perils of early aerial navigation was Capt. William Matteray, who recounted his experiences in an airship over Green Bay in another issue of *Popular Mechanics.*

Matteray, making an exhibition flight at the fair grounds at Octonto, Mich., was carried out over the bay

Model of a glider used by Octave Chanute on the Lake Michigan dunes.

The "Aeriator," built by George A. Lawrence of Sayre, Pa., flew for 200 feet in 1908.

Orville Wright in the twin-propeller plane developed by the brothers in 1908.

Seat and motor of the Wright airplane of 1908. The levers controlled the front and rear rudders and the warping of wings.

Roy Knabenshue, an exhibition flier, dropped confetti "bombs" on Los Angeles in 1909.

by winds which proved more powerful than his airship's tiny gasoline engine.

"I saw several big vessels and got within 50 feet over one big fellow. I called to a man on deck to catch the anchor rope, but he replied he was not in the catching business. It would have been an easy matter to have pulled me down then. The next time I landed I got up to my hips in water and had to throw out some more ballast.

"I had thrown the engine out shortly after I started, as I wished to save the lighter ballast to make a landing if I got a good chance. The third time when I arose I got the higher atmosphere and my wet clothes froze to my body. The big gas bag was dripping and as soon as we struck the higher air it was covered with a thick coating of ice. I expected to get killed any moment, but made up my mind I would stick till the finish, but was going to cut the ropes from the framework of the ship and float with the gas bag if the worst came. The framework is so frail that one misstep would have thrown me out into space. I was

Wright airplane at Fort Meyers, Va., in 1908. An Army requirement was that it "could be transported in an escort wagon."

On May 23, 1908, as 15,000 Berkeley, Calif., spectators gasped, this huge airship collapsed and fell 300 feet. All the 16 passengers, including the inventor, C. A. Morrell, were hurt.

hungry and thirsty from being in the high air and nearly frozen, and became exhausted, so I made a net out of the landing rope across the frame of the ship, tied myself to it and fell asleep. I must have slept a long time, for I was awakened by the basket striking on a tree. I untied myself and made a lasso out of the drag rope and, after striking several trees, finally got the rope over one and fastened it, climbing down to the ground and pulling the ship with me. I unfastened the canvas rudder, made a bed out of it at the foot of the tree and went to sleep. I was awakened in the night by a big black bear which came sniffing around, but did not attempt to do any harm. I saw all kinds of wild animals and dozens of deer, which would give a stare at the big thing in the air and run away in alarm.

"I traveled about 250 miles as the crow flies and was over the water most of the way and on an average of 15,000 feet in the air. I arose in the morning and walked around for four hours, covering about ten miles, and found myself at the starting point. I took another start and arrived at Gaylord in an exhausted condition."

Thus the airships, hard to control even under ideal conditions, were completely helpless in high winds. What the aeronauts really wanted was flight in a machine heavier than air, and a number of them were working on the problem.

The most scientific approach, and one that very nearly succeeded, was being carried on by Samuel P. Langley, director of the Smithsonian Institution. Langley was working with models and finally solved the problems of stability and control so that he was able to make his little planes perform as many as three complete circles in the air. Then Langley built a larger plane fitted with a 52-horsepower steam engine, which came very close to being the first plane to be capable of carrying a man in powered flight. The plane was catapulted from a houseboat in the Potomac River.

What happened then has been a historic controversy ever since. Some believe it was faulty design that caused

When you wanted anything in the line of lighter-than-air equipment in 1907, Carl Myers' balloon farm in Frankfort, N. Y., was the place to get it.

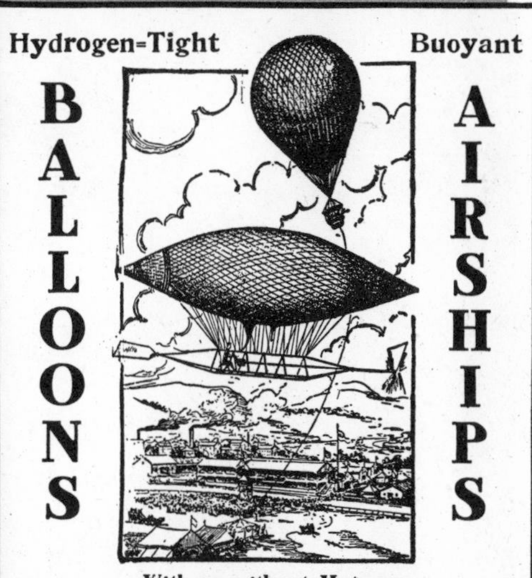

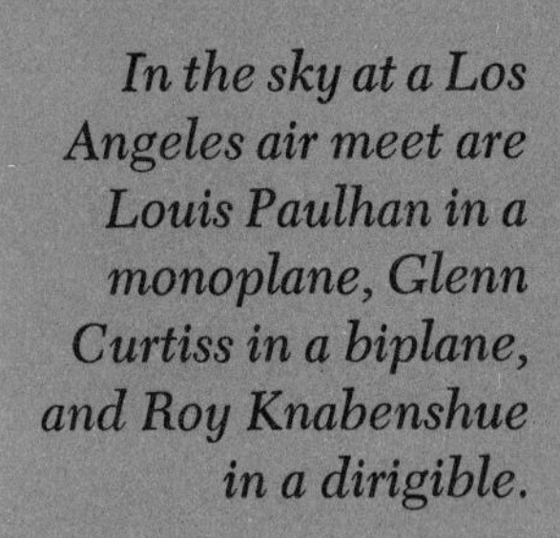

In the sky at a Los Angeles air meet are Louis Paulhan in a monoplane, Glenn Curtiss in a biplane, and Roy Knabenshue in a dirigible.

This airship exploded when the propeller tore the envelope. The operator, a Prof. Moore, died of burns.

the machine to plunge into the river and wreck itself. Others say Langley's plane could have flown; that the frame of the launching platform caught the wings of the machine as it moved along the tracks. Whatever happened on Oct. 7, 1903, happened again on the second attempt a month later. The government, which had been financing Langley's experiments, withdrew support after the second failure.

Popular Mechanics reflected the mood of the public toward Langley when the magazine said:

"The airship was built on the model of a bird, but partakes more of the characteristics of a fish. While the machine refuses to fly, it readily sinks itself in the water, and it is believed that by adding a sufficient amount of cork it would be made to rise to the surface of the water at will, equal to the best government submarine torpedo boats."

The irony of publisher Henry Haven Windsor's comment was inspired by the results Langley had achieved after "years of scientific study and $50,000 of the government's money."

Another school in the search for manmade flight was that of the glider men, out of whose experiments came the first successful heavier-than-air flight. The leading exponent of gliding in America was Octave Chanute, whose

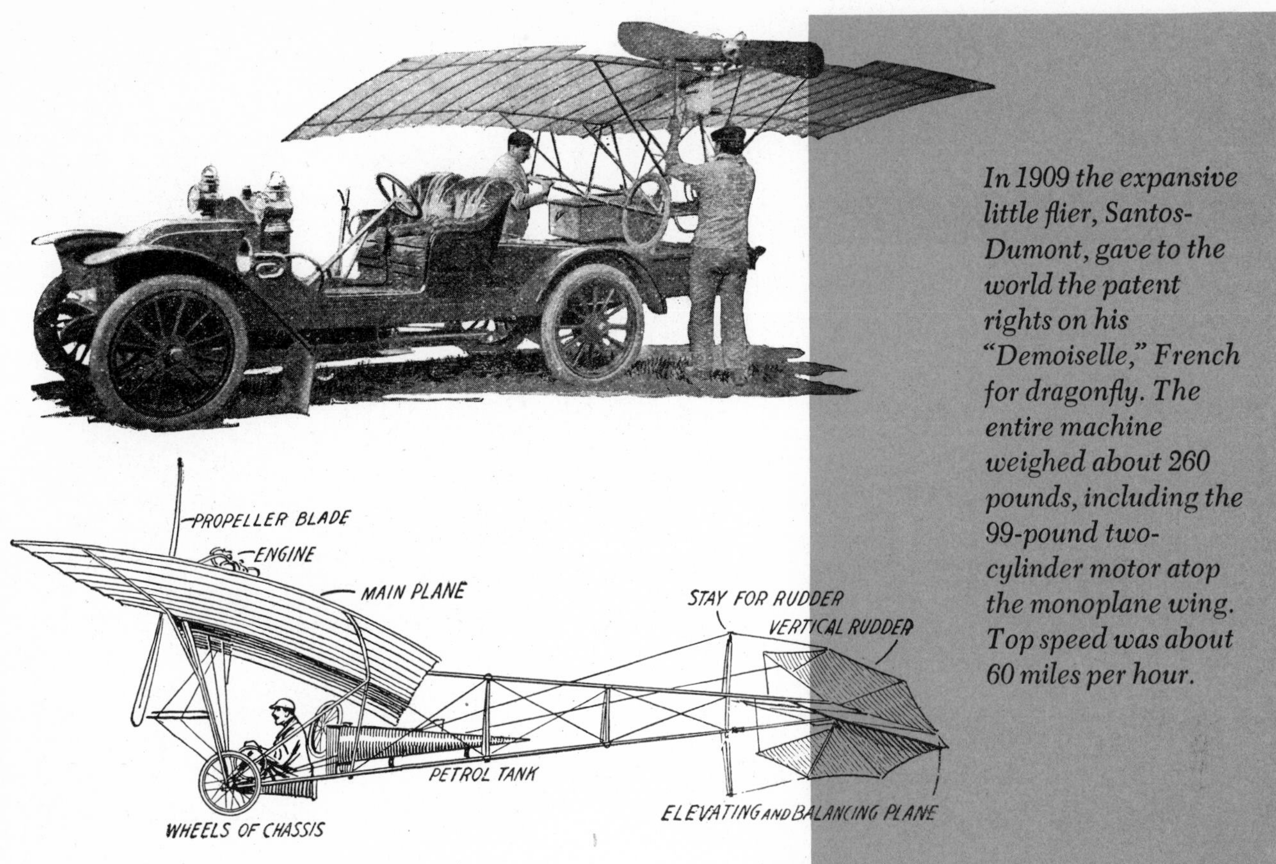

In 1909 the expansive little flier, Santos-Dumont, gave to the world the patent rights on his "Demoiselle," French for dragonfly. The entire machine weighed about 260 pounds, including the 99-pound two-cylinder motor atop the monoplane wing. Top speed was about 60 miles per hour.

knowledge came directly from the notes of Otto Lilienthal of Germany and Percy Pilcher of England. In 1899 Chanute made numerous flights with box-kite gliders on the Lake Michigan sand dunes near Chicago and learned almost all there was then to know about gliding. He learned that biplanes made the best gliders, and with these he was able to make complete turns and to control them in the strongest winds. When the Wright brothers, who were experimenting with gliders in Dayton, Ohio, wrote to Chanute telling him of their interest in his work, he gladly gave them the benefit of all that he knew, thus saving them years of trial and error. Eventually he turned over all of his notes to them.

The Wrights built their first glider in 1900, a biplane with wings measuring 18 by 5 feet, and a primitive elevator in front. In 1900 and in 1901 they flew this and another glider at Kitty Hawk, N.C., where, they had learned from the U. S. Weather Bureau, a steady 18-mile wind blew over the sandy beach. Their flights were rather unsuccessful, and to correct their data, they built the first wind tunnel. It was a square tube with a 16-inch opening widening out to six feet at the other end. In the tube they held tiny sheet metal wings and watched as a fan blew air through the tunnel.

With information gleaned from the wind tunnel, the

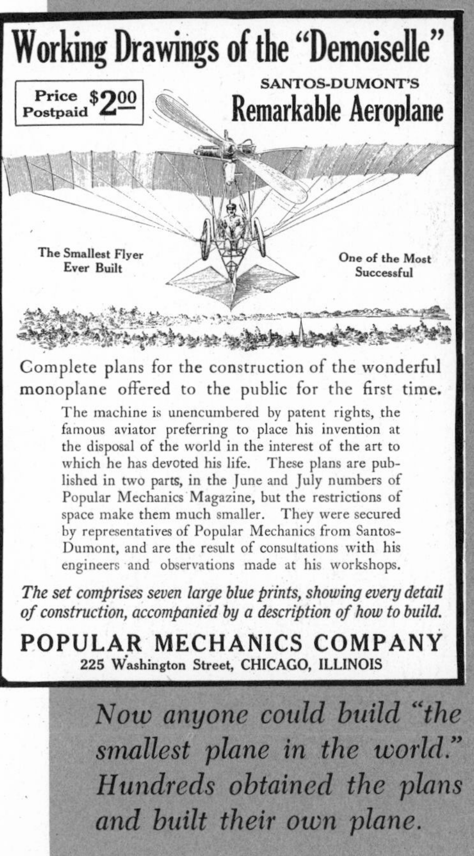

Now anyone could build "the smallest plane in the world." Hundreds obtained the plans and built their own plane.

Arch Hoxsey was killed in this nose-down plunge over Los Angeles in 1911. The accident rate during the early days of flying was staggering, and even a minor accident could be serious when the pilot sat directly in front of the engine of a flimsy wooden airplane.

Eugene B. Ely made the first landing on the deck of a ship in 1911. Note the sandbag-weighted ropes on the deck of the armored cruiser Pennsylvania.

Wrights built another glider and went back to Kitty Hawk in the summer of 1902. This time they were successful. The biplane, equipped with wings 30 feet long and 5 feet wide, made over 1,000 flights, staying up more than a minute sometimes and gliding as far as 600 feet.

The next step was to add power. In the fall of 1903 they showed up at Kitty Hawk once more, bringing along a very odd-looking contraption. Except for its wings, the plane looked like a wrecked piano crate wrapped with wire. There were two vertical rudders at the rear and two horizontal planes mounted out in front to raise or lower

The Paterson, N. J., inventor who designed this strange plane said it could not acquire an angle in descent that would result in a fall. Unfortunately, the plane itself would not fly.

the airplane as it flew, and the wing tips were capable of being warped to obtain lateral balance. Two curved landing skids protruded forward from beneath the plane. In the center of the craft was a wooden platform on which the pilot lay on his stomach beside a homemade, four-cylinder gasoline engine. The pilot grasped two levers which operated the rudders, elevating planes, and wing-working mechanism. With this ship, which arose under its own power from a launching rail, Orville achieved the first sustained, level, heavier-than-air flight in history.

The Wrights were quiet about their triumphs for several years, probably because they wanted to be sure before they told the world about it. By 1905 they were able to fly 24 miles in circles above Dayton, and they announced their flights to the Aeronautical Society of Great Britain. They did not receive Patent No. 821,393 for a "flying machine" until May 22, 1906.

In France, aviators were blissfully unaware of what the

Even in the mountains of Carter County, Kentucky, aviation experiments went on. This "quadraplane" was built in 1911.

A canopy-top airplane built by a Hackensack, N. J., florist. The canopy was intended to act as a parachute in emergencies.

In 1911 the Wrights went back to Kitty Hawk to experiment further with gliders, in an effort to improve their powered designs. Orville is shown at the controls of the 1911 glider. (A) joints in wings; (B) vertical stabilizing fin; (C) adjustable weight for balancing.

The biplane glider hovering in a 50-mile-an-hour wind. Note the extreme use of wing warping to obtain lateral balance. The rudder was wrecked (below, left) when the wind turned the glider over on its back.

Wrights had accomplished. In 1908, Henri Farman claimed a record for a mile circular flight; and two years before, Santos-Dumont had thought himself the first man to fly when he succeeded with a small engine-driven plane. Wilbur went to France to set the record straight and made one flight of 90 miles in 2 hours and 29 minutes.

While Wilbur was breaking records in France, brother Orville put through its paces a machine the Wrights had been commissioned to build for the United States Army. Circling the field at Ft. Meyer, Va., more than 50 times in an hour and two minutes, Orville won acceptance of the plane in its first demonstration. But tragedy struck a week later as the experiments continued. One of the propeller blades caught on a loose rudder wire and the plane crashed, killing the one passenger, Lieut. Thomas E.

Selfridge, and injuring Orville. The tests were completed without further accidents, however, and this plane became the first government-owned airplane in the world.

Wilbur, meanwhile, had returned from his European triumphs. Late in 1908 New York State decided to celebrate the hundredth anniversary of Robert Fulton's first successful steamboat (a little belatedly, since the *Clermont* was launched in 1807). Wilbur lent a modern touch to the celebration by flying man's latest "folly," taking off from Governor's Island, circling around the Statue of Liberty, flying over the Hudson River celebration to Grant's Tomb and then back to the Island. Wilbur was probably the best flier in the world on that day. But he showed the limits of his confidence in himself and his plane by carrying a canoe in his plane as a precaution against this over-water flight!

The greater part of the aircraft of this day were powered by engines made in Hammondsport, N. Y. The guiding genius of that engine factory was Glenn Hammond Curtiss, a motorcycle racer who in 1907 had whirled a 40-horsepower cycle over the sands of Ormond Beach, Fla., at 136.36 miles an hour, making it for the moment the fastest thing on earth.

Curtiss became interested in aviation by a natural chain of events. As a designer of light but extremely powerful engines, Curtiss was the one Capt. Thomas Baldwin had turned to when the United States Army built its first dirigibles. Curtiss went up with Baldwin to handle the motors and was bitten by the flying bug.

In 1908, in a self-built plane he called the "June Bug," Curtiss won a trophy put up by the *Scientific American*. The motorcycle-rider-turned-flyer achieved the then startling speed of 40 miles an hour in the air. Later that year Curtiss fitted another plane with pontoons, the

An early Curtiss pusher (top), and an unidentified tractor monoplane. In each of these planes the danger to the pilot in the event of a crack-up is apparent. That any of the early airmen lived through those years is surprising.

The hydroplane developed by Glenn Curtiss in 1912. Note the propellers and engine rising out of the bow of the pontoon.

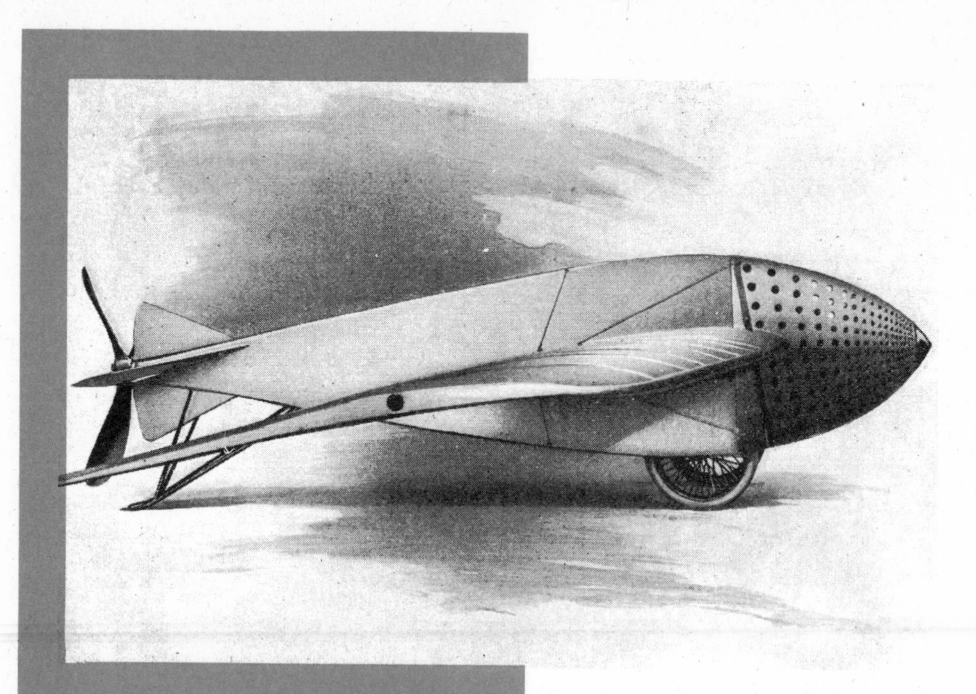

An aeronautical show in 1912 featured many planes which had not yet been flown, including this amazingly streamlined "Bullet" with propeller in rear. Its flight tests were not successful.

A Curtiss flying boat of 1912. Glenn Curtiss had long been experimenting with seaplanes but this one was a radical departure from the others. The wing was mounted directly on the hull, as were the tail planes, which, instead of being out on booms, were an integral part of the hull.

world's first seaplane, and made experimental takeoffs and landings on the water.

In 1910 Curtiss won the *New York World* prize of $10,000 for a flight between Albany and New York City in two hours and 51 minutes. In 1912 he won the annual award of the Aero Club of America for a true flying boat.

Although the Wright brothers used Curtiss engines, their relations with their designer had always been strained and in 1910 the Wrights sued Curtiss for patent infringement. Curtiss contended that Samuel P. Langley has used the same principle in the ill-fated plane that failed its Potomac River tests in 1903. To prove his point, Curtiss rebuilt Langley's original plane, added pontoons, and flew it successfully in 1914. Curtiss insisted the changes were only minor, but the Wrights won their suit.

While the Wright brothers were distinguishing themselves in the field of airplane design and Curtiss was contributing his engineering genius to aviation, another man was demanding public attention as a stunt flier. He was Lincoln Beachey, who began his career as a lad of 17, handling the ropes of catwalk airships in Oakland, Calif., in 1905. The following year young Beachey joined Roy Knabenshue's troupe of aeronauts and distinguished himself by flying around the dome of the national capitol.

In 1911, disdaining the clumsy airships, Beachey enrolled in a flying school Glenn Curtiss had established at Hammondsport. He soon was outflying his instructors and left school as a member of a Curtiss exhibition team.

Improvising freely, Beachey became the star of the troupe. On Jan. 23, 1912, his name hit the front pages with

Another product of 1912 which never survived actual flight tests. Its North Carolina inventor expected this plane to carry seven passengers.

Silas Christofferson made history in 1912 by taking off from the roof of a building in Portland, Ore.

A nonstop record of 1913 was made in this Moisant monoplane by C. Murvin Wood. He flew from Hempstead, L.I., to Gaithersburg, Md., 287 miles, in 265 minutes.

A young law student in Chicago dreamed up this steam flying boat in 1913. He planned to fly the Atlantic in 31 hours and went so far as to build the hull. Engines were two 150-horsepower steam turbines.

The hull of the steam flying boat. Its young builder named it "Napoleon."

The eight-cylinder engine of the Curtiss flying boat (on the opposite page). It was equipped with a self-starter.

the "death dip," a series of screaming, near-vertical dives.

Beachey's flirtation with Niagara Falls was his first great air exploit. On June 27, 1912, he skimmed over both sides of the falls, swung out over Canada and headed back for some real fun. He dipped sharply down into the deep gorge below Niagara with his motor revved wide open, buzzed up the course of the rapids, and zoomed up over the rock lip with just a couple of feet to spare.

After that Beachey became a free-lance stunt flier and performed at fairs and exhibitions. In 1913 he made the first loop-the-loop. But doing tricks high in the air was too tame for him and his awesome specialty became flying close to things without quite hitting them, such as flying between two trees growing so close together that he had to turn his wings up vertically to get through. For awhile he traveled with Barney Oldfield, the famous racing driver. Oldfield would drive madly around the fairground tracks while Beachey flew just above, sometimes bumping the autoist's head with his front landing wheel.

Beachey died stunting at the Panama-Pacific International Exposition along San Francisco Bay in 1915. First one wing, then the other, ripped off his brand new monoplane as he went into a screaming, twisting dive at 2,000 feet. The wingless fuselage plunged into the blue waters of the bay, bearing with it the man whose reckless courage had done so much to win public acceptance of aviation.

Most of these early planes were biplanes and almost all were open-fuselage. The pilot sat strapped to his seat with the wind billowing through sleeves and trousers, with only a few struts, wires, braces, and poles between him and infinity. Two persons were the absolute maximum carrying capacity. Small wonder that the new device offered no threat to other transportation in its first decade!

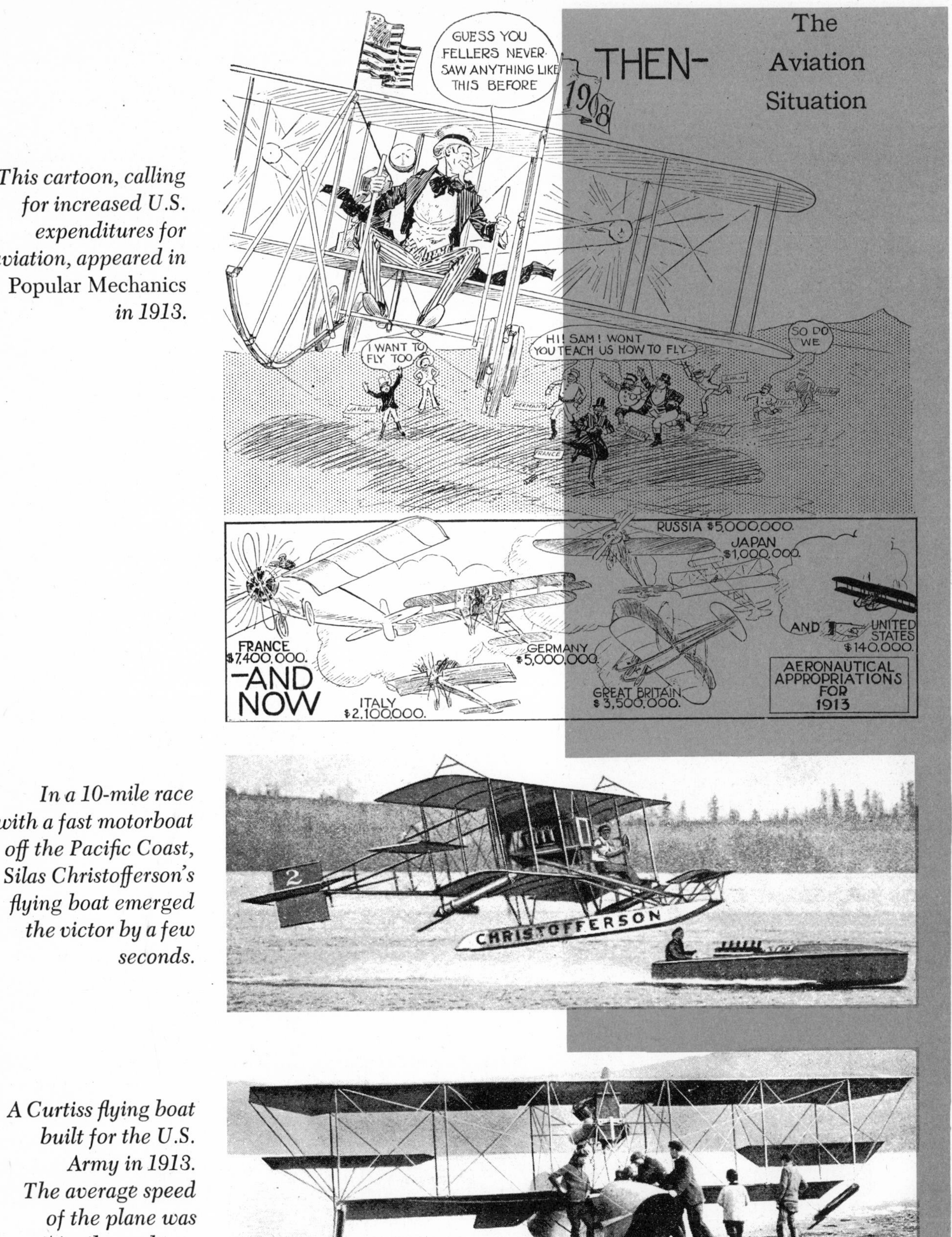

This cartoon, calling for increased U.S. expenditures for aviation, appeared in Popular Mechanics *in 1913.*

In a 10-mile race with a fast motorboat off the Pacific Coast, Silas Christofferson's flying boat emerged the victor by a few seconds.

A Curtiss flying boat built for the U.S. Army in 1913. The average speed of the plane was 54 miles an hour.

A pause in the Munsey Tour of 1908 at the end of a covered bridge allows an autoist and a horse to glare at each other with mutual contempt (right).

The Packard limousine of 1908 ignored the driver's comfort, but it had a door high enough so that passengers could walk in standing almost upright.

There were more than a few feminine members of the tour groups that became konwn as "motomaniacs." (1909 Maxwell)

ALTHOUGH automobile designers made steady improvements on their earliest models, it was Henry Ford who really changed the situation in 1907 with his Model T which, it has been said, "set the world on wheels."

In 1903, the year Ford's third company was founded, the total production of all motor vehicles in the United States had climbed slowly to 11,235. The following year more than 22,000 passenger cars and 700 trucks were built, showing the pace at which the automobile industry was expanding. In 1905 production went up only 2,000 but it jumped to 34,000 in 1906. Thus the infant industry struggled for a foothold. In 1907 43,000 passenger cars and 1,000 trucks were manufactured. In 1908, the year of the first Model T, the industry jumped production almost 50 per cent, making 65,000 vehicles. And then the auto deluge really started. Production for 1909 doubled, hitting

An "ocean to ocean" tour of 1908. These cross-country caravans enjoyed quite a vogue in the early 1900's.

Hard-derbied to a man, the judges of an early road race assume an informal pose as they await the arrival of the leading cars.

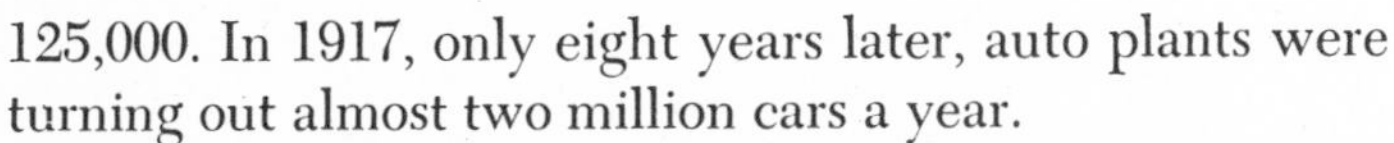

125,000. In 1917, only eight years later, auto plants were turning out almost two million cars a year.

Production was curtailed briefly during World War I. Then, in the '20's came the "automobile boom" which saw the price steadily decrease, the quality increase and the production figures rise from the wartime low of about 1,000,000 to 5,000,000 cars a year by 1929. These, of course, are only new-car production figures. Actually far more cars than that were in circulation at all times. By 1924, midway in the postwar automobile boom, one passenger car was operating inside the U. S. for every seven persons. Ford himself sold 15,000,000 Model T's before the last "tin lizzie" rolled off the Ford assembly line on May 26, 1927. It was replaced by the Model A. Ford did not want to make the change but public demand forced him to abandon his favorite model. His capitulation

The Packard of 1909 was beautifully proportioned and quite dashing, with its flaring fenders and glistening brass.

Hill-climbing tests were important in the days when engines were underpowered and axles likely to break.

marked the end of the automobile's infancy and his surrender to a sleek, modern machine—as General Motors, Chrysler, Dodge, and many others had previously done—marked the end of an era. The public no longer wanted their automobiles to look like buggies. As the years progressed, the desire for a low slung, streamlined car which approached the famed "tear drop" design had to be met.

The Model T had three features. In the first place it was cheap. It entered the world priced around $800, and the price went steadily down to a low of less than $300, briefly, during the postwar depression of 1920-21. (In 1921, when everyone else was curtailing production, Ford increased his and brought out 55 per cent of the industry's total output.)

Secondly, the Model T was so simply designed that anyone could repair it, which highly recommended the car to the isolated American farmer. And in the third place, it was specifically designed to meet the farmer's needs. It looked high and awkward, but it could sail easily over deep ruts and fair-sized rocks and stumps. It seemed

The birth of an American tradition — the roadside picnic. This "buffet tender" was offered motor tourists in 1910.

In 1910 means of transportation and motive power overlapped greatly. Here are oxen, mules, horses and an automobile at the service of a farmer in Michigan.

fragile, but its weight was so light in relation to its motor that it could run through swamp, sand, and mud. With the coming of the Model T the main resistance to the automobile began to melt, for the farmers had been the backbone of that resistance and they began buying Model T's as fast as they could get the money together.

General Motors was founded the same year the Model T appeared, 1908. It expanded to a capitalization of over $1,000,000,000 in the following 14 years and since the early '20's has been the giant of the industry. The first Chevrolet, which later became G.M. property, came out in 1912 and retailed at over $2,000. It was the Chevrolet of the '20's, brought out to compete with the low-priced Model T, that was the primary reason why Ford had to give up his pride and joy.

Roads remained the automobile's worst hobble until the '20's. For three hundred years, the colonies and then the nation had spread slowly along the Indian trails, the waterways, and later the railroads. Since land had been the main inducement in the western movement, farms

The 1909 Carter used this large disk and a sliding, friction-faced wheel to obtain variable speeds.

Pennsylvania, leader in the "good roads" movement, provided this stretch of improved highway in 1909.

"The Sealed Bonnet" was a famous trademark of the Mova. It was based on an 8,000-mile trip made with the hood sealed against repairs or adjustments en route. In addition to the "Racytype," Mova made a more conventional "Tourer," seen at the upper right.

A curious, motorized revival of the sedan chair that appeared on New York streets in 1910.

were a mile or so apart in most of the country. Towns dotted the land 10 miles or more apart, each as isolated as if it were in another continent, unless it was on a river or a railroad. The cost of hauling farm produce to market in the U. S. was $1,000,000,000 in 1908 and most of this was due to bad roads.

Yet the improvement of roads had to wait until the automobile's popularity had grown to a point where millions of people clamored for good highways. This was not too long in happening. By the eve of World War I, car owners had begun to "see America first." Indeed, the national fondness for roaming the country, even though part of the time was spent hub-deep in mud, gave the "touring car" its name. Automobile advertisements recognized this appeal and, for many years, the principal "selling" message was some variation of the happy owner scanning the Rockies with field glasses or snapping a bear in Yellowstone National Park with his Kodak, his wife and children beaming gaily from the car. Reality was considerably sterner than this but despite breakdowns, flat tires, and poor roads, the number of tourists increased steadily.

Alexander Winton's 800-mile trip from Cleveland to New York in 1897 was the first long overland journey in an automobile. No one bettered it until 1901 when Roy Chapin drove 900 miles from Detroit to New York in seven days. This trip was considered impossible to make, and as a matter of fact, Chapin had to drive on the hard-beaten Erie Canal towpath to make it.

Both these trips were by professionals. Winton was recognized as "National Track Champion" by the Automobile Club of America. Roy Chapin, who later became head of Hudson Motors, was a mechanic and demonstrator for Ransom Olds when he made his Detroit-to-New York tour. But in 1904 two "civilians" showed that anybody could do it—providing he had an iron constitution, lots of luck, bulldog determination, and was insensible to insults. The two who demonstrated all these qualities were Mr. and Mrs. J. F. Miller, who drove a two-cylinder Rambler from Chicago to Syracuse, N. Y., and back, a distance of 2,000 miles. In Illinois stones were hurled at them by crowds of roisterers. In New York a farmer threatened them with his shotgun and in Pennsylvania road blocks were built in their path. Miller later wrote, however, that roads were his biggest obstacle. "This country scarcely knows the meaning of the word," he said.

In 1900 the United States Office of Road Inquiry, established many decades before but until then inactive, began

By 1910 neat concrete bridges had begun to replace the romantic but dangerous covered bridges.

1911 Brush station wagon. It sported coil-spring suspension on all four wheels, but had no place for the driver to put his feet.

In the cities and towns began to appear streets of macadam: finely broken stone kept smooth with oil.

The Octagon, an eight-wheeled auto built in 1911 by a Columbus, Ind., inventor who claimed easier riding and minimized tire wear.

This 1911 patent was one of many unsuccessful attempts to find a substitute for the pneumatic tire.

pressuring the various state governments to take action on road building. That year seven states set up highway departments. Information on road building was gathered and passed on to town and village authorities. Agricultural colleges, with wide contacts among the farmers, were enlisted in the cause. Their main job was selling the taxpayers on the necessity for spending money to improve roads. Public lectures, pamphlets, and other promotional activities were used to persuade the public.

In 1904 the Office of Road Inquiry was reorganized as the United States Office of Public Roads. It published the first American road census that year, revealing that America had 2,000,000 miles of roads between farm, village, and town. Of these only 150,000 boasted surfacing of any kind, most of that being gravel. Aside from city streets, there were only 250 miles of paved or surfaced roads in 1905. The first complete mile of concrete highway was built in 1908, when Detroit paved a strip of Woodward Avenue. This stretch drew motorists from miles about like flies to honey and after they had savored the sensation of soaring smoothly over a concrete surface, they helped spread the word for roads. With the increase in automobiles and the popularity of touring, a number of states now began giving way to the pressure. Massachu-

Packard touring car of 1911.

setts appropriated $5,000,000 a year for roads, New York about $6,000,000 and Pennsylvania $6,500,000.

An article in the August, 1908, *Technical World* showed the change that was taking place. The article was appropriately called "Roadless America in Transition."

"From every part of the country comes the same encouraging news," wrote the author, C. F. Carter. "Sixteen states now have highway commissions. . . . At one extreme is New York, which in 1905, voted to expend $5,000,000 in building roads. The state will build and maintain 3,332 miles connecting the principal cities and pay one-half the cost of 4,700 miles of local roads to be built by counties.

"At the other extreme is Iowa, the third state in the Union in extent of road mileage, which doles out an annual appropriation of $5,000 to defray the expenses of the state college faculty while acting in the capacity of highway commission."

Even this, Carter said, was producing results, for the college men were setting up a series of road schools. He then summed up what was happening in the rest of the country, remarking with satisfaction that convicts had been set to work on roads in the South. New Mexico had also used convicts to build a scenic highway from Santa Fe to Las Vegas. The convicts, he claimed, "fairly begged

1912 Packard limousine.

Another inventor proposed brushes to sweep glass and nails away.

In 1913 Chicagoans proposed parking space under Grant Park. But it took 40 years for the plan to bear fruit — ground was broken for the project late in 1952.

A collapsible rim for tires.

A 1913 solution for glare.

for the privilege of working on the road." California was planning a highway across the state and Colorado had organized an association to build a great national scenic highway from Yellowstone Park to the Grand Canyon.

Michigan was also coming to life. Mecosta county had decided to spend $10,000 a year on roads for the next 15 years. "The copper country will spend $100,000 for roads this year," the *Technical World* writer went on. "Wayne county, in which Detroit is situated, will spend $90,000 this year on roads that are to be armored with a tar-macadam compound to render them automobile-proof.

"Louisiana," he went on, "mortified over having lost the Glidden automobile tour on account of its frightful roads, has set to work with energy to remedy this shortcoming." The first road was to connect New Orleans to Baton Rouge, a distance of 125 miles, which Carter described as "too soft for wheeled vehicles, but not quite thin enough for boats."

Maryland, he reported, planned to spend $5,000,000 and Pennsylvania was raising her appropriations to $6,000,000. "California, finding Alameda county's Magnolia Avenue more famous than the orange groves of Riverside, and the Kearney drive at Fresno of greater renown than its raisins . . . is plunging on good roads."

Indiana also was joining the parade. It was the custom throughout the country for farmers to join forces once a year and "work the roads" so they could move their produce to market. By 1908, the state was planning to spend $8,000,000 for gravel roads.

Better roads were found to increase property values, just as the coming of the railroad had done. Daviess county, Kentucky, spent $200,000 for 25 miles of roads, and found that the property value along the roads had increased a million dollars.

This 1913 electric roadster was designed to look like a gasoline-powered auto.

The kind of paving material also came in for scrutiny. Since the automobile pounded gravel and even some macadam to pieces very quickly, this was a big problem for early road makers. At first it was thought that 8 to 12 inches of crushed stone was the minimum for a macadamized foundation. "But now," the *Technical World* author wrote, "the road engineers of the United States recommend road beds as thin as possible. Three inches has been found to be the least practicable depth, while anything over 6 inches is declared unnecessary. In any case, the road must be smooth, hard and impervious to water."

The cost of macadam road in those days ranged from $3,500 to $5,500 a mile for a width of 15 feet. Carter believed that 12 to 16 feet was plenty wide enough, if shoulders of three to five feet were provided. Twelve feet, he maintained, gave room for two vehicles to pass. "On a 16-foot roadway," he concluded, "two automobiles may pass with a team standing partly on the shoulder at one side." There was no doubt in the motorist's mind about which, horse or automobile, should stand and let the other pass—an attitude American motorists since have transferred to the pedestrian.

Roads and automobiles advanced together, each influencing the other. As more automobiles were bought, the

Studebaker introduced electric lights with the 1913 "35" Tourer.

Partly convertible – 1913 Packard.

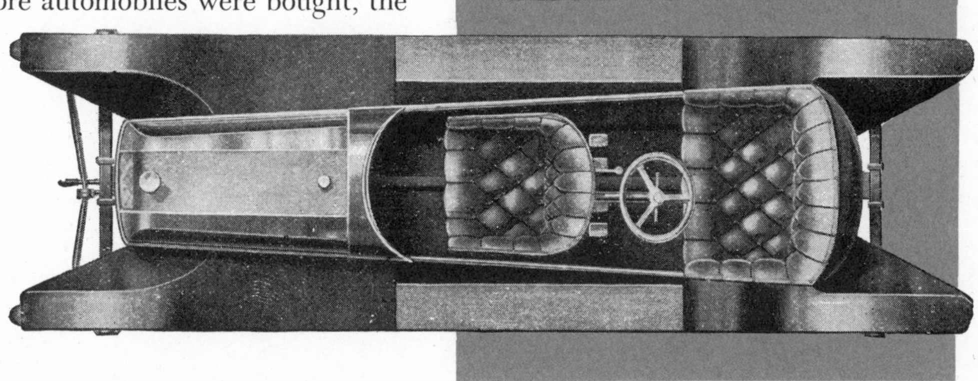

A 1914 curiosity was this "cyclecar," a two-passenger tandem with the driver's seat in the rear.

The sturdy, simple Model T was a favorite of farmers for 20 years.

No matter how beat up or worn out a Model T became, it could always be wired, tied, kicked, hammered, bent, or propped up and be made to run again.

pressure increased for better roads. Better roads made more people want automobiles.

The automobile underwent remarkable improvement in performance and appearance between 1903 and 1913. In 1904 the first White bus appeared and the Stevens-Duryea Company began making four- and six-cylinder cars, with a unit construction of engine, clutch, and transmission housings. This was the first "unit housing plant." That same year the Detroit YMCA established a school for automobile mechanics, while Henry Ford and William K. Vanderbilt, Jr., each drove a racing car more than 90 miles an hour. The shock absorber was introduced by E. V. Hartford, and many new models came out with demountable rims. Light at this time consisted of acetylene gas lamps.

The first Glidden Tour was conducted in 1905. These jaunts were followed with keen interest by the country at large and did a lot to show the superiority of the new machine over the horse under all sorts of adverse conditions. Every automobile manufacturer of repute entered the tours and longed to win them for the publicity that

There were many uses for the wide running boards of touring cars. Here a family lunch box is mounted on the running board for roadside picnics.

would result. Pierce-Arrow won the first four tours.

The Society of Automobile Engineers was formed in 1905. Side entrance to tonneaus began taking the place of rear-entrance bodies and new accessories included the Gabriel exhaust horn, Weed tire chains, Goodyear universal rims, power tire pumps, and ignition locks.

In 1906 Buick became the first to include a storage battery as standard equipment. A few cars appeared with front bumpers. Adams-Farwell introduced three- and five-cylinder rotary engines.

By 1907 many states were eyeing the automobile as a source of tax revenue, and the Association of Licensed Automobile Manufacturers presented a formula for figuring horsepower which was adopted by many states as a taxing basis. Oldsmobile began substituting nickel plating for brass trimming. Speeding was a problem in many communities. Glencoe, Ill., built humps in the streets to slow the motorists down. Ford made more than a million dollars that year, and a Franklin was driven from New York to Chicago in 39 hours, 36 minutes. Buick installed a sliding-gear transmission.

In 1908 C. Harold Wills developed the use of vanadium steel for Ford. The Fisher Body Company and General Motors joined the roster of automobile giants. The first successful four-wheel drive was developed by Otto Zachow and William Besserdich. Other innovations for 1908 included the magnetic speedometer, sleeve-valve engines, silent timing chains, motor-driven horns, baked-enamel finishes, and helical gears. By this time, all auto manufacturers had moved the steering wheel to the left side of the car.

In 1909, Hupmobile featured a transmission clutch in unit with the motor and a fuel-reserve valve in the gasoline tank. W. S. Seaman and Company built the first auto-

Directional indicator suggested in 1916 was a pivoted hand, operated by a cord.

Dodge Brothers offered one of the first closed cars. The price was $1265, compared to $835 for the open touring car or roadster.

The automobile and our national parks grew up together. Here are part of the 500 cars laden with vacationists who swarmed into Glacier National Park for the opening of the 1915 season.

During the "gasless Sundays" of 1918, Glenn Martin equipped his auto to burn natural gas.

Two-way radio car in 1919.

1920 midget never got to market.

mobile bodies in Milwaukee. Fabric tops appeared and Graham trucks came out with overdrive transmissions.

The year 1910 saw further clutch improvement and the beginning of selling cars "completely equipped." Cadillac came out with an electric starter. Several three-ton trucks were manufactured. In 1911 Cadillac combined its electric starting with a generator-battery lighting and ignition system, while Oakland and Hupmobile brought out the first all-steel bodies. In 1913 wire wheels became standard equipment on many cars, and the Bendix drive for electric starters was shown for the first time. Packard introduced forced-feed lubrication and the first Chevrolet assembly plant was opened.

In 1914 Cadillac built the first American eight-cylinder V-type high-speed engine, Packard developed spiral bevel gears, Pierce-Arrow incorporated headlights in the fenders, and Horace and John Dodge started making the car that bore their name. The following year demountable rims replaced clincher types, and Packard brought out America's first 12-cylinder engine. Cadillac came out with tilt-beam headlights, and Oldsmobile offered top and windshield as standard equipment.

Mack Truck brought out its famous "bulldog" in 1916. Hand-operated windshield wipers, stop lights and rear-view mirrors appeared as standard equipment on a few cars. In 1917 Paige brought out a coupé with the first rumble seat, and Studebaker adopted the internal manifold hot spot.

By 1918 Sunday driving had become so widespread that the government had to curtail it for the duration of World War I in order to conserve gasoline. In 1919 Studebaker made its last carriage and turned wholeheartedly to auto production. G. A. Schacht perfected "two-range" transmission, and indirect dashboard lighting appeared.

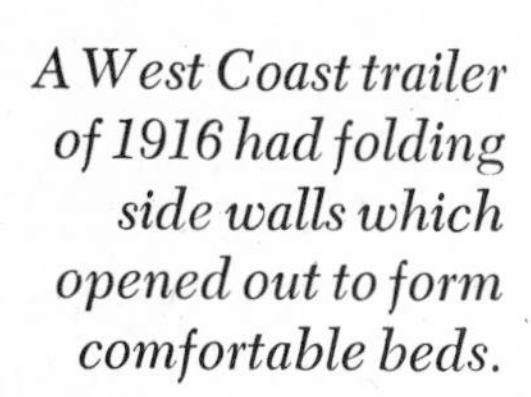

A West Coast trailer of 1916 had folding side walls which opened out to form comfortable beds.

By 1920 the Model T had lost all its fancy brasswork, but it was still attractive because of its selling price – $550.

Springfield Moto Cycle Club, one of the first, met nearly every Sunday for a ride in the country on its Indian motorcycles of about 1900.

THE MOTORCYCLE was an important means of rapid transportation in Europe as early as 1890. But in America, largely because inventors here were concentrating on the automobile, motorcycles did not appear in numbers until after the turn of the century.

Probably the first successful motorcycle in the United States was that of W. W. Austin of Winthrop, Mass., who in 1868 suspended a steam boiler in back of the seat of his bicycle. Piston rods were connected to cranks on the rear wheel. But this was a machine far too heavy for the average cyclist's taste, and Austin's invention went no farther than a few city blocks around his house.

Gottlieb Daimler, German inventor of the four-cycle gasoline engine, hitched one to a bicycle sometime between 1885 and 1890 and his machine is considered the first true motorcycle.

In 1899, when six-day bicycle racing was at the height of its popularity, Henri Fournier brought a motorcycle from France to pace one of the French teams in a race at Madison Square Garden. But the motorcycle was so slow that the French racers finally pedaled on ahead of their sputtering pacemaker, which then was pulled off the track amid the jeers of the crowd.

One man didn't jeer. He was Carl Oscar Hedstrom, a top-ranking professional rider. He alone saw possibilities

An electric motorcycle of 1911 that ran over 75 miles on a single charge (above), a 1908 no-seat motorcyclet (above, right), and a 1910 drawing forecasting the machine of 1912 which, among other things, was to have adequate splash guards and crank starting (right).

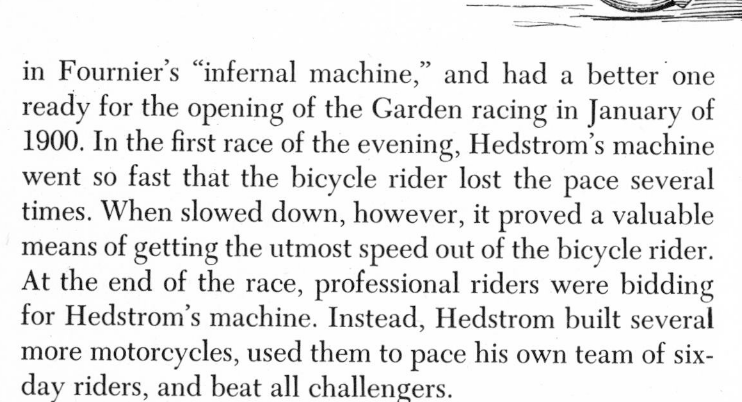

in Fournier's "infernal machine," and had a better one ready for the opening of the Garden racing in January of 1900. In the first race of the evening, Hedstrom's machine went so fast that the bicycle rider lost the pace several times. When slowed down, however, it proved a valuable means of getting the utmost speed out of the bicycle rider. At the end of the race, professional riders were bidding for Hedstrom's machine. Instead, Hedstrom built several more motorcycles, used them to pace his own team of six-day riders, and beat all challengers.

At the end of the 1900 racing season, however, Hedstrom signed a contract on the back of an envelope with George M. Hendee, builder of the then popular Silver King bicycle. The contract called for Hedstrom to build a single-cylinder motor-driven bicycle that could be produced in volume, not for pacemaking, but for everyday use by the general public.

The newspapers of Springfield, Mass., which a decade before had heralded the Duryea automobile, carried an item on June 1, 1901 announcing the public demonstration of a motorized bicycle at the foot of Cross Street Hill. A great many Springfield residents turned out to see a machine that could conquer the 350 feet of 19 per cent grade that most of them had toiled up on foot.

Hedstrom's first charge at the hill topped it with ease.

Motorcycle daredevil in a dash between two trains. He reported missing the cowcatcher of one by about six inches and feeling the other graze the rear tire.

"Hurdling" a motorcycle over a four-inch wooden beam was one concern's method of testing its front-fork strength.

A flexible sidecar developed for motorcycles in 1914 eased riding rough roads.

He started up the grade at 25 miles per hour and went over the top at about 12 miles per hour. On another ride he approached the hill at only five miles per hour, then advanced the speed lever to open up the engine to its full 1¾-horsepower, a maneuver which a Springfield newspaper reported made him "jump forward to the crest of the hill with an abundance of speed and power."

The new vehicle was named the "Indian." Motors were made by the Aurora (Ill.) Machine Company, while the frames and the final assembly were made in Hendee's Springfield bicycle factory. Only three Indians were made in 1901, but 143 were produced in the following year. By 1902 the Indian already had competitors: the Marsh, DeLong, Holley, Royal, Auto-Bi, American, Mitchell, Hercules, Kelecom and Orient were among those advertised. But an Indian won the first motorcycle race in New York City late in 1902.

What was to be the most serious competitor to the Indian was developed in 1903—the Harley-Davidson. It was the product of two young machinists, William Harley and Arthur Davidson, who began working on their first

Despite poor roads, cross-country cycle riding was popular in 1915.

The famous "Harvey Girls" of the railroad restaurant chain pose with motorcycle speedsters at the Dodge City (Kansas) races.

A 1914 Harley-Davidson in messenger service. (Far right) Displaying the popular "habit" of the day, two feminine enthusiasts prepare to ride on their 1913 tandem motorcycle.

Erwin G. "Cannonball" Baker, a colorful figure of motorcycle and auto racing, prepares to break another record at the Cincinnati Speedway on Aug. 15, 1914. He drove 1,534 miles in 24 hours, which included two hours and 23 minutes stopping time.

Kicks were made at full speed in a 1925 motorcycle version of football.

Held by centrifugal force to the steeply banked walls of wooden bowls called "motordromes," cyclists thrilled state fair throngs.

machine in 1901. It ran so well that the boys began making others for friends in 1903 in a 10- by 15-foot shed on the outskirts of Milwaukee. Prophetically, the shed door was crudely lettered, "Harley-Davidson Motor Co." By 1906 this had become a real business. Fifty Harley-Davidsons were produced that year. But Indian, which appeared as the first twin-cylinder motorcycle in 1905, continued to be the best-selling machine.

In 1908 the big talk in motorcycle circles concerned the endurance contest scheduled by the Federation of American Motorcyclists for June 29 and 30, starting in Catskill, N. Y. Riding for Harley-Davidson was Walter Davidson, who had joined brother Arthur and William Harley in the firm and had become its president. Outriding the nation's best professionals, Walter won the diamond medal first prize and secured for Harley-Davidson its first important victory in motorcycle competition.

The early motorcycles were either belt or chain driven. At first they had to be pushed to start their engines; later a clutch-and-pedal mechanism was added. The rear wheel was jacked up on a stand and the engine turned over by a foot-kick lever. The cycle was then eased off its stand as the clutch was engaged.

In 1907 the motorcycle became, briefly, the fastest thing on land, sea, or in the air. Glenn Hammond Curtiss, riding a motorcycle of his own manufacture (eight cylinders with a horsepower rated at 40), sped over the sands at Ormond Beach, Fla., at the rate of 136.36 miles per hour. This was considerably faster than the current speed records of the fastest locomotive, automobile, or airplane.

In 1913 motorcycle production in the United States reached 70,000, the most ever produced in one year for

By 1918 motorcycles had varied uses, including taxi service.

The Los Angeles aqueduct was used as an emergency motor highway by John Edwin Hogg in 1918.

This acrobatic troupe of 1932 developed a balancing act on a motorcycle for outdoor performances.

civilian consumption. Feeding this demand were the motorcycle clubs which, like the bicycle and automobiling clubs before them, sprang up in every city and town. These riders called for more comfort and safety rather than higher speeds. In 1916 Indian brought out a more efficient side-by-side valve arrangement, and the same year Harley-Davidson brought out a model with three-speed transmission and full electric ignition and lights. The small seat borrowed from the bicycle became a spacious saddle, and motorcycle frames rested on cradled springs and forks to absorb road shocks. Long wheelbases and floorboards gave comfort to riders' legs and feet for long rides. New starter mechanisms turned over the engine with one press of the foot.

The sidecar, which first appeared in 1905, made it possible for one passenger to accompany a rider. After 1910, the sidecar also was developed for small package deliveries. Because the motorcycle is economical to operate and presents fewer parking problems than the smallest automobile, its use for city deliveries of small packages increased sharply during the '20's and has continued to the present day.

During World War I the American Expeditionary Forces used a number of motorcycles for scouting expeditions and dispatch carrying. The Army's experiences with motorcycles resulted in their adoption for various phases of city and state police work after the war.

The increasing number of special uses to which motorcycles were being put resulted in a wider variety of models. Harley-Davidson brought out its first twin-cylinder model in 1920, a 74-cubic-inch piston displacement model for commercial use, and followed in 1926 with a 21-cubic-inch single-cylinder model designed especially for sport. In 1928 Indian acquired manufacturing rights to

"Broadsiding" was racing on a dirt course without banked curves. Spills and pile-ups were all part of the attraction.

Battery-operated cycles kept appearing from time to time; here's one made in 1941 (above). Dual controls (left) lessen fatigue.

the Ace, a four-cylinder machine, and marketed it as the Indian Four, the only American-made four-cylinder motorcycle until 1941.

During World War II, Hitler demonstrated that the motorcycle could be used for military missions other than dispatch work. Units of Nazi motorcycle troops, armed with rifles and machine guns and protected by armored shields, made break-throughs behind Nazi tanks and probed deep into enemy territory. Similar motorcycle units were developed by the American Armed Forces—Harley-Davidson alone contributed more than 20,000 armored cycles. Their use was continued in Korea.

After the war new designs continued to flow from the drafting boards of the motorcycle companies. A search for lighter machines and more efficient cooling resulted in

Semi-diesel cycles of 1940 claimed 150 miles per gallon.

A modern Army cavalryman in a pose reminiscent of the Indian War days when mounts of flesh and blood were used in this same way.

New motor scooter has soft coil springs on front wheel and seat, gets 75 miles per gallon, and will go 50 miles an hour.

cycles with aluminum cylinder heads. Additional riding comfort was provided by hydraulic front forks. Shaft drive replaced the chains which had for so long transmitted power to the wheels. The engines ranged from one to four cylinders, rated between 10 and 12 horsepower, and piston displacement was from 30 to 74 inches. Many models appeared with two-wheel brakes; the conventional, pedal-operated, internal-expanding brake on the rear wheel and a front-wheel brake operated by a hand lever on the handlebars.

One revolutionary vehicle of 1952 was the Indian Patrol, a three-wheeled vehicle which had full automotive electrical equipment, a reverse gear, self-starter, hydraulic brakes, and shaft drive. Designed primarily for police work, it was soon available for commercial use.

British Vincent cycle, left, has 80 horsepower, did 156 miles an hour in 1950. Owner later added the egglike shell to cut air resistance to a minimum.

Equipped with two-way radio, the general handiness of this service-cycle traffic control makes it the work horse of many police departments.

Electric trucks at first were the favorites of businessmen because of their simplicity of operation. But gasoline trucks, like this Rapid, soon demonstrated superior power.

It was not long before businessmen began to wonder whether cars could not be used to carry something besides men and women in dusters and goggles.

A few merchants bought passenger cars and converted them into delivery trucks by having carpenters build special bodies for them. For awhile, all trucks used in this country were converted passenger cars. Then manufacturers realized that if autos were to be used for delivering heavy loads, the chassis must be stronger and larger and the engine more powerful. The manufacture of trucks began.

For a time trucks were used only for deliveries in cities. But here and there, as early as 1907, men with trucks offered to carry goods between nearby cities and thus intercity trucking was born. Around the larger towns, trucks were used to carry farm goods to market.

The advantages of the truck were apparent from the start. A farmer located 20 miles from town could ship his load of apples by train or interurban, but to do this he would have to haul the apples to the station in his wagon. There they must be transferred to the train. At the city they must be unloaded from the train and carted to the buyer. The truck, on the other hand, could go straight to the farmer's barn, load the apples, and carry them directly to the buyer. By truck the number of handlings was reduced from four to two, and usually the truck was a bit cheaper than the railroad.

AMERICAN ELECTRIC VEHICLE COMPANY

Their Automobiles Are World Leaders.

THEY got the HIGHEST AWARD and the only GOLD MEDAL given at the Paris Exposition for American Automobiles.

They are the highest exponents of Automobile Construction now before the public.

They are unequalled for speed, endurance, economy, comfort, and general serviceableness.

They are in use or on order by more leading business houses than any other make.

For PLEASURE or BUSINESS--ANYTHING.
WE HAVE GIVEN EXTRA THOUGHT TO DELIVERY WAGONS

Representatives Wanted — Write for Catalogue

General Offices and Repository

132 West 38th St., Near Broadway
NEW YORK

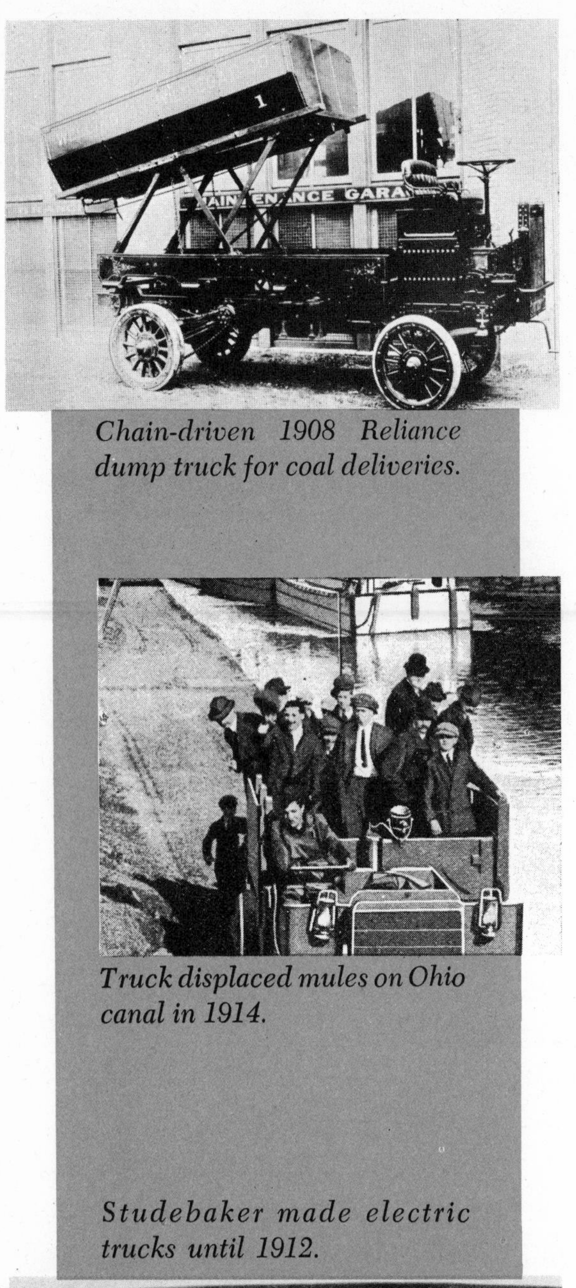

Chain-driven 1908 Reliance dump truck for coal deliveries.

Truck displaced mules on Ohio canal in 1914.

Studebaker made electric trucks until 1912.

But then, even as now, the home owner had seldom visualized the importance of the motor truck to his well-being. The motor truck transports the materials that his home is constructed of, the fuel that keeps it heated, the commodities that enable him to exist—milk, vegetables, meats, etc.—and all these are handled with a flexibility and a swiftness that contribute much to a family's health and comfort.

Until World War I, the use of trucks was confined to towns and short intercity lines. The roads were too bad for long-haul interstate trucking.

But the war created more freight business than the railroads could bear. It was necessary to move men and goods from city to camp and from camp to port. Lumber and supplies had to be transported to camp sites and farm products carried to the seaboard for shipment to our growing expeditionary force. Freight houses in cities became so congested that trains had to dump their bales and boxes along the tracks outside of the city.

There was only one answer to this problem, of course. President Wilson appointed a Highway Transport Committee and put the Detroit automobile man, Roy Chapin, in charge. This was the same Roy Chapin who, at the age of 21, made the first long-distance automobile tour in 1901.

Chapin knew that the government had ordered some 30,000 trucks for delivery to France, where trucks were all-important in distributing food, clothing, and ammunition to troops. Ordinarily these trucks would have been loaded on railroad flatcars and shipped to the Atlantic Coast.

Instead of that, Chapin had them driven to New York, Boston, Philadelphia, and other ports. Nor did they go empty. They were loaded with clothes, guns, helmets, and other war supplies. These trucks, lurching over bad rural roads to the Atlantic, demonstrated on a large scale the practicability of long-haul trucking.

One of the first companies to establish a truck fleet on a regular schedule was the Goodyear Tire and Rubber Company of Akron, Ohio. During the war Goodyear ran seven trucks regularly over a route between Akron and Boston, 740 miles. Instead of going the direct route through New York State, the trucks went through Pennsylvania to New York City and up the coast because the bridges on the New York State route were too flimsy for heavy trucks.

Goodyear Company officials had two reasons for establishing the route. They wished to test their big pneumatic tires by giving them actual road service—at that time most trucks were using solid tires—and they wished to deliver tires to eastern dealers.

1910 electric truck, used for lumber in Cambridge, Mass., had a three-horse-power motor in each wheel.

A 1916 street department truck for flushing or oiling macadam surfaces.

A 1913 truck with a power-loading mechanism. The driver's seat was beside the hood, rather than in back of the motor.

1910 Reliance gave a hard ride to a still-famous cargo.

Chicago's South Water Market in 1926, showing that the horse-drawn produce wagon had entirely disappeared.

Akin to the early road engines is this 30-wheel truck train hauling magnesium ore to a railhead in the Southwest.

This truck, built in 1923 to ride on rails or the highway, had flanged wheels for its railroad journeys.

Since comfort was no requisite for its passengers, this police patrol of 1925 had only solid rubber tires.

Within a year, these big trucks were making the trip each way in four days and giving regular service. Here was another practical demonstration of long-haul trucking.

Thereafter, the trucking industry grew rapidly. In 1915, the second year of the World War, there were only 136,000 trucks in the country. Five years later, the war over, there were a million trucks. In 1950 there were 8,238,000 of all types.

Until about 1920, most heavy-duty trucks were chain driven because this type of transmission was more powerful than the gear transmissions then available. Now the mechanism of a truck is similar in structure to that of an automobile except that the parts are heavier. Small commercial vehicles are sometimes made on standard automobile frames, with larger bodies and perhaps oversize water pumps, clutches, brakes, springs, and a lower gear ratio. There are literally dozens of types of these small commercial vehicles. In growing popularity is the square-bodied sedan which can be used as a small truck simply by folding the rear seat forward. A small business owner or farmer thus can have an attractive family car and truck all in an easily converted unit.

The biggest trucks, when fully loaded, will weigh 60,000 pounds, or 30 tons. Without loads, these monster trucks will weigh between 11,000 and 13,000 pounds. Between these extremes are many types of trucks, with chassis and bodies built to carry a wide range of cargoes and to meet all kinds of highway conditions.

(Below) No load is too heavy or too ungainly in shape for a modern truck to handle.

Trucks brought vital supplies to New York City despite a 26-inch snowfall in the winter of 1947.

Sliding tanks move milk from flatcar to trailer. 65 percent of the five million quarts New York uses each day is brought in by truck.

The Washington Street Market truck terminal in New York City.

Two general types of intercity trucking are now carried on. Fleets of trucks are maintained by private companies to carry their goods. And there are the common carriers who, like the railroads, will carry anybody's goods for hire. Of these, truck engines are commonly gasoline fueled; however, many are of the Diesel type which first began to appear about 1929 along with the first tractor-trailer units, joined together by a huge shoe coupling.

Among the private fleets are the great tank trucks belonging to the large oil companies, delivering gasoline and oil to service stations. There are the large dairy companies delivering butter, cheese, and milk to retail stores and collecting milk from farmers. You have seen their oval tank trucks rumbling over the highways. Packing companies have fleets of refrigerated trucks to carry their dressed meats all over the country. Chain-store systems use trucks to restock their stores.

Among the common carriers are the freight haulers and movers whose giant vans operate throughout the United States. There are 15,000 of these companies, small and

This mammoth rig with a wrecking boom easily handles an 18,000-pound load. Driver, above, makes coffee right in the cab.

large, operating about 50,000 vehicles, and they carry the respectable total of 8 per cent of all commercial freight.

Trucks have become especially useful in carrying certain kinds of goods. A furniture van with a capacity of 1,400 cubic feet will back up to the front door and swallow within its padded sides all the furniture and goods of a large house. It is not necessary to crate the furniture. The moving company's men will load it, take it across the country, and place it in your new house. It is estimated that 90 per cent of all office and household furniture is moved by truck.

Trucks have replaced railroads as the chief means of transporting livestock from farm to stockyard. Where in 1916 less than 2 per cent of all livestock was moved by truck, now 55 per cent is thus carried.

Milk used to be brought to the city creamery by the milk train. Today only 18 per cent of milk is carried this way. Oval tank trucks are doing the job. A single tank truck may carry as many as 2,600 gallons of milk in its glass-lined thermos bottle container.

Turbine-powered truck built in 1950. The engine, shown next to the man, weighs only 200 pounds, but develops 175 horsepower.

Hydraulic-lift "chuck wagon" brings meals to a Northwest Airlines plane.

A single cable on a block and tackle dumps the load from a new truck-trailer.

Coal trucks operating from mine to city, refrigerated fruit and vegetable trucks rolling from farm to market, tank trucks, bulky vans, stock trucks carrying livestock to the packing plant, specially built vans taking race horses from city to city, traveling libraries, traveling groceries, traveling dental offices—all these form a colorful and important part of our transportation.

Present trends are toward uniform state laws as regards sizes and weights, toward axle-load regulations instead of gross-weight laws, better lighting equipment, compulsory inspection, uniform licensing laws, strict federal regulations on interstate movements by the Interstate Commerce Commission, higher-speed vehicles, and lighter chassis and body weight in relation to pay load.

A railroad train can go only where the tracks lead and it costs money to build a track to a new town. A truck can go anywhere that there is a highway and it can change its route at will. Only the airplane can approach this flexibility, and it is handicapped by airport and airway limitations and much higher operating costs.

At present, there are an estimated 50,000 communities served by trucks alone; percentagewise, this means that trucks carry 10 per cent of all our commercial freight traffic. Without the truck lines, our transportation system would be incomplete. With it, we have freedom of trade such as the world has never seen over so large an area.

The truck and semi-trailer combination is now the standard long-distance hauling unit.

An Army airplane was successfully launched from a Navy blimp by releasing it from the end of a 100-foot cable over Rockaway Beach, L. I., in 1919.

IT WAS DURING WORLD WAR I that the airplane became really practical. When war began 11 years after Kitty Hawk, the average speed for an airplane was between 70 and 80 miles per hour and 7,000 feet was the very best altitude attainable. Four years later, when the war ended, the average speed had more than doubled to 150 miles per hour and the ceiling was up to 30,000 feet. The average engine more than doubled in efficiency, weighing 1.9 pounds for each horsepower developed as compared to 4 pounds earlier. By improving the wings and plane design, the wing-loading capacity was increased from four to eight pounds per square foot. The fuselage was covered, undercarriage simplified, the tail assembly was complete, and the efficiency of the airframe had been improved about 200 per cent.

With few exceptions, the postwar planes were biplanes, not so much by preference, but because of the structural limitations of wood and fabric. It was easier to brace the thin wings against each other than it was to guy, by means of wires, the necessarily longer wings of a monoplane.

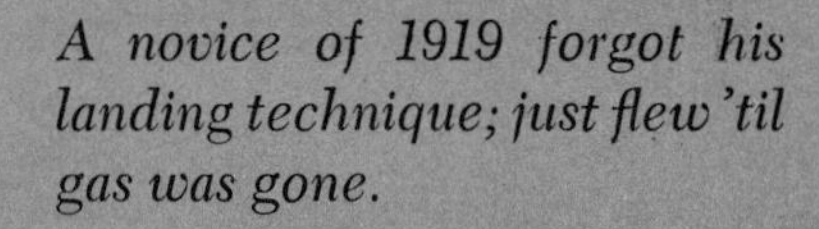

A novice of 1919 forgot his landing technique; just flew 'til gas was gone.

The first World War I De Haviland with the famous Liberty 12 motor. In 1919 it was sent to the Smithsonian Institution.

Equipped with a turbine-supercharged Liberty engine, this Le Pere biplane of 1919 set new speed and altitude records at Dayton, Ohio.

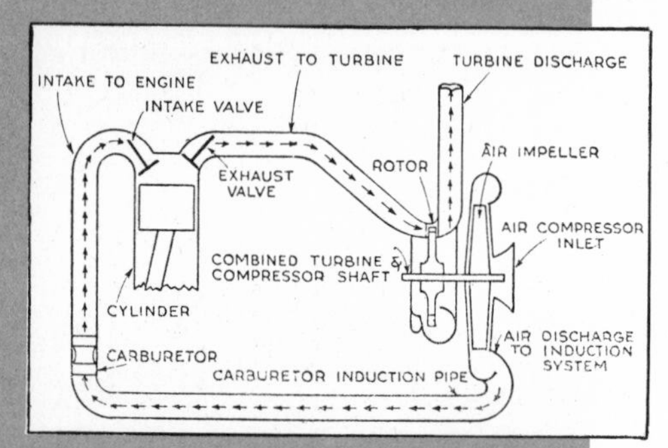

The supercharger operated on the same principle as those used on planes of World War II. Above, schematic drawing.

Part of the improvement in performance came from enclosing the fuselage, which eliminated much drag. There were yet no cabin planes. Only the two-seaters were able to carry an extra passenger.

So far, then, the airplane had been used for sport and exhibition before the war and as a military weapon during the conflict. Now, in 1920, it was ready to enter the field of transportation. The British and French were first with the establishment of daily service between London and Paris on Aug. 26, 1919. The following year the first passenger service in the U. S. began with regular runs between Key West, Fla., and Havana, Cuba. In 1922 a passenger air route was established between Los Angeles and San Francisco to make *two* trips per day. Flying time

Curtiss Jn-4D-2, popularly called the "Jenny," was the standard trainer of the First World War. Here is one with the fabric stripped off to show the construction.

This tandem-type, multiple-wing plane was one of the unsuccessful efforts of airplane designers to improve the breed at Langley Field, Va., in 1920.

between these cities—a distance of 400 miles—was five hours, or 80 miles an hour. The planes were three-seaters carrying *four* passengers on each trip. One-way fare was $50.

The average citizen, however, continued to regard the new machine askance and preferred to keep his feet on "good old terra firma," as he expressed it forcefully and often. Nor should the citizen of a later day consider him a yokel whose timidity held back progress. There were sound reasons for his attitude. The planes were fragile still, and dangerous. A lot was still to be learned of aeronautics. For one thing, planes of those days had a tendency to go into spins on slight provocation. The pilots themselves were a daredevil breed, glamorous heroes at

An airman of 1919 was unhurt when his Jenny biplane crashed into the top of a tree.

The "Bullet" of 1919 was then the "fastest thing with wings." This strutless biplane with flexible wings reached a top speed of 195 miles per hour.

Chicago was horror-stricken in September, 1919, when this dirigible exploded in mid-air over the Illinois Trust and Savings Bank in Chicago. The flaming engines plunged through the bank's skylight into a rotunda where 150 bookkeepers and typists worked. Thirteen persons were killed and a score injured in the explosion and fire that followed in the wake of the crash into the building.

county fairs and such, but not men in whose hands a sober citizen would care to place his life.

Thus airplane production in the U. S., which reached 411 planes in its greatest prewar year, 1916, dropped to 263 in 1922. The wartime peak of 14,000 in 1918 was almost entirely for military use. And almost all of the 263 planes made in 1922 went to the government for mail or military service. There simply was no civilian market worth mentioning. The barnstormers who performed at fairs and exhibitions usually bought surplus war planes.

The federal government played the greatest part in keeping aviation alive during these years. In May of 1918, the government established airmail service between Washington, Philadelphia, and New York. In 1920, the Post Office began regular airmail service between New York and Chicago. On August 21, 1923, airmail planes left Los Angeles and New York on the first legs of relays to a rendezvous in Cheyenne, Wyo. These flights covered 2,680 miles in 26 hours and some of the legs were made at night. A string of giant 5,000-candlepower lights placed three miles apart guided the airmen on their way. Emergency landing fields every 25 miles were lit with 5,000,000 candlepower and regular airfields were lit with 500,000,000 candlepower. Regular service was begun by the Post Office the following year.

Barnstorming inspired a Popular Mechanics *artist to predict aerial tournaments.*

None of this, however, could keep the youthful industry in a healthy condition. A civilian market was necessary, and to get that, civilian acceptance of flying itself was the prerequisite. Accordingly, in 1922, the Aeronautical Chamber of Commerce was formed to sell commercial aviation to America and to promote research. The problem had three aspects: publicity, safety, and speed. Research would increase the last two; aviators themselves took care of the first. For the next few years, aided directly or indirectly by the ACC, a number of aviators performed headline-making feats.

Miss Brassac was put into a bag and air mailed in 1920.

Several historic flights already had been made when the ACC was formed. In May, 1919, three Navy NC-4 planes braved the Atlantic. Breaking the isolating grip of oceans had from the start a dramatic effect on the imagination of men. This first flight called for stops in the Azores, at Ponta Delgada and Lisbon, then a flight north to England. A string of 66 warships dotted the route. Only one of the planes, flown by Lieut. Albert Cushing Read with a five-man crew, finished the flight which required 15 days.

A month later, on June 14, John Alcock and Arthur Witten Brown flew nonstop across the North Atlantic from Newfoundland to Ireland in 16 hours, 12 minutes. In 1923 Lieut. O. G. Kelly and J. C. MacReady flew a Liberty-

This Lawson airliner began service from Milwaukee to New York and Washington and return in 1920. The 95-foot plane carried 20 passengers at an average speed of 110 miles an hour.

Helicopter research continued in 1921 despite the doubts of experts. This machine proved to be capable of lifting its own weight, but it was unstable.

engined Fokker monoplane on a nonstop 2,516-mile flight across the U. S. They took off from Roosevelt Field, N. Y., on May 2, and arrived in San Diego 26 hours and 50 minutes later. In 1924 Russell Maugham flew solo from Roosevelt Field to San Francisco, 2,540 miles, in 21 hours and 41½ minutes, making only three stops for fuel.

Along with these headline-making flights, another activity was going on which helped, slowly but surely, to win acceptance for the airplane simply by making it part of the everyday scene. Hundreds of fliers were trying to make their ruling passion their bread and butter as well.

The bulk of commercial air service of this period was conducted by free-lance pilots, most of them former World War I fliers. They were of a race of adventurers who found it hard to settle down to mundane jobs when they returned home. These Army and Navy pilots were convinced that the airplane would have as dazzling a future as the automobile.

"Jersey" Ringel, typical of the barnstormers of the 20's, hangs from his plane by his knees over Newark, N.J.

Even as late as 1922, plane designers were trying to obtain advantages from the multiple wing. This triplane, built to carry freight, also anticipated the "flying boxcar."

Their activities were two-sided. Some took up where the barnstorming pilots and balloonists of prewar days had left off. The ear-splitting voice of the airplane exhaust was heard again in the land as airplane exhibitions became feature events at fairs and carnivals across the country. The pilots thrilled the crowds with barrel rolls, outside loops, screaming dives, and every other maneuver possible to execute with the plane of the day. When the repertoire of maneuverability was exhausted, they took to walking on wings, changing planes in mid-air, stunting on rope ladders suspended from the planes, changing from racing automobiles to racing planes and vice versa. These antics also helped keep the airplane before the public eye. By the late '20's the American public, having barely recovered from the shock of the automobile, was already speaking of the "Air Age," although this same public still preferred to keep its feet on the ground.

In addition to stunt flying, airmen established an un-

Inventors Peter Cooper Hewitt and Francis Bacon Crocker came up with a two-propeller helicopter in 1920. This system, with added features, is used by some present-day machines.

Army pilot C. C. Moseley just missed attaining a speed of three miles a minute in winning the Pulitzer trophy race with this plane in 1920.

Despite the disastrous record of dirigibles during the 1920's, the search continued for safe and speedy airships. This was a drafting-board dream with wings.

The Fokker monoplane used by Macready and Kelly in establishing the 1923 endurance record. They circled non-stop for 36 hours at 75 miles an hour, enough to have crossed the Atlantic.

1923 aircraft engine made a record-breaking run of 573 hours, enough to fly 60,000 miles with the throttle wide open.

counted number of one- or two-man companies across the country to conduct what charitably might be called businesses. Equipped with the surplus war planes and sometimes joined by their service buddies or idolizing youths whom they taught to fly, scores of ex-service pilots settled on rented cow pastures on the outskirts of small towns and villages. They made a living of sorts by flying sightseeing trips over the nearby countryside, giving flying lessons to the more bold of the townsfolk, and flying businessmen to neighboring towns or further.

Seldom did their business operations achieve the settled dignity of regularly scheduled flights. Generally both lessons and flights were arranged in advance. The passenger, or sometimes, passengers, sat in an open cockpit as did the pilot, strapped to the seat and wearing goggles. It was a favorite sport of pilots in those days to perform a few stunts in the course of the day's flight, whether for business or sightseeing, especially if they had a customer who

Delaying the opening of his parachute for a quick drop, Dick Cruikshank beat a diving airplane to the ground in 1923. The race to earth started 1,500 feet in the air.

was making his maiden flight. Passengers who had been victimized considered this a finely humorous thing to pass on to later novitiates, so that for a time an informal initiation rather like that which attends a ship passenger's first crossing of the equator came close to being institutionalized among aviation folkways. Most pilots still flew by the "seat of their pants," following railroad tracks and highways and checking their course by familiar landmarks.

Until about 1922, most airplanes were made of wood. At first this was an advantage, for it was a time of much experiment in shape and design and wood was easier and cheaper to experiment with. It was also very light and strong for its weight. But improvements in the engine soon made it clear that no type of wood would be able to take the strain the engine was going to be able to put on the plane in the near future. Both government and private manufacturers began experimenting with metals. Aluminum alloys seemed to give the most strength for the least weight. In the early '20's, German manufacturers demonstrated the first Duralumin planes in the U. S.

During the '20's, the appearance of the airplane was in constant evolution. Each year saw more and more streamlining, with more and more drag eliminated. By the end of the decade almost all planes were monoplanes, with shapes ever more birdlike. The variable-pitch propeller was perfected, which greatly increased the cruising speed and shortened the takeoff run. With a sharp "bite" at the air, the planes could accelerate more quickly on the ground. Designs were also constantly changed to get the load distributed more evenly and to reduce air resistance and strengthen the structure. This allowed an increase in the pay load and made possible the coming of the giant cargo and passenger ships of the '30's.

Safety aids were replacing stunts in importance. Radio men kept track of flights; expert mechanics began to replace tinkerers.

Daily airmail service between New York and San Francisco marked a new era in aviation in 1924. The eastbound flights spanned the continent in 32 hours.

As air service became regular, flights were linked with other forms of transportation; this motorbus transferred passengers to a plane for a flight — to a mountain resort.

Revolving beacons stabbed the sky as night flying increased.

The Dayton-Wright variable cam gear and the Handley-Page slotted wing increased the load per square foot of wing area, while permitting a further reduction of take-off and landing speeds. The thick section or "high lift" wing also added to the lifting power.

Air resistance was reduced by smoothing the surface to a glassy gloss and by streamlining the shape and getting rid of all the struts and braces of wire, metal, and wood which had held the early planes in one piece. By using metal, designers were able to strip the framework down to the bare essentials and to develop the cantilever wing, whose internal structure removed the need for external bracing. All external parts or protuberances were either teardropped by means of cowls or were retractable. The retractable undercarriage had also been developed. All these improvements, however, represented refinements rather than basic innovations from the planes of the Wright brothers.

Army experiments, though sometimes far-fetched, helped the cause of civilian aviation. Here a blimp carries a messenger plane. The name "blimp" originated in the Balloon Corps of the British Army before the First World War. Airships having a framework and gas bags, like the famous Zeppelins, were called "rigid." Those without framework were called "limp." One of their favorite limp models was designated "B." B-Limp was soon contracted to blimp, and the name stuck.

Meanwhile the fliers kept up their ceaseless activity, breaking into newsprint with feat after feat. In 1924 came a flight that really made the world take notice—a flight around the world. Eight fliers in four Douglas biplanes with Liberty engines took off from Clover Field, Santa Monica, Calif., on March 17, 1924. Two of them landed in Washington, D. C., 175 days later, having circled the globe in spite of almost incredible difficulties. They had flown up the West Coast to Alaska, then across and down the Asian coast to Shanghai, over India and the Middle East, and across Turkey to Europe, coming home by way of England, Iceland, Greenland, Labrador and Nova Scotia. The fliers encountered curious natives who almost wrecked the planes, desert sandstorms, icy gales off Alaska, and even ran into a swarm of storks. The flight was for the Air Age what Magellan's voyage had been to the Age of Exploration, and the 25,000 mile flight caught the public fancy.

How the tiny airplane was anchored to the car of the dirigible.

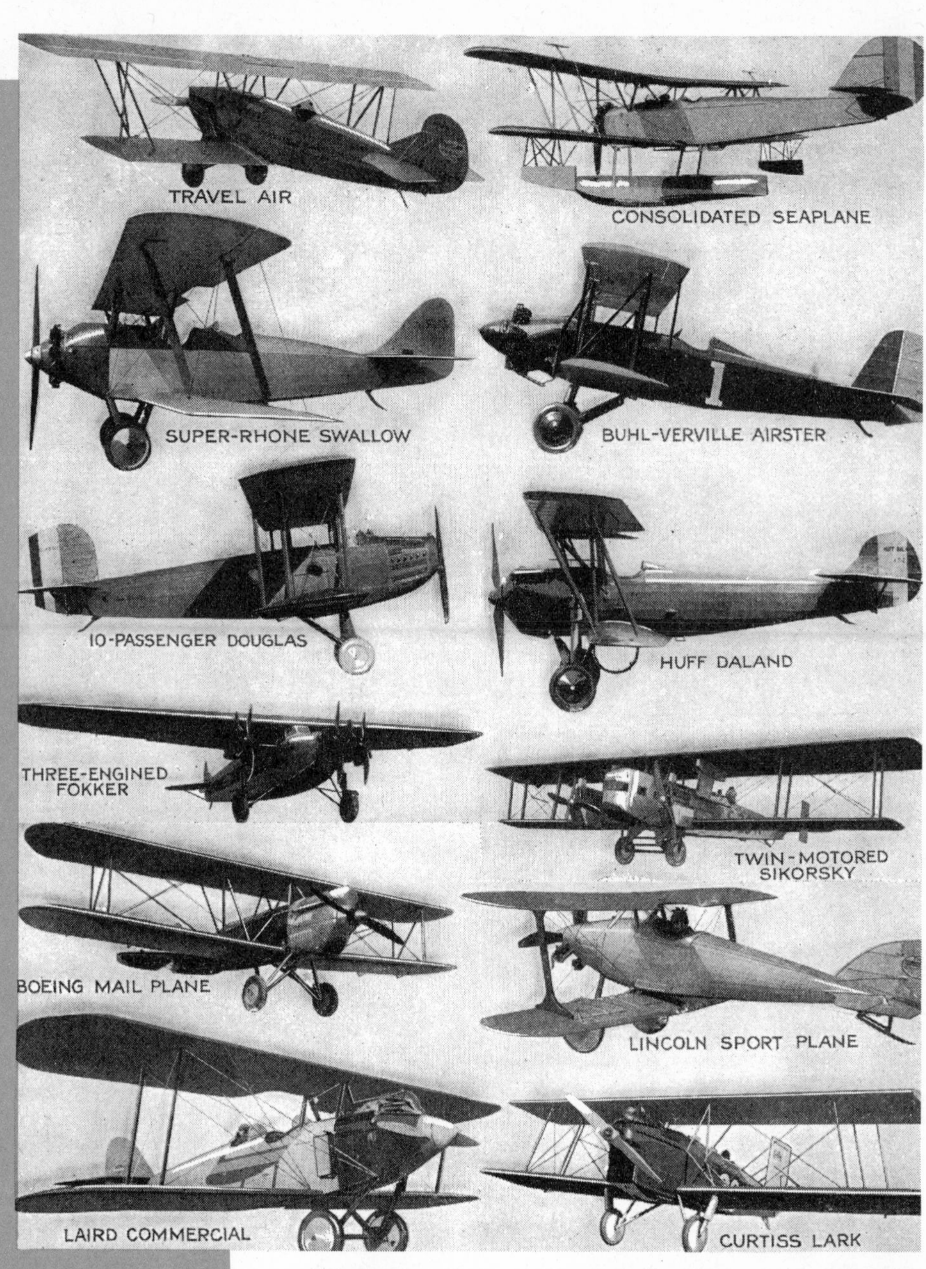

Some outstanding planes of the middle 20's. Biplanes predominated largely because of the limitations imposed by wood, fabric, and wire construction. It was simpler to brace two short wings, one against the other, than one long one.

A giant bombing plane overshadows with its mighty wings a tiny private plane of 1925.

Ground crew struggling to get the unwieldly Los Angeles *into her hangar at Lakehurst, N. J. On this particular effort in 1925, which took 12 hours, $6,000 worth of helium was lost. She was dismantled in 1939.*

Casualties of ocean flights were (top to bottom) Capt. William P. Erwin, who dove into the Pacific in the Dallas Spirit; *Paul Redfern, who was last seen off South America; Lloyd Bertaud, who took* Old Glory *on her last Atlantic flight.*

The government also had not been idle in fostering aviation. In 1926 an aircraft board was formed under the Department of Commerce, while Congress passed the Air Commerce Act, which helped the aviation industry fully as much as the government's interest in highways helped the automobile.

The Air Commerce Act began to bring order out of the existing confusion by providing for: (1) the establishment of air lands and air traffic rules; (2) the supervision of airports; (3) the inspection and licensing of planes and pilots; and (4) regular weather information.

Appropriately enough, 1926 also marked the beginning of the first air passenger service over any considerable distance in the eastern part of the country. The Kelly Act gave the Postmaster General authority to award contracts for airmail to private companies. When this act went into effect, seats also were sold to private passengers for the mail flights between Detroit and Chicago, and Cleveland and Detroit. The government withdrew altogether from operating mail flights on August 21, 1927, after having also inaugurated express-hauling service on these mail planes. On Sept. 1, 1927, a large system of air express was organized, combining (in use, not in financing) the routes, equipment, and personnel of a great number of small lines, and working with the American Railway Express Agency. This might be said to be the real beginning of commercial aviation.

320-pound plane of 1926 flew 35 miles on a gallon of gas. Cruising speed was 85 m.p.h.

A sleeper plane of 1927, tried out first in Germany, then put into service on a few longer runs in the United States.

"The Lone Eagle," Charles A. Lindbergh, captor of a nation's imagination with his Atlantic flight.

By 1926, airplane production had risen to 4,346 ships. But only about 6,000 passengers were carried over some 8,000 miles of the domestic routes. Many flying boats and light planes for private use were brought out that year, and Juan de la Cierva unveiled the Autogiro. Then began the dream and search that continues today: for a "flying auto" that would carry commuters to work and housewives to shopping centers by air. The "flying flivvers" came and went and none lived up to their inventors' promises. But light private planes did make it possible for aviation to become a popular sport for thousands of Americans. Flying clubs appeared around the nation in the wake of the cycling and automobile clubs of another day. By 1929, more than 5,000 planes were manufactured for private use. The bulk of private flying was done in the great western plains of Texas, Oklahoma, and the states in the wheat belt, where the vast distances and good flying weather were favorable factors. Oilmen, cattlemen, and wealthy farmers took gratefully to the small planes being developed. Almost every community, however, had its small band of amateur flying enthusiasts.

But the event which probably did more to sell aviation

Lindy when he was just "Slim," an airmail pilot, posing with the Spirit of St. Louis *before the epoch-making flight to Paris.*

A Monocoupe, in the 1928 Ford Reliability Tour. This two-place personal cabin plane cost less than $2,700.

to the public than any other single flight took place in 1927. Until then, while the man in the street followed the flights, endurance and speed records with interest, on the whole he still preferred to walk and ride on Mother Earth.

What aviation needed was a new type of pilot, who would retain the glamour of the barnstorming stunt pilot, yet would inspire confidence in the competence and safety-mindedness of the average aviator. A man was needed who would look like a man not given to dramatizing himself, yet who could rise to heroic achievement.

History has often fumbled these problems in paradox, but this time her performance left absolutely nothing to be desired. In 1927 a 25-year-old graduate of the Army Air School at Kelley Field, Tex., Charles A. Lindbergh, decided to try for the prize Raymond B. Orteig had offered for the first nonstop flight from New York to Paris. Since 1919 a number of fliers had tried it, none successfully, and several lost their lives.

Lindbergh was flying airmail between St. Louis and Chicago at the time and he found a number of St. Louis citizens who believed in him enough to help finance his effort. In gratitude, he named the plane he had designed

Amelia Earhart's Friendship, *first plane with sea pontoons to fly the Atlantic (the NC-4 was a flying boat).*

The Fairchild monoplane with folding wings that John Henry Mears used to fly around the world in 1928.

Transatlantic flights inspired many engineering dreams. This was a proposal for floating emergency landing fields. Most of the early visualizations of ocean flying were of this nature. Few men anticipated the amazing advances which actually occurred in navigation techniques and in planes themselves to make intercontinental flying safe.

This aerial taxi was used by a German liner at West Indian ports.

the *Spirit of St. Louis.* It was a Ryan monoplane with a 46-foot wing span and an air-cooled Wright engine which produced 225 horsepower. The cockpit was enclosed and to see ahead the pilot either tilted the plane in flight and looked out through the side through a window or peered into a periscope that looked forward. The flight did much to establish the superiority of the monoplane and the air-cooled engine. Without fanfare, Lindbergh blazed a new transcontinental speed record with this plane, setting it down in New York 21 hours and 20 minutes after leaving San Diego, having made one stop at St. Louis en route.

This feat did not attract wide attention. Records were being made and broken often and Lindbergh was never a publicity chaser. Besides, he found a number of aviation celebrities already at Roosevelt Field preparing for a try at the Orteig prize and these were getting most of the newsmen's attention. Richard Byrd was there with a crew, working over a three-engined Fokker monoplane; Clarence Chamberlain and Charles Levine also were making feverish preparations.

A Wright pusher plane alongside a trimotored cabin plane of 1928. The old Wright plane was still in flying condition at this time.

Sikorsky led the field in flying boats during the 20's. In addition to military planes, they also made amphibians for commercial service. This one provided transport around Long Island in 1929.

Lindbergh went among them quietly, the only solo flier scheduled for the flight, and stayed just long enough to recheck his plane and engine thoroughly and to get some good weather. On May 20, the tenth day after he had arrived, Lindbergh took off and headed out over the North Atlantic. Thirty-three hours and 39 minutes later, he broke out of the night above Paris and landed at Le Bourget Airfield, having flown 3,900 miles. He was given an ovation equaled in France perhaps only by that given Napoleon on his return. When he arrived at home he received the greatest welcome ever extended by this nation to anyone. Broadway was white with confetti and ticker tape the day Lindy rode up it; smiling shyly.

The suddenness of his amazing feat, his modesty, quietness, and youthful good looks, went home to the nation's heart as few things have. After the "Lone Eagle's" flight the public went crazy over aviation. No barnstormer in the old tradition, Lindbergh inspired not only hero worship but confidence. He was a transition in the aviator breed, marking the beginning of a more sober type of pilot.

Interior view of a 785-foot airship designed for the U.S. Navy in 1929.

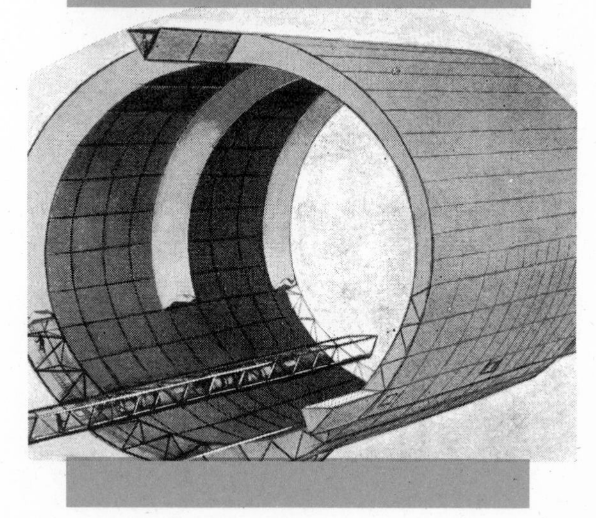

Diagram shows the six-day flight of the Question Mark, *which established a new endurance record off the California coast in 1929.*

In 1928 Eddie Stinson (in plane) and George Haldeman stayed in the air for two and a half days.

Now new markets opened and bankers, who had regarded the airplane with that same jaundiced eye they had turned on the automobile 25 years earlier, opened their purses a bit. In 1929, aviation manufacturers sold over $70,000,000 worth of planes and parts.

Lindbergh helped things along by granting interviews to magazines in which he talked of the future of commercial aviation. In *Popular Mechanics* he made some amazingly accurate predictions, including the time that would be required to establish commercial aviation, which he put at 5 to 10 years.

Lindbergh's flight was followed by a rash of other Atlantic flights. Chamberlain and Levine took off on June 4, 1927, landing at Eisleben, about 100 miles from Berlin. Levine had the distinction of being the first transatlantic airplane passenger. Byrd followed on June 29, but he missed Paris and flew back to the sea and landed off shore at Vur sur Mer. Amelia Earhart became the first woman to cross the Atlantic in an airplane when she went along

The Fairchild 21, a low-wing monoplane designed as a training ship in 1929.

Streamlined even to its landing wheels, this plywood plane of 1929 was flown at 200 miles an hour and climbed to 1,000 feet within a minute.

with Wilmer Stutz and Louis Gordon in their flight that same year. Other flights were attempted, none of them getting to the exact destination hoped for, and only a handful coming close. One woman and 18 men lost their lives.

The public had its attention compelled back to aviation again and again as pilots challenged barrier after barrier which had bound man in time and space since his appearance on the globe. On April 12, 1928, Baron Guenther von Huenefeld, Captain Hermann Koehl, and Captain James Fitzmaurice flew the Atlantic from east to west for the first time. They flew a single-engine all-metal Junkers monoplane from Dublin to Greenly Island, Labrador, where they crashed and were rescued. The Pacific also was a challenge and on May 31, 1928, Sir Charles Kingsford-Smith, Captain Charles T. P. Ulm, Harry W. Lyon, and James Warner took off from Oakland, Calif., for Australia in a trimotored Fokker. They arrived in Brisbane on June 8 by way of Hawaii and the Fiji Islands.

In 1929 airlines used Fokkers, Sikorskys, Loenings, Keystones and Fords, such as this one.

Larger planes meant special handling equipment. No longer could the pilot and a mechanic push their plane about

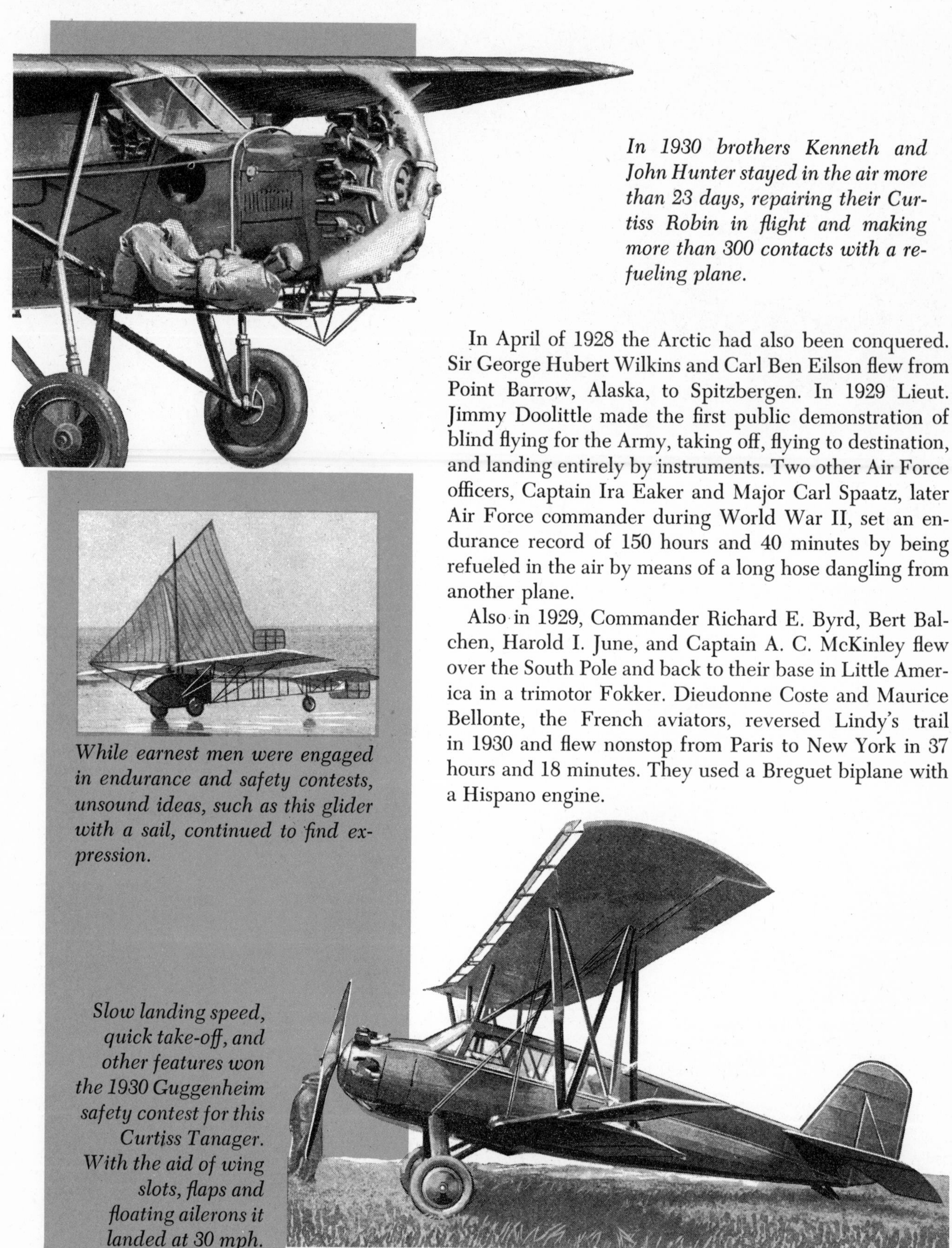

In 1930 brothers Kenneth and John Hunter stayed in the air more than 23 days, repairing their Curtiss Robin in flight and making more than 300 contacts with a refueling plane.

In April of 1928 the Arctic had also been conquered. Sir George Hubert Wilkins and Carl Ben Eilson flew from Point Barrow, Alaska, to Spitzbergen. In 1929 Lieut. Jimmy Doolittle made the first public demonstration of blind flying for the Army, taking off, flying to destination, and landing entirely by instruments. Two other Air Force officers, Captain Ira Eaker and Major Carl Spaatz, later Air Force commander during World War II, set an endurance record of 150 hours and 40 minutes by being refueled in the air by means of a long hose dangling from another plane.

Also in 1929, Commander Richard E. Byrd, Bert Balchen, Harold I. June, and Captain A. C. McKinley flew over the South Pole and back to their base in Little America in a trimotor Fokker. Dieudonne Coste and Maurice Bellonte, the French aviators, reversed Lindy's trail in 1930 and flew nonstop from Paris to New York in 37 hours and 18 minutes. They used a Breguet biplane with a Hispano engine.

While earnest men were engaged in endurance and safety contests, unsound ideas, such as this glider with a sail, continued to find expression.

Slow landing speed, quick take-off, and other features won the 1930 Guggenheim safety contest for this Curtiss Tanager. With the aid of wing slots, flaps and floating ailerons it landed at 30 mph.

A canvas-top bus of 1912 on the turntable at Inspiration Point, Colorado. Pikes Peak in the distance.

An early "rubberneck" bus which carried 16 passengers through Rainier National Park in 1912.

IN 1914, in two quite unalike sections of the country—the iron-rich Mesabi mining range of Minnesota and the movie-mad community of Los Angeles—a new form of transportation developed, the motor bus.

It is true that intracity motorized common carriers had come much earlier. The Fifth Avenue Coach Company had put a 24-passenger, double-decked motor bus into service along with the company's horse-drawn omnibuses as early as 1905. This first bus and subsequent additions were so popular that by 1908 all the company's horses were sold at auction.

In 1912 the Cleveland Street Railway became the first electric line to operate gasoline buses when it purchased

Bus believed to have run somewhere in the East in 1904.

Probably the earliest scheduled intercity motorbus line was Eric Wickman's, in Minnesota, started in 1914 with a Hupmobile. By 1919 Wickman had added several Packard Twin Sixes, and extended his lines to Duluth (facing page).

Motorbuses ran in Chicago as early as 1917.

three to serve an outlying district. There was no rush to follow Cleveland's lead: as late as 1920 there were only about 60 motor buses operated by 10 electric railways in the entire country.

In Minnesota, the first intercity bus line was established in 1914 because an auto dealer found business slow. He was Eric Wickman, who established a Hupmobile agency in Hibbing. Finding difficulty in getting rid of a seven-passenger Hupp, Wickman sold it to himself. There was much traffic between Hibbing and the town of Alice (now South Hibbing), and the only means of conveyance was by the local taxis, which charged from $1.50 to $3. Wickman and a partner, Charles Anderson, decided to run the unsalable Hupmobile on a regular schedule, charging 15 cents one way and 25 cents for the round trip. By carry-

This converted auto ran over an old stagecoach route from San Diego to El Centro in California's Imperial Valley in 1914.

ing the overflow on the running boards and fenders, the partners were able to transport from 15 to 18 passengers. Business boomed and within a few months Wickman and Anderson were able to purchase a second car. By 1916 they had five buses and several routes.

While Wickman was running his Hupmobile from Hibbing to Alice in 1914, new subdivisions of sprawling Los Angeles were built far beyond the limited streetcar service there. More or less casually, the owners of private automobiles began picking up passengers. Some of them found their riders were glad to pay five cents for a ride; "jitney" was slang for a five-cent piece, and thus the jitney was born.

The jitney craze spread rapidly and these unlicensed and unregulated common carriers were soon in operation

By 1919 some upper decks were roofed on Fifth Avenue.

In 1922 one enterprising bus operator on the Pacific Coast offered his patrons music with their miles by equipping his vehicles for radio reception.

Greyhound's first bus, grandiosely labeled "Supercoach," stands beside its 1952 counterpart. The body of the 1916 model was built by a cabinet maker and mounted on a White truck chassis.

Mary Pickford, "America's Sweetheart," christened the first bus to run from Hollywood to San Francisco in 1924. Because of prohibition, Mary used grape juice.

all over the country. The jitney operators developed such low, cunning maneuvers as driving just ahead of the regular run of a streetcar, easily diverting patrons to the novelty and greater speed of their conveyance. These tactics soon had transit line attorneys in the courts, purple-faced from shouting for injunctions. In some cities they were successful in holding that the jitneys were dangerous and their operators financially irresponsible; in others they were not.

The feeling in many cities was the same as that expressed in a report of the Public Utilities Committee of the Los Angeles City Council:

"We hold as a sound economic principle that every mode of transportation in operation prior to the advent of the motor bus should sustain its appeal to popular favor and profit-making upon its intrinsic merit and not upon protective legislation."

(The jitney has risen sporadically to plague public transportation systems wherever service has been felt inadequate or rates excessive. The Chicago Transit Authority was having difficulties with South Side jitneys in 1952.)

Thus far, most buses were simply converted autos. Two brothers, Frank and William Fageol, were the builders of the first bus designed from the ground up for that particular purpose. This was at Oakland, Calif., in 1920. As far back as 1899, Frank had driven a steam-operated auto between downtown Des Moines and the Iowa fairgrounds. The memory clung for 15 years and when Frank saw the jitney craze sweep California, he sat down to a drawing board. The result was the Fageol Safety Coach. It was built close to the ground, giving it a low center of gravity and an entrance step. The springs were a great improvement over those in the truck chassis then widely

This Pacific Coast bus of 1927 had a "pilot house" for the driver and an observation deck, kitchen and dining facilities, and washrooms.

Double-deck motor buses carrying 53 passengers were another innovation on the Pacific Coast in 1930.

Night coach of 1933 had compartments containing berths.

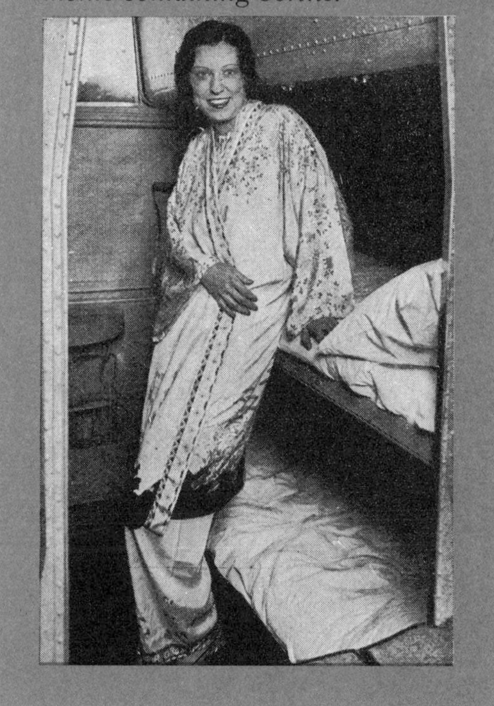

used for buses. The Fageol engine was more powerful and the interior fittings attractive. Altogether it was such an advance over previous designs that it became standard not only in the United States but in much of Europe.

Two rival bus systems had grown up in the early '20's. One, the Pioneer Yelloway System headed by W. E. Travis, was a direct outgrowth of the old Western stagecoach lines. Travis' father had been one of the pioneer stagecoach operators of the West, handling a number of government mail contracts. The son early saw the possibilities in buses, and established his lines over the old stagecoach routes operated by his father. The rival line was Pickwick Stages, operated by Charles F. Wren. These two soon were joined by the Southern Pacific Railroad, one of the first rail lines to establish bus feeder systems.

Early in 1928 these three lines were merged as the Pacific Greyhound Lines and soon operations were extended east of the Mississippi to the Atlantic Seaboard. The next step toward a nation-wide system was the acquiring of an interest in the Southland Transportation Company, operating lines in Texas, and the changing of

Huge, yet light and strong buses are made possible by the modern, lightweight alloys.

Many long-haul intercity buses are air-conditioned by automatic, under-floor units.

Drivers are well trained and are required to observe rigid safety rules.

the name to Southland Greyhound Lines. Bus lines of the Great Northern were induced to join the national system as Northland Greyhound Lines; the Colonial Motor Coach Company, operating in northern New York State, became Eastern Greyhound Lines. Purchase of the Gray Line between Boston and New York in the fall of 1929 made the national bus system a reality except for the Southeast.

A southeastern network was added to the Greyhound system in 1931, after the Pennsylvania Railroad had bailed the bus lines out of financial difficulties under an arrangement whereby the Pennsylvania and the Greyhound Corporation each received 50 per cent of the stock. By 1952 the Greyhound Corporation owned or directly controlled 17 operating companies. Minority interests in the stocks of other Greyhound companies were owned by five railroads. Although Greyhound-owned routes make up the largest percentage of bus lines there are competing independent companies in almost every region.

In city transportation, buses and a mechanical cousin, the trackless trolley-bus, are replacing more and more streetcars every year. In 1920, street-railway men felt the bus could do the whole transit job for cities under 50,000 population. Soon they raised the figure to 75,000. Then it became 100,000. Today, almost all large cities have already changed or are changing to an all-bus system.

Designers consulted the posture experts on comfortable seating. Reclining seats are now standard on intercity buses.

Both "streamlined" and "articulated" was this highway bus of 1934. The power unit was self-contained, while the coach proper was a trailer.

Newest city buses carry 30 to 50 passengers. Most have underfloor or rear diesel engines with torque-converter transmissions, which relieve driver from shifting gears.

Deck-and-a-half intercity buses are again gaining in popularity, as they were in the early 30's. They allow greater baggage space and increased passenger visibility.

RAILROAD LANDS

VERY CHEAP

FREE TRANSPORTATION

To quickly build up population along the Washington & Choctaw Railroad in new reservation just thrown open, I will sell a little of our 100,000 acres of $25 and $50 lands for $17.50 per acre.

Magnificent opportunity for settlers, investors and speculators. Easy terms, as low as $1 per month. Any size tract from ten acres up. Gulf Coast lands the most productive in the world—ten acres will yield an income of $5,000 a year. Sweet, pure water; cool, pleasant summers and mild, balmy winters; beautiful lands, adapted to farming, truck and fruit growing, or live stock, poultry, bees and dairying; no swamp, no stones, irrigation not needed; only part of the United States absolutely free from local diseases. Sixty miles from the coast; 21 hours from St. Louis; 29 hours from Chicago; with best shipping facilities. Don't buy lands anywhere until you investigate this, Send me your name, a postal card will do, and I will send you complete details, also a railroad pass free, on Washington & Choctaw R'y, whether you buy or not.

M. G. WINEGAR, General Manager,
6171 Times Bldg., St. Louis, Mo.

Special terms to live land agents capable of buying two sections or more for spot cash.

·V·

Transportation in Our Time

In 1902 the New York Central belatedly greeted the new century with a new train—the Twentieth Century Limited. She had a locomotive built for speed, which pulled cars containing new comfort, luxury, and services for passengers. She sped over the country from New York to Chicago in 20 hours, scooping up water from trackside troughs to save precious minutes. The New York Central thought it had the scoop of the century, but while the Limited was being built with great fanfare, the Pennsylvania secretly was completing an almost similar train, which was put on the New York-Chicago run at about the same time.

The introduction of faster and heavier crack passenger trains meant reduction of grades, elimination of sharp curves, a larger amount of double-tracking and the re-

The fastest train on rails in 1902 was the New York Central's Twentieth Century Limited.

A Burlington train amazed the countryside in 1904 as it chuffed over the Nebraska plains towing a courthouse.

building of many miles of roadbed to accommodate the 50 per cent heavier engines.

In 1916 the American railroad network reached an all-time peak of 254,000 miles. Since that year the abandonment of branch lines has exceeded the new mileage built. These lines were abandoned not only because of the increasing competition from truck lines, but also because of the exhaustion of timber, coal, iron, and other natural resource areas.

During the decade after 1920, when the public was beginning to travel in its own cars or in buses and the

As America began to feel her industrial oats, there was much emphasis on the "largest in the world," and it is true that engines were being built which made the eyes of old railroad men pop.

THE LARGEST ENGINES IN THE WORLD

Keep CHICAGO & ALTON Trains
On Time Between
CHICAGO · ST. LOUIS · KANSAS CITY.
"The Only Way"
GEO. J. CHARLTON, GENERAL PASSENGER AGENT. CHICAGO.

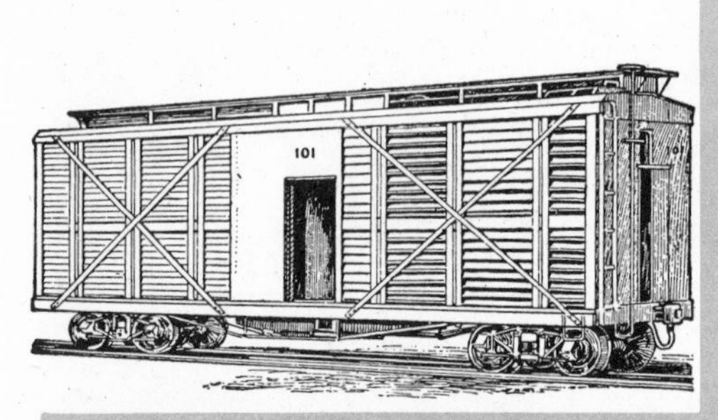

Special poultry car of 1909 was built with adjustable shutters forming the side sheathing.

Motorized handcars, able to carry 15 men at 15 miles an hour, began to appear in 1905.

A remarkable feat of railroad engineering in 1904 was the 8,000-foot Santa Susana tunnel.

railroads made no perceptible attempt to prevent it, people said the railroads were obsolete. And it is true that not until the depression years following 1930 did the lines start making gestures of good will to the passenger public.

Vanished, save from secondary lines, were the red plush seats, the brass trim, and the cement floors. Instead, with the talents of such designers as Raymond Loewy, the railroads and the Pullman Company created within the steel walls of coaches and sleepers, appointments of grace, comfort, and palatial elegance. Deep-piled carpets softened the floors; featherbed-soft chairs, masculine in size, sat beside roomy divans; "conversation corners" and even fireplaces appeared.

The new trains hurled themselves across the wide spaces of America, hardly swaying as they dashed through cities and forests, taking only 16 hours between New York and Chicago.

Another indication that the railroads were not going to give in to the motor and air age without a struggle rode

No. 1, first locomotive used by the Great Northern, and weighing 55,400 pounds, stands alongside a 1909 model, 10 times as heavy.

The first section of Florida's 128-mile, island-hopping railway to Key West was completed in 1912.

Freight cars with end doors for automobiles were used by Chicago, Burlington and Quincy.

A third rail instead of flanged wheels was proposed in 1907, but the idea did not get very far.

across the flatlands of the Midwest in 1934. It was the Burlington's streamlined diesel Zephyr. Instigated by Ralph Budd, head of the C B & Q, the Zephyr was the first determined effort to retrieve some of the passenger business.

From that point on streamlining advanced rapidly, sometimes in conjunction with diesel engines, as in the complete streamlined train unit; again simply by streamlining cars operating with steam locomotives sheathed to look like torpedoes. The whole affair caught the public fancy, and a dozen years later the public was still captivated by Zephyrs, Comets, Meadowlarks, Meteors, Super Chiefs, and Flying Yankees.

As for the diesel itself, it seems certain of an even greater advance. Like the steam and the gasoline engines, it is a machine for turning heat into power. Of those two types of engines, the first burns fuel to heat water into steam, then works the steam in a cylinder. The second mixes gasoline and air in a cylinder. The mixture is ignited

Cars were equipped with a non-telescoping device in 1910.

with a spark and the great heat developed expands the gases which drive the piston down. The diesel draws raw air into the cylinder. This air is heated by compression to the point where fuel oil, injected directly into the combustion chamber, is ignited spontaneously. The diesel gets four times as much work out of a pound of fuel as does the steam engine; and perhaps twice as much as does the gasoline engine. Of some 120 streamlined trains in service in 1952, approximately three-fourths were drawn by diesel locomotives.

The first diesel built specifically for freight work was put into service in 1941 by the Santa Fe, and before the end of that year other freight diesels had been ordered by the Great Northern, the Southern, and the Milwaukee.

The trend to diesels was accompanied by a trend toward much faster freight trains. The day seems not far when there will be little difference between the speeds of main-line passenger and freight trains.

Five years before the diesel engine was invented, railroads had begun using electricity as motive power. The first electrified train service opened on June 28, 1895, on the short Nantasket Branch of the New York, New Haven & Hartford. Two months later the Baltimore & Ohio electrified the 3½ miles of its track that ran through the Baltimore tunnel. Fifty years later, 20 Class 1 line haul railroads had electrified 6,495 miles of track.

The largest car in the world in 1907 – the Pennsylvania's all-steel postal car.

Passenger train speeds increased. In 1930 the number of miles operated each day at speeds of 60 miles an hour or better was 1,100. Ten years later daily runs at such speeds averaged 75,000 miles, and 10 per cent of the runs were made at more than 70 miles an hour.

After World War II, the railroads could no longer use "emergency" to excuse shortcomings which became apparent during the war years. The carriers were on the spot again, a spot hotter than ever, for now both airlines and truck and bus lines were after the customers in a big way.

In 1945 the Burlington Route captured the public fancy with the first panoramic view car, in spite of its rather

A compressed air buffer for locomotives appeared in 1908 "to end all wrecks."

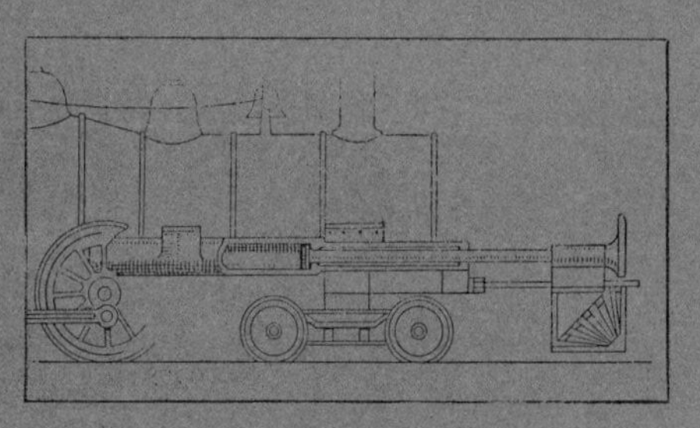

An engine suspended by nothing more solid than the rails after a bridge wash-out in Colorado.

A head-on collision between two freight trains on the Ann Arbor railroad in 1908. One engineer and both firemen were killed.

An engine fitted for receiving wireless orders was an experiment which did not meet wide acceptance in 1910.

The train "butcher" with his pack of refreshments appeared to be doomed when an eastern railroad introduced a lunch-counter car in 1914. This car was run on trains that also carried standard dining cars.

Tethering animals with a slip-line in 1918 made life happier for both farmer and trainman along the Illinois Central lines.

A railroad in Kansas, short on funds, transformed a touring car into a locomotive in 1914. It carried over 100,000 tons of freight in 15 months.

A dramatic seesaw at Grayville, Ill., in 1918, caused by a confusion of signals. A fast freight entered the revolving bridge just as it started to open. The locomotive and three cars went down, but no lives were lost.

awful name of "Vista-Dome Car." Basically it is of caboose architecture, with a dome of double-laminated safety glass. A short stairway leads up to the dome compartment in which some 20 passengers have a 180-degree view of the countryside—as fine a view as had any tramp sitting on a gondola end or a brakeman in the dome of a caboose.

We have approximately 230,000 miles of railroad, or 30 per cent of the world's mileage. Texas has the most mileage of any state with 16,700; Illinois is next with 12,000; and Pennsylvania is third with 11,000. Our passengers and freight are carried by 42,000 passenger cars and 2,000,000 freight cars, with 50,000 locomotives to do the pulling.

Let's take an imaginary trip on a crack cross-country train. The car in which you are sitting is built of steel. The air inside the car is filtered and washed clean of dust and soot as it is drawn from the outside. In summer it is cooled by being passed over cold-water pipes, and in the winter it is heated by steam pipes running along the sides of the

New gas-electric coaches were built primarily to carry mail and baggage in 1928. They were capable of 70 miles an hour.

Gasoline-driven cars were operated by the New York and New Haven Railroad as early as 1922.

car close to the floor, the steam being supplied by the locomotive and being carried from car to car by hose connections.

Electric lights are supplied with current from a generator driven by one of the axles. The generator not only lights the car but fills a storage battery so that the car will remain lighted when the train is stopped.

There are 12 sections in your Pullman, each section consisting of an upper and lower berth. In the daytime a section is two comfortable, upholstered seats facing each other. But at night, part of the curved ceiling is lowered to form the upper berth and the cushions of the facing seats are rearranged to form a lower.

Our train has, in addition to Pullmans, a baggage car, a day coach with individual reclining seats for passengers who don't wish to pay for a Pullman berth, a diner, and a club car.

The Northern Pacific's half-block-long, 34-wheel (including 12 on the tender) engine weighed 1,000,000 pounds. It was built in 1929, and burned 22 tons of coal an hour.

Even with five locomotives pushing and pulling, progress was slow on steep grades in the Utah mountains.

As we pull away from large cities, we may pass commuters' trains consisting entirely of day coaches, carrying businessmen and office workers to the city from outlying suburbs. Some of these suburban trains are electrified.

At our first stop, we walk along the platform and take a look at our train from one end to the other.

The engine may weigh as much as 300 tons. The first engines built in this country for the B. & O. weighed three and one-half tons. The Stourbridge Lion, imported from England, weighed seven tons.

But we can't spend all our time at the engine. Back of the tender, which also carries extra water for the locomotive's boiler, is the baggage car. It may also be a mail car. In it, our extra baggage is stored – also our dog if he's along. My ticket, and yours, entitles each of us to carry 150 pounds of baggage free of charge.

Many trains carry a separate mail car that is a miniature

Traveling from one flatcar to another, a power shovel unloads an entire trainload of boulders used in making a breakwater.

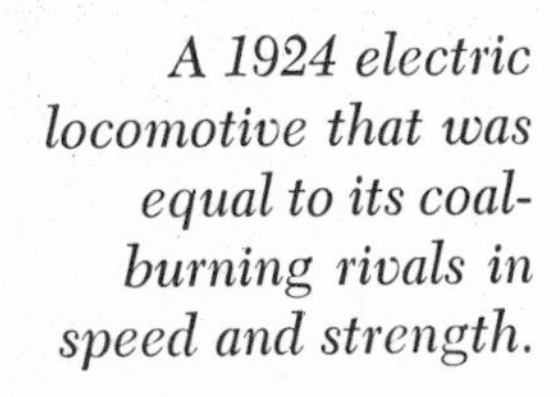

A 1924 electric locomotive that was equal to its coal-burning rivals in speed and strength.

A monorail was considered by the Pennsylvania Railroad in 1931. It was to be capable of a speed of 150 miles an hour.

traveling post office inside which a mail clerk sorts out letters and packages for the various stations while the train is on its way.

Back of the mail-and-baggage car are the passenger cars, diners, club cars, observation cars, day coaches—whatever equipment the traffic demands. There may be a Pullman consisting entirely of staterooms, with a narrow aisle running the length of the car on one side. Each room is equipped with an upper, a lower, and a washstand.

Looking between the cars, we see two python-like hoses. One carries compressed air from car to car for the air brakes. The other carries air for the conductor's whistle. Near these two hoses is the metallic pipe connection that carries steam from the locomotive boiler to the heating systems of the cars. Also between the cars are two big metal castings clasping each other like cupped hands. This is the automatic coupler that has replaced the link and pin.

Look at the track upon which the train wheels rest. It is made of rolled steel and weighs about 100 pounds per yard. The heavy rails rest on crossties of creosoted wood and the ties in turn rest on a crushed rock, gravel, or

An 1882 engine contrasted with the oil-burning Hiawatha, *the oil-burning* 400, *the diesel-electric* Zephyr, *and the steam-driven* Abraham Lincoln *of 1935.*

Disk wheels on locomotives were cheap and light, but trials in 1933 proved them impractical.

The original Zephyr, *which started streamline styles for the Burlington Route, is contrasted with its big brother, the 1936* Denver Zephyr.

cinder bed called ballast. Rains soak quickly through a porous roadbed of this type, thus preventing washouts.

Let's take a look at the adjoining track, over which a long freight train is moving. A single engine may pull a train of 100 cars nearly a mile in length and in that length we see cars of every kind and belonging to many railroads.

Here are yellow refrigerator cars. Unlike most boxcars, they don't have sliding doors. They have swinging doors that may be tightly shut. The sides of the cars, built of two layers of wood or steel with hairfelt or corkboard in between, insulate the inside of the car from the summer heat. The car is cooled either by circulating brine or by ice tanks at either end of the car.

The refrigerator car may be carrying dressed meat from a Chicago packing plant to an eastern city. Before the development of the refrigerator car by Gustavus Swift in the 1870's, meat could not be carried any considerable distance without spoiling. There had to be a packing plant in every town.

But in a refrigerator car meat can be safely shipped thousands of miles, thus making it possible to concentrate large packing plants in a few centers like Chicago, Omaha, and Kansas City, close to the farms from which the livestock comes.

The refrigerator car may carry other things: fresh apples from Washington or New York; oranges and grapefruit from California or Florida; fresh vegetables and butter from truck gardens and dairy districts.

The refrigerator car made it possible for Minnesota and Wisconsin to become dairy states. Today, whether you live in California or Maine, you may be putting Wisconsin butter on your toast tomorrow.

As your eye runs down the line of rumbling freight cars, you see many devoted to a special purpose. There are

The Union Pacific's 1934 streamliners had vertical beams to warn motorists of their approach.

The upkeep of an old iron horse is an arduous and complex task. The workman is replacing the seamless boiler tubes.

hopper cars with trapdoors in the bottom, each carrying 50 to 70 tons of coal from a Pennsylvania mine to a big city coalyard. Other hopper cars may be loaded with gravel for concrete construction or iron ore for a steel mill.

There are plain wooden boxcars with sliding doors, loaded with canned goods, clothing, furniture, groceries, and grain.

You may see cylinder-shaped tank cars filled with oil, gasoline, liquid chemicals, molasses, or mineral water.

Stock cars with slatted sides, filled with cattle, roll by. Some of these cars are fitted with two floors for sheep or hogs.

There are flatcars—simple platforms on wheels—loaded with steel beams or huge machines. There may be a container car, consisting of a number of separate metal sections each containing an odd-lot load of goods from a single shipper. At the arrival point, each metal container may be put on a separate truck and taken directly to the buyer.

At the end of the freight train is a caboose containing bunks for conductor and brakemen. There is a cupola sticking up from the roof of the caboose with windows on all four sides.

Freight cars, like locomotives, have grown larger. The average capacity of a freight car today is 48 tons, where once it was less than 10.

Our train may pass a great freight yard with scores of tracks and switches. Perhaps you wondered when you saw that 100-car freight train carrying all types of goods going to scores of separate destinations, just how a railroad made sure that each car went to the right town.

A locomotive with a steam-turbine power plant was clocked at two miles a minute in 1939. The turbine is used to generate electricity for six driving motors.

Big Boy, *built in 1941, was another giant freight locomotive. It weighed 755,000 pounds and had 16 driving wheels. Below is a diagram of the weight distribution.*

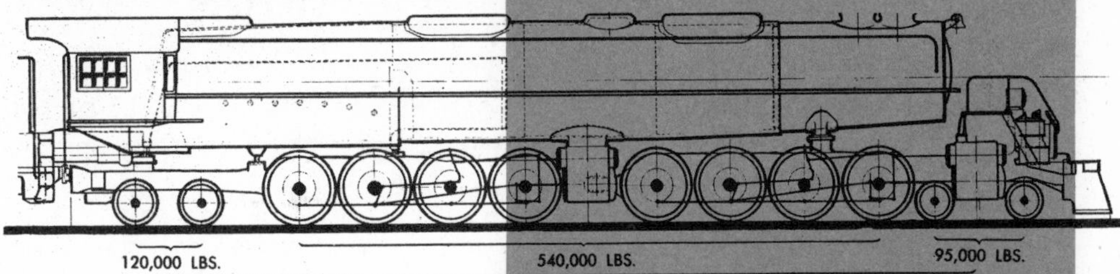

The puzzle becomes clearer when we think of the freight yard as being divided down the middle. One half is for freight bound in one direction. The other half is for freight bound in the other direction. Each half has its own receiving yard, classification yard, and departure yard.

Watch that freight train coming into the receiving yard. A switch engine pushes it along the track and up an artificial hill called a "hump." At the top of the hump a yard man climbs to the roof of the head car. The car is uncoupled and coasts down the other side of the hump. At the bottom of the hump tracks branch out and the car takes one of these tracks, coasting along until it is braked to a stop.

Other cars will be left along this track. Then a switch engine will come and take them all away to the freight house in the city where boxes and bales will be unloaded and carried away by trucks to the grocery and department stores and other buyers.

The next three cars going over the hump may be flatcars loaded with machinery. They will be switched onto a different track and taken from there to one of the city's factories.

A muscle man" demonstrates the smoothness of roller-bearing railway car wheels.

A 1942 mountain climber hauling a load of freight that would have required from three to five engines 20 years before.

The four-track, Harrisburg diesel heavy-repair shop replaced the old roundhouse.

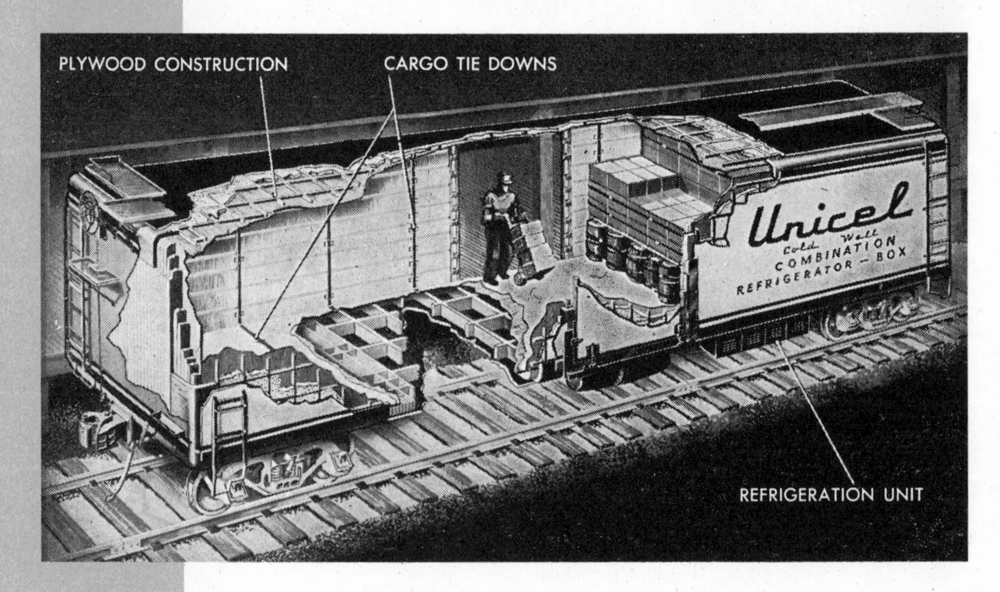

Cheaper to make, lighter yet stronger than the conventional freight car, the 1951 "Unicel" could be used either as a boxcar or as a refrigerator car.

The next few cars may be coal hoppers bound not for this city, but a town farther down the line. They coast down the hump onto still another track where they are attached to a through train to continue their journey.

Thus, in the freight yard, cars are sorted and sent to industrial sidings, freight stations, and on to farther destinations. A Chicago freight yard can handle 10,000 cars a day, or 200 trains of 50 cars each.

Our transcontinental flier has now reached a speed of 70 miles an hour but on another line a silver-colored train, going in the same direction, is overtaking us. At a speed of 90, perhaps 100 miles an hour, our own train looks slow.

It is a beautiful, different-looking train—more like an artist's dream of the future than a real train. It is lower. Its cars are fitted together so that the entire train seems to be one continuous, unbroken line. The engine has no stacks and domes. It has a rounded front with a window panel high up and a headlight at the very top. We are looking at one of the new lightweight, streamlined trains.

The first of these trains specifically put into service for passengers was by the Union Pacific and was called the M-10001. In October, 1934, this train ran from Los Angeles, Calif., to New York City, a distance of 3,248 miles, in 56 hours and 55 minutes. It attained a maximum speed of 120 miles an hour and ran 506 miles at an average of 82.7 m.p.h. Later this train, called *The City of Portland*, was put into service between Portland, Ore., and Chicago, doing the 2,272 miles in 39¾ hours.

Let us take a quick walk through one of the 12-car Zephyrs. The first two cars are power cars, the front one having two 900-horsepower units and the second a 1200-horsepower unit. One-half of the third car generates power for air conditioning and lighting and the other half is a traveling post office. The forward half of the fourth car is devoted to baggage and express, the rear half to a cocktail lounge. Then come two coaches, accommodating a total of 102 passengers in individual reclining chairs.

1947 double-deck Vista Dome car gives travelers a broad view of the passing landscape.

Home-like comforts and modernization were first on the railroads' list of "musts" after World War II.

An Army big gun, weighing many tons, cradled on an oversized, 12-wheeled flatcar for a long journey.

Present-day steel catcher arm for mailbags still resembles those used in 1907.

Hundreds of wheat-laden freight cars in Kansas City ready to deliver the goods.

Behind the coaches is the dining car. Then three 12-section sleepers. The next to the last car is the latest thing in railroad comfort: an all-room car containing six bedrooms, three compartments, and a drawing room. You can, if you wish, have a two-room suite with meals in your room. The final car is an observation lounge.

This train, 883 feet long, will take us 1,034 miles between Chicago and Denver in 938 minutes. The safety of the trip depends on the automatic electric block signal. All our main lines are divided into short sections called "blocks." At the beginning of each block is a tower with a movable arm called a semaphore.

This arm has three positions. When it is vertical, the engineer knows that the track is clear for two blocks ahead. When the semaphore is in a diagonal position, the block ahead is clear but the second block has a train in it. When the semaphore is horizontal, the block ahead is occupied and the train must come to a stop, after which it may go ahead slowly. In addition to the arm position, the signal shows green, yellow, and red lights. The signal is wired to the tracks so that a continuous current is flowing through the block. As the train entered the block, it short-circuited the current, causing the signal to change to the stop position automatically.

The train disappears down the track and shortly we see the semaphore arm swing to the diagonal position. The train has entered the second block ahead. After a short wait the arm swings to the vertical position. The track is clear for two blocks ahead.

The railroad in America is a little more than 100 years old. It overtook and passed the stagecoach and canal in merely the time required to lay the rails, and for the next 75 years it dominated inland travel and transportation and it still does today. What its position will be 20 years hence is in the realm of prophecy, or the last chapter of this book.

The old and new ways of switching. Modern operator has a push-button panel resembling a map of the yard.

The Pioneer, *first locomotive to roll out of Chicago in 1848, stands alongside a modern diesel locomotive to contrast over 100 years of railroad progress.*

Used-car dealers and old-car scrap heaps were established institutions by 1923.

A scene in downtown Bowling Green, Ky., in 1922, showing an automobile density that was to become a real problem later.

Overhead crossings to avoid congestion on Chicago's Outer Drive were constructed in 1927.

The Model-A *Ford appeared in 1927. It sold for $495 and ran 30 miles on a gallon of gasoline.*

In 1920 motor car production was 1,905,560 passenger cars, 321,789 trucks and buses. By now the automobile had begun to lose the remaining vestiges of its carriage look. The new vehicle was an established part of the American scene and a vast industry had been built around it. That year Alemite chassis lubrication was introduced, and Duesenberg appeared with the first U. S. straight-eight engine and four-wheel brakes. Packard introduced the Lanchester vibration dampener.

In 1921 Studebaker developed nickel-molybdenum steel for commercial use, and Hudson offered an adjustable front seat. Hudson also offered something else that year which showed that the automobile had reached a turning point in its history. Up to this time the motorist had either bent his head grimly into wind and rain, sitting exposed on the seat, or pulled up the stiff collapsible top of his touring car, expending several hundred foot pounds of energy and then snapped on the canvas sides, equipped with celluloid strips for windows. There had been closed sedans and coaches, of course, but they were too expensive for most citizens. Now Hudson brought out the Essex, a coach which sold for only $300 more than the touring car. This was the beginning of the closed-car era in which, once the roads were in shape, weather was no consideration.

In 1924, passenger car production was over 3,000,000 vehicles and almost half a million trucks and buses were made. Balloon tires became standard equipment. Two-filament bulbs, permitting use of both direct and diverted light, appeared in the headlights of a few cars. Ford produced his ten millionth car. The auto statisticians paused for breath, counted up, and discovered to their amazement that there was an automobile for every seventh person in the United States.

Automatic transmission and power brakes were tried as early as 1922.

An electric heating pad was proposed for autos in 1927.

The Duesenberg, with 325 horsepower, was famous for speed and power in the 30's. This 1933 model was driven by Alan Ladd in the movie, The Great Gatsby.

A 1935 Hudson sedan featured an eight-cylinder engine which developed 113 horsepower.

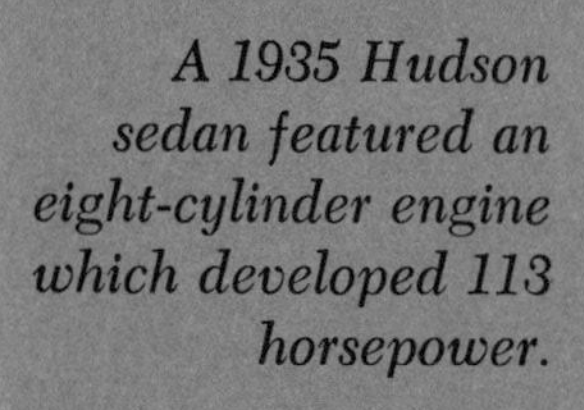

A New York engineer proposed a foot-operated vacuum gearshift in 1930.

Road building kept pace with this rush. A guiding spirit was Carl G. Fisher, founder of the Prest-O-Lite Corporation, promoter of the Indianapolis Motor Speedway, and the spark behind the development of Miami Beach. Fisher saw that the hit-or-miss road building being done by the various states, counties, and villages across America was by no means keeping up with the need.

In 1912, Fisher proposed a coast-to-coast highway to the leaders of the automobile industry. He put his project before Roy Chapin, Henry Ford, Henry Joy, Frank Sieberling of Goodyear, and others. Fisher asked the automobile industry to raise $10,000,000, roughly a tenth of what was needed. The automobile men, at Henry Joy's suggestion, named the project "Lincoln Memorial Highway," and started out to sell the nation on its worth.

A huge caravan rolled westward from Indianapolis on July 1, 1913, and reached San Francisco on August 3. The publicity given the caravan captured the national imagination and before it was well under way, mayors, councilmen, and governors were fighting to have a place on the route. Local officials and civic leaders met the caravan at

The Cord of 1929 was the lowest car on the road, made possible by front wheel drive. It was also one of the handsomest, with extremely long front fenders.

The Willys coupe of 1933 featured fender-recessed headlights, a sharply sloping hood, and a rugged 4-cylinder engine.

By 1933 the rumble seat was such an institution that some had tops.

every town along the route and the trip was a tremendous triumph. So successful was the publicity that alternate routes had to be established to pacify several states. The main route ran from New York through Jersey City, Philadelphia, Pittsburgh, Fort Wayne, Chicago Heights, Joliet, Clinton, Cedar Rapids, Council Bluffs, Omaha, Denver, Cheyenne, Salt Lake City, Reno, Sacramento, Oakland, and San Francisco.

From then until 1927 the nation was enlisted in the cause of the Lincoln Highway. A contribution became a patriotic duty. Even schoolchildren were asked to contribute nickels and dimes. The highway was completed in the early 20's, and the association disbanded in 1927. By then many other good roads were available or being built.

Another spur to road building was the Federal Road Act of 1916, giving $75,000,000 to be divided among the states for five years. To be eligible a state had to have a highway department. The Federal Highway Act was passed in 1921 to continue this work. By then there were enough roads to make necessary a system of road marking. Federal highway systems were designated by a shield, state high-

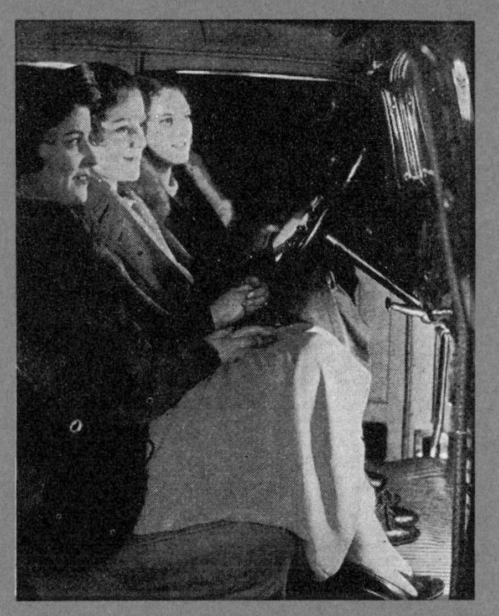

Reo introduced an authentic automatic transmission in 1933.

A 1935 trailer with welded-steel frame and duralumin body. It had two compartments.

Taxicabs with sliding roofs were a sensation in 1936.

ways by a circle, and both were numbered. This in turn made possible the development of road maps. Up to this time, motorists had used route guides or tour guides, consisting of minute listings of familiar landmarks every two to three miles, with the distances between them. A page of fine print was required to guide the motorist 20 or 30 miles. At that, he had to have somebody with him to watch the road and the route guide or he would lose his way the first time he overlooked a warning such as, "turn left at the abandoned water tower."

At the edges of the highways there began to appear the filling station, which was joined by eating spots, general stores, motels, and tourist cabins. In the beginning, motorists bought their oil and gasoline at the general store and carried it out to the car by hand. If they were wise they strained the gas through a cloth, for it had received only the coarsest refining. The first gas pump was set up by Sylvanus P. Bowser at Fort Wayne, Ind., in 1885, but it was well into the 1900's before there were enough automobiles to justify very many. With the growth of touring and the development of roads, however, filling stations

The 1937 Ford offered an all-steel body with one-piece steel top and new cable brakes.

A genuine economy car was introduced by Powell Crosley in 1939. A two-cylinder engine ran the 925-pound bantam at 45 mph.

began to dot the highways of the 20's like red, yellow, and orange beads. For miles, signs informed the driver that he would soon be at Joe's Filling Station, where Highway 56 met Route 7. At first only gasoline and oil were sold, but soon the attendants were offering repairs, battery recharges, and tire changes.

It was an easy jump from gas and oil to other items to refresh the weary motorist—soft drinks, candy, sandwiches. Fruit and vegetable stands began to appear alongside the filling stations, and by 1930 there were 110,000 roadside stands, almost all of which had expanded from filling stations. That year roadside marketing amounted to $500,000,000. There were 317,000 filling stations in all. About 6,000 of them were owned and operated by the large oil companies like Standard, Shell, and Phillips and many of these also distributed tires through the stations. Auto parts also were available at some stations.

For awhile it seemed that the roadside markets, some of which grew into enormous supermarkets where almost every merchandisable item including clothing was available, would eventually supplant city shopping. However,

Oldsmobile had further perfected the automatic gearshift by 1937.

Hudson's 1939 Country Club sedan was an evolutionary stage in auto design. Running boards were optional equipment.

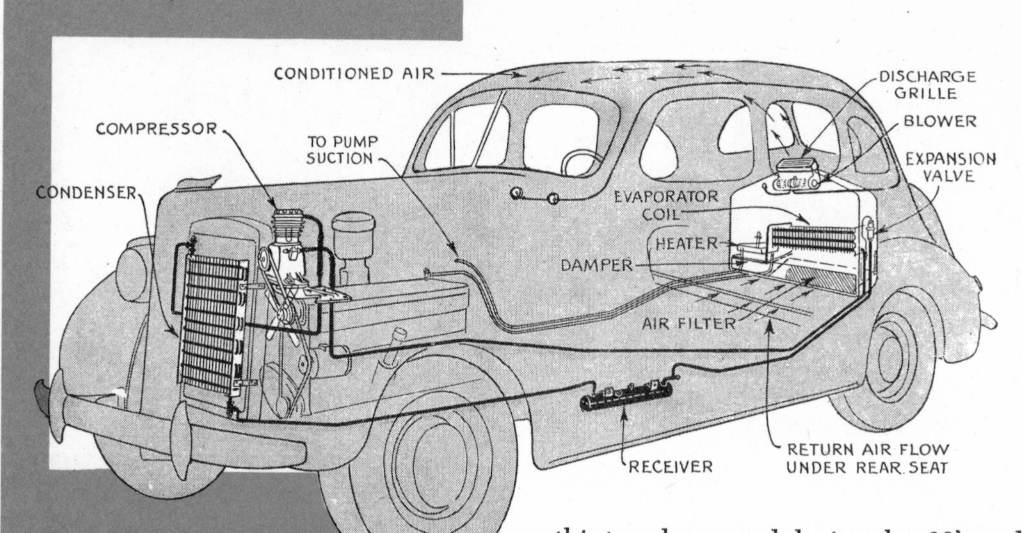

Packard was a leader in the development of fully air-conditioned automobiles. This is an outline sketch of the system in the 1940 Packards.

Lines of a 1930 model sketched over photograph of a 1940 car show how shape evolved.

1941 Packard "Clipper," had narrowed but familiar grille.

this trend reversed during the 30's and 40's. The number of filling stations dropped to 200,000 in 1950, although the volume of business rose to about $6,500,000,000 a year. The principal reasons for this reverse were that there were fewer breakdowns on the roads and the gas tanks could hold more gas, making fewer stops necessary.

Around 1920 the federal government had stimulated the state highway departments by paying half the cost of new mileage on up to 7 per cent of the roads of each state. About 28,000 surplus motor vehicles built for the armed services during World War I were distributed among the states for use in road building work.

At that time the state highway systems totaled about 200,000 miles. By 1940 this had risen to 329,000 miles. Local roads were woven into state webs and state systems synchronized with the national network. Between 1920 and the outbreak of World War II the U. S. paved about 220,000 miles of highway. Technical schools and highway engineers experimented with concrete, macadam, gravel, and other surfaces and learned the best way to use them. The roads were smoothed, "polished," straightened and strengthened. Three-, then four-, then six-lane highways came into being. Over-and-under crossings were built,

The 1940 models were exciting news. Upper left, nose of the Hudson touring sedan. Center, detail of Packard radiator and fender. Right, a view of Cadillac streamlining of 1940.

1941 Plymouth ploughing through mud pit on test track is typical of tests that experimental cars must undergo before production is begun.

and in many places large sums were spent just to landscape the scenery.

During the 20's, the automobile changed radically in appearance. The high, blunt bodies became lower and longer each year, but true streamlining as we know it today was still a long way off. Assembly line techniques were universal in the industry, paced by Henry Ford, who could roll 9,000 automobiles a day from his lines by 1925. Some 25,000,000 cars had been made by now, and a nationwide chain of drive-yourself stations was established. Oldsmobile introduced chromium plating in 1925.

The internal-combustion engine never approached the smooth transition of power possible with the steam engine, and for that reason new types of transmissions continued to be brought forward hopefully year after year. Hot-water car heaters were introduced in 1926 and by now the automobilist was beginning to roll in solid comfort.

Chrysler came out with rubber engine mounts in 1927, greatly reducing vibration. Cadillac tried out synchro-

Straightaway on the Pennsylvania Turnpike, "The Dream Highway."

In 1941 accident prevention became a major goal throughout the country.

Out of the World War II jeep (top) developed a civilian utility car. Umbrella stand (above) was neat touch on the '42 Pontiac.

mesh gears in 1928, Ford offered shatterproof glass as standard equipment, and four-speed transmissions were revived. Cord pioneered a front-wheel drive the following year; Klieber Motor experimented with Diesel-engine trucks, Chrysler adopted the downdraft carburetor.

By 1930 a number of striking innovations were made. Studebaker introduced free wheeling and a carburetor silencer; Graham-Paige brought out rubber-cushioned chassis springs and aluminum pistons with Invar struts; Pontiac tried out tin-plated pistons and pressed-steel axle housings. Police cars were being equipped with radios.

In the following few years four-cylinder cars virtually disappeared, and the six- and eight-cylinder engine became practically universal. Windshields were slanted to eliminate reflections and decrease air resistance. In 1932 the first full-skirted fenders appeared and inside visors further decreased wind resistance. In 1933 manufacturers began combining the starting mechanism with the accelerator pedal so that the motorist could start with but a single motion of his foot. Valve inserts, independent wheel suspension, and reflex glass tail lights were adopted.

Chrysler and DeSoto came out with their radical airflow design in 1934, as well as automatic overdrive. Cadillac began the use of generators with controlled current to keep the battery fully charged for extra loads. Reo put the gearshift on the dash where no more knees would be knocked against it.

Ford's first postwar model made its bow in 1946. It represented the greatest change in Ford models since 1932.

The 1947 Studebaker Champion was among the first whose fenders had been streamlined into the body.

In 1935 sloping side windows and built-in windshield defrosters made their appearance. Coil springs for rear-end suspensions and steering-column gearshifts came out in 1937. Batteries were moved from beneath the floor-boards and placed under the hood, where mechanics or owners could get at them easily. Chevrolet brought out a vacuum-assisted gearshift in 1938.

By 1939 automatic overdrive was available on several different makes of cars, and the Oldsmobile came equipped with all-coil-spring suspension, four-way stabilization, and knee-action front-wheel suspension. Automobilists, whose every gesture was being studied by car makers, now could turn on their car radios by pushing a button. Hudson came out with "airfoam" cushions and

Postwar trailers had every comfort.

A 1949 Flagship trailer with all living facilities, including a roomy sun deck.

Pride of Willow Run was the long awaited 1947 Frazer sedan. Less expensive companion was the Kaiser.

Preston Tucker, designer and builder of an ill-fated automobile demonstrates how the front end is used as a luggage compartment. Engine at rear was a horizontally-opposed, 150 horsepower 6, which drove through two torque converters directly to the rear wheels.

"Autopoise" front-wheel control, with the hood hinged in front and the lock for it under the dashboard.

Cadillac made "Hydramatic drive" available on all its models in 1940, while Dodge, DeSoto and Chrysler equipped their cars with fluid drive. Chrysler also introduced the safety-rim wheel. Sealed-beam headlights were introduced.

For the next four years, 1942 through 1945, the automobile industry was enlisted in the greatest war production effort of all time. America and her allies had good reason to be grateful for the men and circumstances which had created this gigantic production plant in about 40 years. Tanks, planes, jeeps, half-tracks, artillery, guns, shells, and countless other implements of war poured from the automotive capital in ever-increasing torrents. An awed world agreed when it was said by high officials that "if Hitler had had Detroit he could have won the war."

Another fact emerged under the impact of the war. The entire economy had become geared to the automobile. Farmers delivered their produce to market, doctors made calls, workers drove to factories, all in automobiles. The automobile had also made it possible for cities to "explode" into the suburbs, expanding ever further from their industrial centers, and millions of jobholders were dependent

Olds 98 four-door sedan of 1952 had hydramatic superdrive transmission and hydraulic steering.

on their automobiles to get to work. If the automobile had been suddenly removed from the country, transportation would have been practically paralyzed. A Michigan survey showed that of 850,000 workers in the state, 635,000 depended on cars to get to work. Exhaustive surveys by government and business showed that of the 29,000,000 automobiles in the nation at the time of Pearl Harbor, at least 20,000,000 would have to be kept in operation. This was an absolute minimum! That much had the automobile molded the nation around itself.

By the fall of 1945 all restrictions on manufacturing had been lifted, and the following year the converted industry offered over 2,000,000 cars to a car-starved market. Passenger car production rose to 3,500,000 in 1947, while bus and truck output went over 1,000,000.

Marvelous changes had been promised the postwar car buyer, but most of them failed to materialize at once. Except for minor changes in styling, the automobile remained much as it had been—except for the virtual disappearance of the low-priced small car. Emphasis was on what some critics called "dream boats," with the car several feet longer than its working parts required, hanging over in front and back in the interest of appearance. Expensive, hard-to-housekeep chrome was lavished on the bodies. Lifting the broad, low hoods of the less expensive cars revealed the relatively small motor surrounded by areas of empty space.

In 1947 two symbols of the auto industry died: Henry Ford, the monkey-wrench engineer who established the production line; and William Crapo Durant, whose adventurous finance promotion created General Motors.

Production in 1948 reached a point just short of four million new cars. Oldsmobile introduced its Futuramic as the company's golden anniversary model, and Pontiac offered Hydramatic drive as optional equipment. The Tucker Corporation displayed the first models of what was to be the most revolutionary auto ever offered by the industry, then became involved in a searching court investigation of its finances which resulted in dissolution of the company.

Chrysler pioneered power steering on its deluxe models in 1951 and extended it throughout the line in 1952 as Cadillac, Oldsmobile, and Buick followed suit.

There was a trend toward the smaller car again. Nash started it with the Rambler, and Kaiser-Frazer followed with the Henry J. Sears Roebuck, the mail-order house, entered the automobile lists for the first time since the turn of the last century with the Allstate, distributed on a limited scale in 1952. New-car production neared the five million mark.

In 1913, assembly lines like Ford's (top) turned out 400 cars a week. Today's equivalents produce 140,000 weekly.

Sunday afternoon — and part of America's 35,000,000 cars.

Dr. Hugo Junkers, one of Germany's foremost plane manufacturers anticipated many of the features of present day aircraft design. His 4-engine approach to the flying wing was very advanced for 1930.

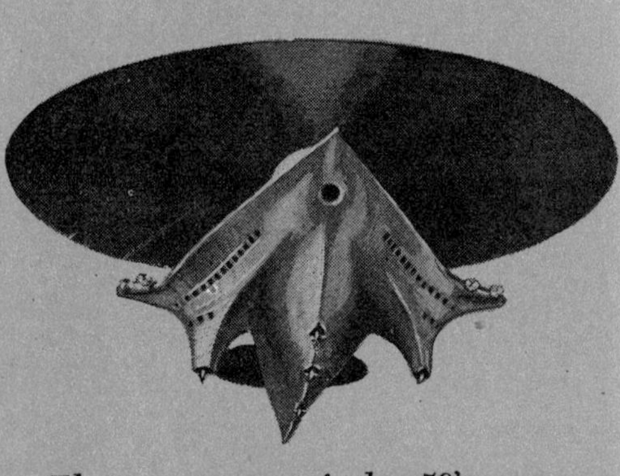

Flying saucers of the 50's were anticipated in 1930 on the drawing board of Guido Fallei. His flying boat with rotating wings was never built.

IN 1931 THE AIRPLANE and its basic engine had improved enough for a nonstop Pacific flight to be attempted. Hugh Herndon and Clyde Pangborn flew from Japan to Wenatchee, Wash., over 4,000 miles, in 41 hours and 13 minutes.

The year 1932 saw three more firsts, two of them involving women. Amelia Earhart became the first woman to fly the Atlantic solo. James Mollison made the first east-west Atlantic flight. Ruth Rowland Nichols became the first woman airline pilot in the world when she went to work for the New York-New England Airways. She held three international records at one time for speed, distance, and altitude.

In 1933, only nine years after the Army fliers had made their halting way around the world in 175 days, Wiley

Daily flights between New York and Buenos Aires were inaugurated by these 20-passenger Sikorsky flying boats in 1930.

Lockheed "Sirus" plane being launched before the Lindberghs' flight to the Orient.

Post and Harold Gatty breezed around the globe in 7 days, 18 hours, 49 minutes, and 30 seconds. (This was almost exactly the time—8 days—which *Popular Mechanics* had prophesied for the next round-the-world flight back in 1924.) Post flew a Lockheed Vega called the *Winnie May*.

In 1937 aviation suffered a great loss in the death of Amelia Earhart. In 1935 she had soloed from Honolulu to Oakland, Calif., in 18 hours, 16 minutes, which, together with her earlier Atlantic solo, established her as the foremost woman pilot in the world. In 1937 she tried a hop around the world. She made it to Miami, crossed to Europe, flew over southern Asia, and down to Australia safely. With success almost achieved, she disappeared June 2 near Howland Island. The world's ships and planes searched the area for weeks, but no trace of the flier, her navigator, or the plane has ever been found. One theory is that she may have been forced down on one of the small islands of the Pacific which now and then submerge, as the ocean bed is constantly shifting.

All this activity and publicity in behalf of aviation began to bear fruit. By 1928 aviation manufacturing already was on its way to becoming a major industry. That year, for the first time in its history, the industry sold more planes to civilians than to the military. There were now

In 1931, Lindbergh made a "tour" of the Orient with Anne Morrow Lindbergh as his navigator. He flew up through Alaska and across to Japan and from there to China where the plane was wrecked while being hauled aboard a ship.

The search for the "flivver plane" went on. This monoplane was built with wings that could be folded for parking in an ordinary garage.

67 airplane manufacturers and almost two dozen transport companies.

Pan American World Airways began the first passenger service to Europe in 1929, and the first transpacific flights were made from San Francisco to the Philippines. In 1930, cross-continental service was begun between Los Angeles and New York, so that it was now possible to fly from the Philippines to Europe by way of the U. S. The world record for land planes was 250 miles an hour; for seaplanes, 300 miles an hour.

The first transcontinental service, however, was not exclusively by plane since the passengers wanted to make no night landings. Although Doolittle had demonstrated the feasibility of night flying, few aviators had yet learned the art. The public was not ready for it yet anyway, nor were there many airfields lighted properly for night landings. Therefore, the nightly portions of a two-day trip across the nation were made by train, necessitating three transfers. When flying from New York to California, passengers left Manhattan at night by train, took planes at Columbus, Ohio, the next morning, changed back to train at Waynoka, Okla., that night, and the following morning

This unusual helicopter of the 30's had two propellers under the wing in addition to the nose propeller.

The plane that flew "backward" – the inventor claimed more stability came from reversing the wing, rudder and elevator positions.

boarded another plane at Clovis, N.M., flying the rest of the way.

The planes used on this service were forerunners of modern luxury planes. The interior of the passenger compartment looked rather like a narrow bus, with a narrow aisle and a row of single passenger seats on each side. Only nine passengers could be accommodated.

The public's confidence in the future of aviation proved a mixed blessing. The stocks of five leading manufacturers – Aviation Corporation, Curtiss-Wright, Douglas, North American Aviation, and United Aircraft – were objects of so much trading during the aviation boom that their paper value came to $712,000,000. Charles A. Loening, "the Wingmaker," famed builder of the Loening Amphibians, pointed out in his book, *Our Wings Grow*

A Cincinnati inventor made flying tests in 1931 of a plane whose fuselage flared into an air cell which was supposed to provide greater lifting capacity. The inventor claimed the plane could take off within 100 feet and land with a roll of less than 20 feet.

Seeking sometimes they knew not what, aviators continued to experiment. This plane took off from the roof of a speeding automobile (52 miles an hour) at Old Orchard, Me.

As ordinary planes began to climb near 20,000 feet, the inventors began to dream of rocket ships.

As planes became heavier and faster, wing flaps were added to decrease landing speeds.

Faster (Doubleday, Doran & Co., 1935) that the most optimistic estimate of industry-wide earning for 1929 would be about $9,000,000, or a return of little better than 1 per cent on the investment of all these speculators. Yet the aviation bubble grew, and many investors lost heavily when the crash came. By 1932 the price of United Aircraft common stock had dropped from 162 to 6; Curtiss-Wright from 30 to ⅞.

The stock market crash made it difficult for aviation to climb back. For the next 10 years the industry went ahead, improving planes immeasurably, getting new customers and expanding services, but they were not able to get back any momentum for production until the outbreak of World War II. In 1939 the industry was manufacturing only 3,770 civilian aircraft, still considerably below the nearly 6,000 planes turned out in 1928. The following year, because of orders for warplanes from Europe, production went to 6,844 and from there it leaped every year to a peak of 100,000 planes a year during the war.

If fewer planes were made in any one year, they were continually better. From 1930 on they were increasingly streamlined, speeded up, enlarged, and their mechanical wrinkles and bugs ironed out. As engine power was increased, so was the beauty of design. By 1935, fleets of graceful, powerful skyliners were carrying 15 or 20 passengers between our growing number of airports at speeds around 200 miles an hour.

By the mid-Thirties, the huge Martin flying boats, graceful as giant birds, were ranging over routes as long as 3,000 miles, driven by four engines whirling three-blade propellers. The famed Sikorsky Clipper was also in service with its four engines and two tail rudders, looking like a lean greyhound with flashing wings. The supercharger was being used, allowing planes to fly at high altitudes. There were by now about 15,000 American civilian pilots.

Once again, the government's need for airmail had helped the industry weather the storm. In 1939 the Watres Act was passed, providing for 10-year route certificates for handling airmail. The Postmaster General was given great leeway in awarding the airmail contracts. The policy followed was to make it difficult for any but the most stable and experienced companies to get into the bidding, then to grant extensions of the routes and to bring the routes together into some sort of system which could be the basis for any sudden expansion required in the future.

In February of 1934, the government canceled all its civilian contracts after charges of collusion in granting the awards had been made. President Roosevelt gave the duties of carrying the airmail briefly to the Army, with tragic results. In the early years of the depression, aviation

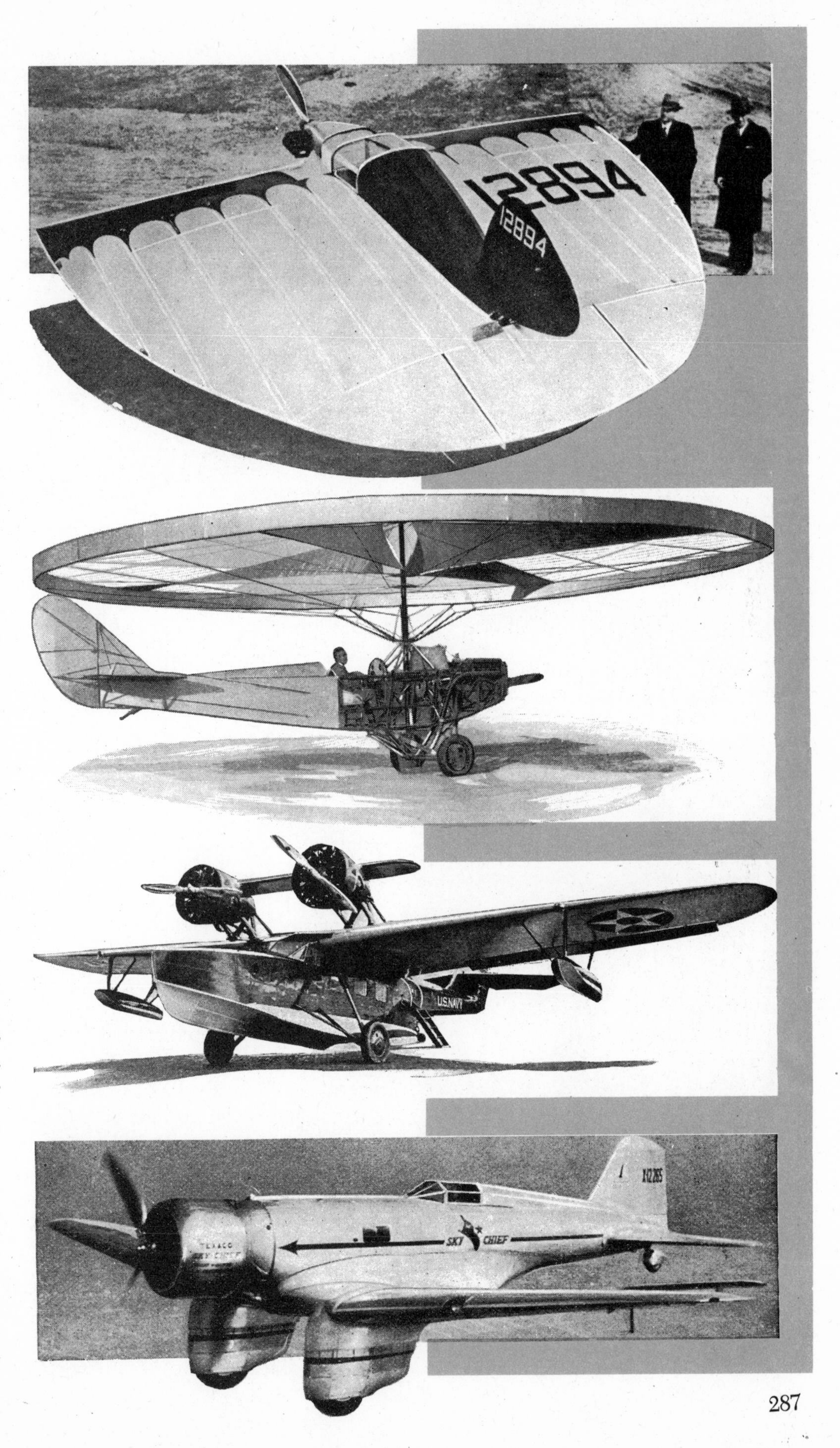

Tailspins and flat spins were declared impossible with this plane with semicircular wings built at South Bend in 1933.

This was one of many attempts to achieve true vertical flight, which only the modern helicopter can do. The four whirling wings of this 1931 "windmill" plane were enclosed by a circular steel band.

First U.S. President to have a personal plane was Franklin D. Roosevelt. In the big, amphibian Mayflower, FDR was flown to many an historic conference.

Frank Hawks, speed record breaker of the 30's, was one of the first fliers to use an automatic pilot.

The amphibian planes ordered by Pan American Airways in 1934 were radical in that the underside was built to act as a runner.

The simple "joy stick" and throttle gave way in the middle 30's to a complicated accumulation of controls and instruments. Here the co-pilot is raising the landing gear by means of a hydraulic pump lever.

appropriations for both Army and Navy had been cut deeply, and the forces were in sorry shape to take on any extra burdens. They did not have enough planes for adequate training. Airmail flying, moreover, required additional training. Moreover, the new duties were assumed on Feb. 9, in one of the worst seasons of the year so far as weather was concerned. The result was that an appalling number of our young Army fliers lost their lives. The public clamored for an investigation; money was promptly restored to air forces' budgets on the one hand and the contracts for mail carrying were given back to private air lines.

In 1929, meanwhile, the first all-metal transport plane in America had been made by Ford, and in 1933 came the first airline plane completely equipped for sleeping, flown by American Airlines. In 1935 Pan American inaugurated regular transpacific service from San Francisco to Manila. The number of international passengers was rising by leaps and bounds from the 18 who made trips in the first year after 1927. By 1938, over 109,000 passengers were carried across the borders of the U. S. That same year, 1,365,000 passengers bought tickets for flights inside the country. In 1930 the airplanes were doing less than 1 per cent of the business done in railroad Pullman fares alone. This rose to about 14 per cent in the following 10 years. Between 1934 and 1938, the aviation industry settled and consolidated, the number of airlines falling from 30 to 20 as the volume of traffic increased.

The planes themselves were made larger to accommodate more passengers. The average rose from about 6 seats

When these Douglas airliners were put into service in 1933, they were the fastest passenger planes in the United States (cruising speed 185 miles per hour).

Accommodations for passengers became luxurious, as proven by this cabin interior of a Douglas airliner of 1935.

Flying became a science – the man in charge of an airliner was part engineer, part navigator and part pilot and captain.

The pride of Pan-American was the Clipper, a 32-passenger Sikorsky amphibian which made an historic flight from the mainland to Hawaii in 1935.

"Broncho" Charlie Miller, last of the Pony Express riders, sends the first copy of his autobiography over his old route by air express in 1935.

to the plane in 1932 to 10 in 1935, 12 in 1937, and 14 in 1939. Inside the plane the furnishings were increasingly comfortable and luxurious. Today the average passenger seat costs the airlines about $500, and during the '30's they were of comparable value. Extra comforts and services for passengers were a part of commercial flights from the earliest days to aid competition with the railroads and buses. Meals have been served free by almost all airlines from the start. At first these consisted of sandwiches, but today such meals include full-course dinners.

Sleeping accommodations have never been too much of a problem in commercial aviation because of the great speed of the airplane. However, they are necessary and available for some flights. The passenger capacity is cut in half on the sleeper planes since the lower berth is made up by adjusting four seats. Uppers swing down out of the ceiling as in railroad Pullmans.

Except for the B-29 superfortress bomber and the P-61

Rocket experiments were conducted by the Guggenheim School for Aeronautics. This flight in 1936 was dignified by a commemorative stamp because the 100-pound "ship" carried a package of philatelists' covers on a 2,000 foot flight.

There was a lull in the search for the "air flivver." Private planes became faster and costlier, like this all-metal cabin plane with two engines.

Howard Hughes (below) dipped into a fortune to develop his personal planes. In 1939 he set a new record (9 hours, 27 minutes) for transcontinental flights.

night fighter, all the airplanes used by the armed forces during World War II were either exact duplicates or extensions of planes that were in use by military or commercial airlines during the 30's. The Martin B-10 and the Boeing Monomail were the early ancestors of our large planes, appearing in the early 30's. These were soon refined, giving way to the Boeing 247 in 1933 and the Douglas DC-2 in 1933. This latter plane was quickly adopted by most airlines, foreign as well as American. The four-engine, long-range planes which appeared during and after the war were refinements of the type first unveiled in the Douglas DC-4 in 1938. This ship weighed around 20,000 pounds and was capable of 240 miles an hour. Other models in favor were the Douglas DC-3, a smaller plane of 5,000 pounds and a speed of 180 miles per hour, and the Curtiss C-46, a 10,000-pound plane that flew 220 miles per hour.

In 1939 regular transatlantic service was started by

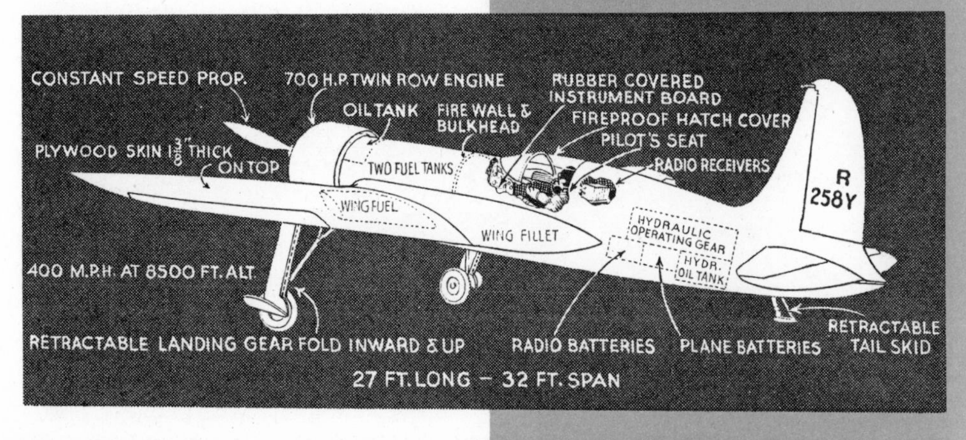

Diagram of the plane in which Howard Hughes flew from Los Angeles to New York at better than five miles a minute.

"Wrong Way" Douglas Corrigan, who flew the Atlantic in a Curtiss Robin cabin monoplane, practically without the aid of instruments, and with tongue in cheek. His de-icing equipment consisted of a long pole, to be stuck out of the window and banged against the leading edge of the wing. He had no legal permission for his flight, and stoutly maintained that he thought he was headed for California, but had read his compass backwards.

Pan American and Imperial Airways between New York City and Southampton, England. During the preceding 10 years the ratio of passengers and freight to airmail had constantly risen. In 1930 airmail made up some 88 per cent of the total. Freight was hardly worth mentioning. By 1938 passengers made up 61 per cent of the traffic, mail about 35 per cent, express and freight together 4 per cent. The ratio is still shifting in the same direction. Today passengers make up about 85 per cent, freight 8 per cent, mail 5 per cent, and express 2 per cent of airline business.

From these figures it is plain that the airplane made deep inroads into passenger transportation. But no such dent has been made in the freight business. The amount of freight carried by the airlines multiplied more than 50 times, rising from 1,900,000 ton-miles in 1936 to around 100,000,000 ton-miles in 1945. However, the latter figure was still a drop in the bucket compared to the staggering amount of freight handled by the nation's railroads, which totaled about 6,500 times as much as the airplane figure.

In overnight passenger traffic, however, the airplane's great speed allowed it to bite deeply into the Pullman business. Today the airlines haul more than a third of the amount of people who buy Pullman tickets, compared to the 14 per cent in 1940.

After June of 1934, when the government hurriedly gave the airmail back to private airlines, the Interstate Commerce Commission regulated the rates of pay and charges. In 1938, the Civil Aeronautics Act was passed, which created the Civil Aeronautics Board and the Civil Aeronautics Authority. All certificates of routes were then reawarded to those companies which already had them and provision was made for future applicants to be investigated and allotted routes. All rates were regulated by the CAA. The airplane, only 15 years before an object of glamorous fearfulness, had achieved solid responsibility. Probably no other machine that man has devised was improved so radically in so brief a time.

The $900 plane, which Douglas put together from spare parts of three other ships, and with it defied authorities by flying it from New York to Dublin.

The flying boxcar was on drawing boards in 1939, a decade before the first freight plane was built.

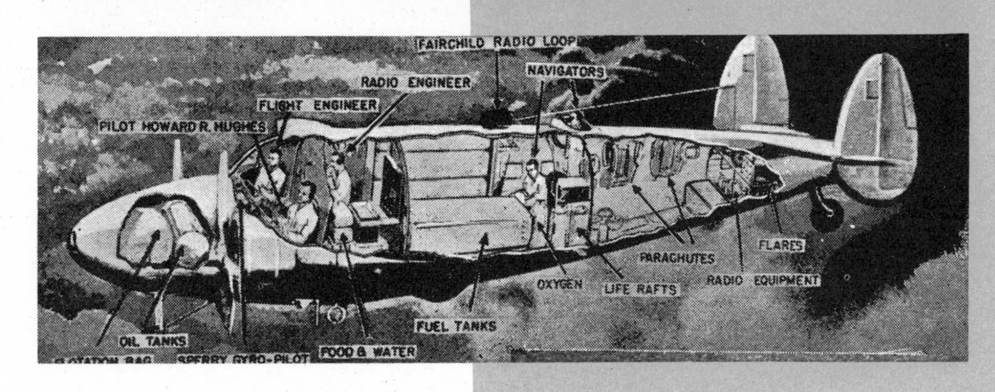

By flying around the world in 91 hours in 1938, Howard Hughes and four companions demonstrated that airplane speeds had doubled since the flight of Lindbergh.

In Denver, one of the last remaining stage coaches rattles along beside an American Airlines Flagship. Less than a century separated the two forms of transportation when this photograph was taken in 1938.

The P59A Airacomet, first American jet plane, made for the Army in 1944.

Airports had become large and well equipped by 1940. Control towers had every electronic and mechanical safety aid.

During World War II most of those Americans who had not already surrendered their fears of flying joined the ranks of aviation enthusiasts. Wartime travel conditions, necessitating endless trips across country by countless individuals; the constant traveling of servicemen on leaves and passes; plus the sudden overloading of other means of transportation, brought it to pass. Everything, it seemed, had gone to war. Railroads, freight cars, day coaches and Pullman cars, automobiles, spark plugs, tires, gas, oil, buses—airplanes too, for that matter. So the tremendous demand confronted a shortage—and at a time when people had more money than they had had for 10 years. People forgot all prejudices, fears, and economies. They tried for seats on the bus lines, the railroads, and the airlines, fought for whatever seat they could get on any means of travel and were grateful for what they got.

By the time the war was over the only thing that kept the average citizen out of the air when he had to make a trip was the price of the ticket. The airplane had taken its place in the nation's transportation system and the nation's psychology. It was still the luxury class of travel or ship-

Giant of the skies in 1944 was the 70-ton Martin Mars, built for the Naval Air Transport Service.

ping, costing somewhat more than other means of transportation. But now all the prospective traveler or shipper considered was the extra money against the time saved.

The armed forces were more interested in the jet planes after the war. Today almost all the fighters are jets, but not until 1946 did the U. S. have enough of the Lockheed P-80's to train squadrons. By 1949 the jet engines were being put on big bombers. Boeing, North American, Douglas, and Martin were all bringing out jet planes. Northrop was working on a flying wing to be powered by the jet engine. In 1947 Consolidated Vultee developed the B-36, an enormous pusher-propeller plane of 150 tons, driven by six 3,000-horsepower piston engines. In 1948 four jet engines were added.

Tail section was 52 feet high.

A fabulous white elephant was Howard Hughes' 200-ton, 8-engine plywood flying boat with a wing span of 320 feet and an overall length of 219 feet. Fully loaded it drew 8 feet of water, and the flight deck was as large as a living room. Although it took off and flew successfully for a short distance, test flights were abandoned in 1948 after $25,000,000 had been spent.

The Boeing Stratocruiser, introduced in 1949, set a new high for luxury in the air, featuring a lounge and berths.

Air mileage rose between 1926 and the eve of World War II from 8,250 miles to over 35,000. Today this figure is around 140,000 miles of routes inside the United States. There are some 173,000 miles of international routes.

By 1950 the U. S. boasted no less than four transcontinental airlines, nine international lines, a number of feeder lines running north and south, and many small regional lines.

In addition to all these scheduled lines there were about 16,000 operators who still conducted nonscheduled flights from a single base of operations in the now venerable tradition of the men who started it all when they returned home from World War I. Many of these returned home from flying in World War II, just as restless as their uncles had been, and equally convinced of the still expanding horizons of aviation.

The Boeing Stratocruiser, an enormous ship which

Where the paths of airplanes and autos crossed at New York's International Airport, this two-level intersection was built in 1949.

General Electric built jet engines for the Air Force and conducted special research into the many problems presented by these new power sources.

soared the skies like a small ocean liner, indicated the trend for the near future. This plane had a double deck, a bar and lounge on the first floor, and accommodations for 80 passengers.

Present-day airships are navigated by stars, radio, radar, and automatic direction finders. Usually the large passenger ships are flown by two officers, while the passengers are served and tended by airline hostesses, who are the prettiest group of girls this side of Hollywood and Vine . . . an ingratiating feature of commercial aviation which has been with it almost from the start.

The planes are increasingly complex, of course. Today there are over 60,000 parts in a fairly large ship, *not* counting the zillions of washers, bolts, screws, pins, nuts, and rivets. A great many of those parts are machine-tooled to microscopic tolerances.

By 1947 there were 92,600 civil aircraft in the United

The military services pushed jet flight along. This Navy flying wing traveled 600 miles per hour in 1949.

The XC-99, a double-decked freighter plane modeled after the B-36, flew a record 200,000 ton-miles on one mission in 1950. The load was 42 airplane engines of 2300 pounds each.

States, of which about 80,000 were single engine, and a few hundred were gliders. No one knows the exact figures on military production.

Since the close of World War II the armed forces had been working on supersonic flight. In 1951 it was achieved. On August 15 William Bridgeman, Navy test pilot, flew a Douglas Skyrocket equipped with four rocket motors past the sound barrier, reading a top speed of 1,238 miles per hour, and an altitude of 79,494 feet, or more than 15 miles above the earth's surface.

Supersonic planes are dropped from the belly of carrier planes, apparently because their design does not permit both normal takeoff and supersonic speed. Of this strange and soundless world, the military has understandably released little information, but the little they have leaves many large questions about the future of supersonic flight.

The difficulties remain of how to design planes so the fantastic pressures on the wing and fuselage at such speeds will not crush the plane, and how to be certain of

Helicopters like these made the best bid for personal air travel. The jet 'copter at the right is tiny compared to the standard-sized model beside it.

With four rocket tubes going, the Skyrocket takes off at 190 miles an hour, leaving the ground within 2700 feet. Normal landing speed was 160 mph.

control. There are as yet unplumbed psychological and physiological factors in man himself which must emerge when he places himself under stresses for which his evolution has equipped neither his body nor his mind. It is highly possible that mechanical flight may one day pass beyond the capacity of a human pilot to control, perhaps even to experience. Much work had already been done on the matter of automatically controlled or guided ships long before supersonic speed was seriously thought of. The first completely automatic flight was made by a U. S. Army C-54, which was flown all the way from Newfoundland to England without a pilot back in 1944. It is possible that something like an automatic pilot or a remote control system—radio or some other means—will do the major part of the flying, with the pilot along as a sort of machine tender to take over in case of failure after the ship falls to a speed where he can handle it.

Meanwhile, back among the ordinary commercial airliners, which seem by comparison as reassuringly old-fashioned as a one-horse shay, the airlines continue to grow in popularity with passengers. By 1948 some 13 million passengers bought tickets for domestic use and over 1,300,000 used the international lines connecting with this country. In the summer of 1952, as a record host of tourists made for Europe, almost half of the 750,000 traveled by air.

The first regular jet airliner flight was made by a British De Haviland *Comet,* and the only American to make the historic, 6,724-mile hop from London to Johannesburg, South Africa, was Aubrey Cookman, aviation editor of *Popular Mechanics Magazine.* It took the 36-passenger jet liner only 17 hours and 16 minutes to make the three-continent flight. One stop was made, at Rome, which was reached 2 hours and 34 minutes after the takeoff from London. The *Comet* cruised at 450 miles

Flying faster than sound was described by test pilot Gene May as "like riding a solid-tire truck over cobblestones." The Skyrocket was sometimes launched from the belly of a B-29 after being carried aloft 30,000 feet. On these flights, which lasted only some 15 minutes from the time of release, the little ship reached speeds almost twice that of sound at around 80,000 feet of altitude. Wide open, the four rocket motors burn a ton of propellant every minute.

The Comet, built by deHaviland in Britain, is the first successful jet airliner.

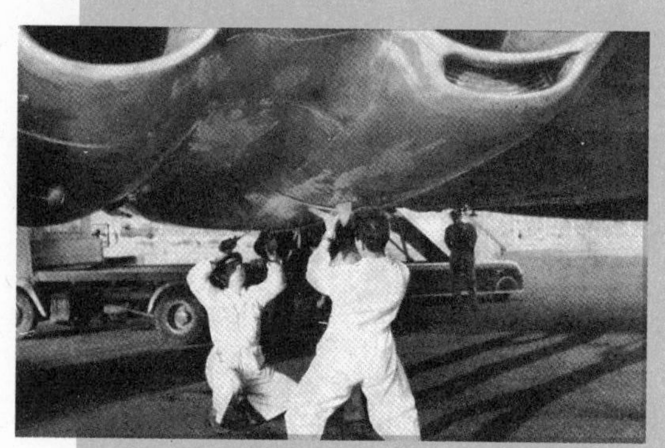

In place of propellors, the Comet has the now-familiar jet air intakes. Engines are close to the ground for easy maintenance.

Cabins are pressurized for eight-mile-high travel, where the plane cruises at almost 500 mph. One crew member always wears an oxygen mask in case of emergency.

per hour and reached top speeds of about 525 miles per hour during the flight.

At the time that this flight was made, no pure jet airliner had yet been flown in the United States, but the British flight pointed the way to jet Atlantic flights in the near future. Editor Cookman's reactions to the flight will be interesting to those whose futures include journeys above the stratosphere at supersonic speeds:

"Fourteen minutes after takeoff my British seatmate, Bert Hardy, reported we were already over the English Channel. This is about half the time it ordinarily takes to reach the Channel. Paris, well behind us, was sighted through a cloud break as we straightened out to make our run for Rome, 48 flying minutes from London. It was 4 P.M. British time.

"By now we had reached the jet's most economical operating altitude, in the neighborhood of 35,000 feet, and the sky I'd always known as blue suddenly was indigo. Stars were visible in the dark reddish-blue sky overhead although it was only late afternoon. You experience an eerie feeling of 'other worldliness' as you glide almost noiselessly high above a cloud carpet that blots out all sight of the earth and water below. It took word from the captain to yank me back to reality.

"It was a message passed back from the cockpit telling the passengers that we were then at 39,000 feet, while the cabin pressure remained as at 8,000 feet, and that our ground speed had moved well above 450 miles an hour. He added apologetically, 'We are now in the stratosphere – the mild turbulence you may have noticed a short while ago was experienced in passing through the tropopause.' We habitually earth-bound creatures were pleased and thrilled by the explanation."

·VI·

Transportation of the Future

IN considering transportation of the future, we do not intend to be conservative—any thoughtful study of the history of invention will show the folly of such a position. We do not wish to align ourselves with the men of yesterday who dubbed a certain boat "Fulton's Folly," or those who shouted, "Get a horse!" at the first automobiles they saw. Nor do we want to join those prudent men of today who doubt that there will be any widespread civilian use of atomic power or rocket ships. We shall be better prophets if we remember that all the mechanical wonders of our modern world once were only daring speculations.

With this in mind, we can only accept as inevitable some kind of transcontinental rocket travel. Dr. Hsue-shen Tsien of the California Institute of Technology already has plotted such a rocket flight between Los Angeles and

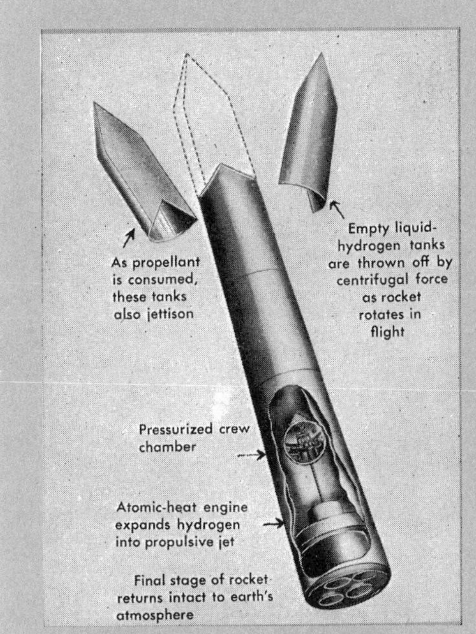

Cutaway diagram of a man-carrying rocket, the basic principles of which will be used for flights into space. Such a rocket would have to weigh about 1500 tons, 80 to 90 percent of which would be liquid propellant carried in huge jettisonable tanks.

From models like this, General Electric rocket engineers obtain data for use in ships that will someday zoom skyward into the stratosphere.

With wing, tail and boom all in one detachable section, this "flying auto" was successfully flown and driven on the road. It cruised in the air at 110 miles an hour.

New York. The time of the flight would be slightly under one hour. Under power only for the first third of the flight, the rocket would rise to a top altitude of 300 miles. The remainder of the flight would be a supersonic glide, gradually lessening to a quite safe landing speed of 150 miles an hour. Passengers, wearing "space suits," would lie down in contour chairs during the powered portion of the flight through the stratosphere at speeds over 4,000 miles per hour. During the gliding portion of the flight, they would enjoy luxury train comfort and freedom.

Transcontinental flights probably will be the shortest trips for which rocket ships will be put to use. Anything less would be comparable to getting the family car out of the garage for a drive to the front gate. But it is possible that during the gliding portion of the rocket ship's flight small planes may be dropped off with passengers bound for intermediate destinations.

Rocket travel will be delayed for at least two or three decades. In the meantime, air travel developments will be in more traditional directions. Commercial airliners will continuously be larger and faster.

These airplanes will be built to cruise at altitudes above 20,000 feet—"overweather flying," they call it, because there are few storms at such altitudes. Because of the constant clear weather and the thinner air which gives less resistance to the ship, air speeds will rise above 350 miles an hour. The passengers will be enclosed in cabins that are literally skin-tight. Air will be drawn into the wings and there condensed to breathable consistency—the same consistency as air at 10,000 feet—and fed through ducts into the cabin. The same air – supercharged, as it is called – will be fed to the engines, which, like human

The "flying auto" is small enough to be parked in the family garage.

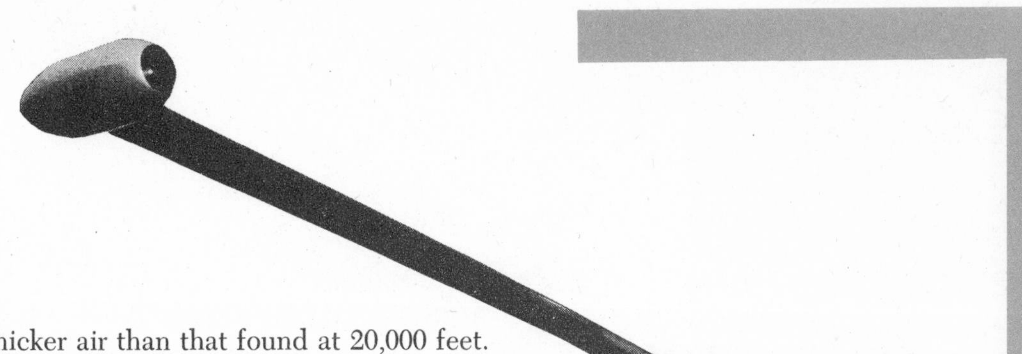

lungs, demand thicker air than that found at 20,000 feet.

To accommodate these ever larger and swifter planes, airports must be larger. Runways a mile and a quarter long will become the rule rather than the exception.

Solar energy has not been discarded as a source of future power: in fact many scientists believe that the harnessing of sunrays is more feasible than widespread use of atomic energy. You may in your lifetime, then, see the sunplane, an aircraft with enormously widespread wings to capture the power of the rays and transmit it into motive power for the plane. Scientists already have moved little machines with solar energy.

The family airplane, which has been predicted for the last 25 years, will become a reality within the next decade. Successful "flying autos," combining the light plane with a roadable car, have been made here and there for the past 10 years. But it is the helicopter, marvelously improved during the Korean war, which will actually become the family "air flivver." There are too many problems involved in the operation and maintenance of an air-land vehicle. Light, economical, and easy-to-handle helicopters already are the answer to personal air travel.

On the railroads, diesel engines will someday be the curiosity steam locomotives are becoming today. Jet pro-

The "Hiller Hornet," a two-place, jet-powered helicopter, designed for the civilian market but given its trials in the Korean campaign. It has a maximum speed of 85 mph. and a ceiling of 12,000 feet.

Flight strips like this one, built along an eastern highway, will be a familiar part of air travel in the future.

A Douglas DC-7 airliner scheduled for service in 1954. The 60-passenger plane will have four 3,000 horse-power engines which will give it a cruising speed of 360 miles per hour.

Reports of flying disks have stimulated serious experiments to determine whether this type of machine is feasible.

pulsion or rocket motors are entirely applicable to fast trains, assuming that roadbeds are built to handle such trains. Railroad mileage probably will decrease a little, as nonpaying lines are eliminated in favor of improved bus and truck services.

Passenger trains will be shorter, fully articulated units with the motive power in the center car—a pancake diesel-electric or gas-turbine engine beneath the floor. The engineer will operate the controls from a forward car, and on the return trip will simply transfer them to the other end of the train, eliminating expensive and time-consuming switching. Runs will be shorter and more frequent; the long-distance trains will be eliminated by air travel within a decade.

The automobile already has been developed, from the standpoint of speed and power, to a point exceeding the capacities of our present streets and highways. The road builders have not kept pace with the auto makers. Experts

An artist pictures the Hudson River lined with small landing fields for the era of helicopters.

Layers of glass fiber held together by plastic glue may form the body of tomorrow's automobile. It will be molded in one piece.

are skeptical of our ability to improve the roads we have within the next 20 years.

But their estimates are based on highway building with the materials and the methods we now use. The pattern of history would indicate that this is a situation calling for radical new materials and methods. Tomorrow's highway may be a marvelous new composition of chemistry, cheap, easy to apply, and resistant to speed and weight. For buses and trucks, special highways are a crying need even now—and need has always been the factor in technical progress, regardless of the apparently insurmountable difficulties.

When the highway hurdle has been overcome, the automobile itself is due for some radical changes. Auto engineers have long been sorrowful about the relative inefficiency of the internal combustion engine. Some form of turbo-jet engine, possibly fueled by atomic energy, will be found for the automobile of the future.

Your car of the future will be less under your control

The glass fiber bodies are molded in forms like this. A special releasing agent prevents the body from sticking when the plastic has set.

The "Scenicruiser" is a two-deck coach developed by Greyhound Lines. The 40-foot, 43-passenger bus goes into service in 1954. It will be air-conditioned and will have rest-room facilities. Buses of this general plan are already in service in the Southwest.

and therefore less subject to faults of human judgment. Electronic automatic pilots will take over on the superhighways, maintaining a constant speed and bringing the car to a stop *before* an emergency.

Automobile bodies will undergo marked change; the indicated direction seems to be toward one-piece, truly streamlined bodies molded in single units of plastic.

Yes, the future, like the past, will see all forms of transportation either die out in their present state or change into something else only indirectly related to the past. Public transportation within cities, for instance, may someday be off the streets entirely, and constantly moving underground platforms may provide the swiftest and most economical transportation of tomorrow. Don't discount too much any prediction of the scientist or transportation engineer. While man is still seeking peace, justice, and freedom, his score in technical development is pretty high. In this field, what man has dreamed, he has achieved.

Nobody knows just what tomorrow's cars will look like, but we can get an idea from some existing experimental models. At right and above is GM's "Le Sabre," which has a 300 horsepower, supercharged engine and a top which raises automatically if it rains. Below is a Chrysler, handmade at a cost of $400,000.

PICTURE CREDITS

EXPLANATION OF KEY SYMBOLS USED

T	Top		R	Right
C	Center	*combined with*	L	Left
B	Bottom		u	upper
			l	lower

WE WISH to express our gratitude to the following individuals and organizations who have given us permission to use the pictures appearing in this book.

I. *Colonial Days*

[PAGES 1–15]

Chicago Historical Society, 10T, 10B
Edison Electric Institute, 14
Museum of Science and Industry, 8B
New York Central Railroad, 13T
Smithsonian Institution, 2T, 3, 4, 5, 6B, 7, 9T, 12B, 15T
Studebaker Corporation, 8C
United States Department of Commerce, Bureau of Public Roads, 9C, 12C
Washington Commercial Company, 1, 2B, 6T, 8T, 9B, 10C, 11, 13C, 13B, 15B

II. *The Westward Movement*

[PAGES 16–84]

Alden Scott Boyer Collection, George Eastman House, 80
American Locomotive Company, 75B
American Waterways Operators, Inc., 42T, 65T
Association of American Railroads, 61T, 68T, 70C, 71T, 72T, 73T, 74B, 76B, 77C
Baltimore and Ohio Railroad, 67, 79, 81C
Chicago Historical Society, 26B
Chicago, Rock Island and Pacific Railroad, 73B
City Art Museum of St. Louis (from *Mississippi Panorama),* 33T, 35C, 35B, 36C, 36B, 39, 40, 41, 43B, 45B, 46, 47, 48T, 49B, 52, 53, 55B
Delaware and Hudson Railroad Corporation, 66B
Edison Institute, 54B
Illinois Central Railroad, 81T
Meine, Franklin J., 38T, 50, 63T
Milwaukee Road, 72B, 75C
Museum of Science and Industry, 20B, 66C
United States Department of Interior, National Park Service, 59B, 61B, 62, 64
New York Central System, 70B, 71B, 74T, 75T, 76, 77T
New York State Engineer's and Surveyor's Department, 65B
Pennsylvania Railroad Company, 68C, 81B, 82B
Popular Mechanics Company, 21T, 37C, 37B
Pullman Standard, 78
Reading Company, 70T
Smithsonian Institution, 18B, 19T, 20T, 20C, 22T, 22C, 27T, 29, 32T, 37T, 54T
Southern Pacific Railway, 82T, 82C
Southern Railway, 68B
State Street Trust Company, Boston, 28, 66T
Studebaker Corporation, 23T
Union Pacific Railroad, 84
United States Department of Commerce, Bureau of Public Roads, 16T, 17, 22B, 25T, 26T, 58B, 59T, 63B
Washington Commercial Company, 18T, 19B, 21B, 24B, 25B, 27C, 27B, 30, 31, 32B, 33B, 36T, 42B, 58T, 60, 62T
Way, Frederick, Jr., 35T, 38B, 43T, 44, 45T, 48B, 49T, 55T, 56, 57

III. *Period of Settlement and Immigration*

[PAGES 85–143]

Alden Scott Boyer Collection, George Eastman House, 85T, 86B, 87B, 104T, 106T, 107C, 108T, 109T, 109C, 110B, 111B, 112T, 119C, 119B, 126B
American Locomotive Company, 116B
Arnold, Schwinn and Company, 133C, 132BL, 137T, 142, 143
Association of American Railroads, 110T, 111T, 116T, 118B, 121T, 124T
Baltimore and Ohio Railroad, 113B, 119T, 120B
Brink's, Inc., 90C
Canadian National Railway, 116C
Chicago, Burlington and Quincy Railroad, 114B
Chicago Historical Society, 89, 91T, 94T, 96T, 99B, 133B, 134B, 136
Chicago Transit Authority, 85B, 86T, 86C, 88, 103T, 103C, 104C, 104B, 105B, 106B, 107, 108C, 108B, 109B, 121B
Cosmopolitan (June 1900), 100T
Edison Institute, 92T, 97C
General Railway Signal Company, 117T, 117C
Indianapolis Star, 130T, 131T
Jones, Vane A., 125T, 127T
McClure's, 92B, 98T, 98C, 137B, 139T
The Milwaukee Road, 114T, 121Cl
Museum of Science and Industry, Chicago, 90B, 91B, 95T, 97B, 132BR, 135C
Newberry Library, 133T
New York Central System, 87T, 113T, 118C, 123, 124B
Northern Pacific Railway, 122C
Pennsylvania Railroad Company, 114C, 121B
Pennsylvania Turnpike Commission, 99T
Popular Mechanics Company, 101, 102, 126C, 129, 134T, 134C, 135T, 138, 139B, 140, 141
Ritter, Bert R., 125B, 128C, 128B
Simons, Richard L., 126T, 128T, 130B, 131B
Smithsonian Institution, 132T
Southern Pacific Company, 112B, 115, 120T, 121B
Studebaker Corporation, 90T, 93, 94B, 95B, 96, 97T, 98B
Union Pacific Railroad, 122B
Washington Commercial, 105T

Picture Credits

IV. *Horseless Carriages and Piano Wire Crates*

[PAGES 144–251]

A. L. Mechling Barge Lines, Inc., 150T
American Waterways Operators, Inc., 147T, 149B, 150B, 151B, 153T, 154C, 154B, 155
Automobile Manufacturers Association, 171B, 172B, 174T, 176TR, 194TR, 194B, 195, 217T
Cosmopolitan (1900), 168C, 170B, 217B
Edison Institute, 164T, 168T, 169, 170C, 173T, 173C, 175T, 175C
Ford News Bureau, 204, 207B
General Motors Coporation, 218T, 219B, 224C
Greyhound Corporation, 246T, 246B
Harley-Davidson Motor Company, 211 215B, 213T, 216B
Indian Sales Corporation, 208T, 212T
Jordan River Line, Inc., 152
McClure's (1896), 166; (1899), 168B
Packard Motor Car Company, 171T, 172Cu, 172Cl, 175B, 194TL, 196T, 201T, 201C, 203Cl
Popular Mechanics Company, 146T, 149T, 156, 157, 158, 159, 160T, 160C, 164B, 165, 167, 171C, 174C, 174B, 176B, 177, 178, 179, 180, 181, 182, 183, 184, 185, 186, 187, 188, 189, 190, 191, 192, 193, 196C, 196B, 197, 198, 199, 200, 201B, 202, 203T, 203B, 205, 206, 207T, 208B, 209, 210, 212B, 212C, 213B, 214, 215T, 215C, 216T, 216C, 218C, 219Cu, 219Cl, 220, 221, 222, 223, 224T, 224B, 225, 226, 227, 228, 229, 230, 231, 232, 233, 234, 235, 236, 237, 238, 239, 240, 241, 242, 243, 244, 245, 246C, 247, 249, 250, 251
St. Louis Shipbuilding and Steel Company, 151T, 154T
Standard Oil Company of Indiana, 148TL
Streckfus Steamers, Inc., 160C, 160B, 161, 162, 163
Studebaker Corporation, 171T, 172T, 173B, 176TL, 176C, 203Cu, 218B
United States Army, Corps of Engineers, 147B, 149C
Way, Frederick, Jr., 144, 145
Wheeling Steel Corporation, 148TR, 148B

V. *Transportation in Our Time*

[PAGES 252–300]

Pennsylvania Railroad Company, 266C
Popular Mechanics Company, 252, 253, 254, 255, 256, 257, 258, 259, 260, 261, 262, 263, 264, 265, 266T, 266B, 267, 268, 269T, 270, 271, 272, 273, 274, 275, 276, 277, 278B, 278C, 279, 280, 281, 282, 283, 284, 285, 286, 287, 288, 289, 290, 291, 292, 293, 294, 295, 296, 297, 298, 299, 300B, 300C
Willys-Overland Motors, Inc., 278T

VI. *Transportation of the Future*

[PAGES 301–306]

Douglas Aircraft Company, 304T
Greyhound Corporation, 305B
Popular Mechanics Company, 301, 302, 303, 304C, 304B, 305T, 308

INDEX

ROMAN NUMBERS REFER TO TEXT; ITALIC NUMBERS REFER TO PICTURE CAPTIONS

Index

Index